+ + +

If You
Love Me
You Will
Do My
Will

+ + +

*STEPHEN G.
MICHAUD*

*HUGH
AYNESWORTH*

A SIGNET BOOK

For our wives,
Susan Harper Michaud
and
Paula Butler Aynesworth

SIGNET
Published by the Penguin Group
Penguin Books USA Inc., 375 Hudson Street,
New York, New York 10014, U.S.A.
Penguin Books Ltd, 27 Wrights Lane,
London W8 5TZ, England
Penguin Books Australia Ltd, Ringwood,
Victoria, Australia
Penguin Books Canada Ltd, 2801 John Street,
Markham, Ontario, Canada L3R 1B4
Penguin Books (N.Z.) Ltd, 182–190 Wairau Road,
Auckland 10, New Zealand

Penguin Books Ltd, Registered Offices:
Harmondsworth, Middlesex, England

Published by Signet, an imprint of New American Library, a division of
Penguin Books USA Inc. This is an authorized reprint of a hardcover
edition published by W.W. Norton & Company, Inc.

First Signet Printing, July, 1991
10 9 8 7 6 5 4 3 2 1

✝ ✝ ✝
Contents

✛ ✛ ✛
Acknowledgments

We wish to thank Stanley Addington and Max Dreyer at the Raymondville, Texas, Historical Museum, as well as Patrick J. O'Connell of Spring Hill College, in Mobile, Alabama, and Fred Bona of W.R. Grace & Company. All were helpful in pulling together the detailed research necessary to complete this book.

Likewise, we are indebted to Katharine Idsal, a daughter of the Wild Horse Desert, and Father Francis Kelly Nemick, who welcomed us to the old Headquarters at La Parra. Thanks also to Elna Christopher, Serena Lisa Kuvet, and Brenda Patrick Wallace, present and former members of the Texas attorney general's staff in Austin.

At St. Joseph's Abbey in Massachusetts we were given vital assistance by Fathers Laurence Bourget and Placid McSweeney. In Colorado, Sister Bernardette Teasdale went out of her way to be helpful. In New York, Lester Glassner ably oversaw photo research, and Anthony Levintow at W.W. Norton kept his head while all about him were losing theirs.

We are especially grateful to our agent, Kathy Robbins, who rescued this project more than once, and to Starling Lawrence, our editor, a person of discernment, fine humor, and rare compassion. It was a privilege to work with him.

✝ ✝ ✝

Dramatis Personae

Henrietta Armstrong Sarita Kenedy East's close friend and ranching neighbor. She believed that the monk Brother Leo exercised a benign spiritual influence over Mrs. East.

Sara Curiel Sarita's Spanish-speaking maid, who allegedly supplied Mrs. East's relatives with tales of her mistress's ardent affection for Brother Leo.

Joe Day Lawyer to a group of Mrs. East's "Mexican heirs," descendants from her Mexican grandmother's first marriage. Day became an expert on Kenedy family history.

Sarita Kenedy East The rich widow and lonely *patrona* of La Parra, her grandfather's remote, 400,000-acre south Texas cattle kingdom, situated over a subterranean ocean of oil.

Tom East, Jr. Sarita's wealthy nephew. East coveted his aunt's ranch land.

Judge Bill Edwards The only jurist to hear the full case against Leo and his codefendant, J. Peter Grace. Edwards found them both guilty of having unduly influenced Mrs. East.

Jake Floyd Sarita's crafty attorney, known as the Snake. Floyd also represented Tom East, Jr., as well as the Alice National Bank.

Dom Edmund Futterer Brother Leo's affectionate abbot. Father Edmund originally sent the monk into the world to raise money for the Trappists' expansion program.

Father Richard Gans The former superior of the Trappist monastery in Chile, and one of Brother Leo's staunchest allies within the order.

Bishop Mariano Garriga Sarita's excitable bishop and the Roman Catholic prelate of Corpus Christi. Garriga regarded the Kenedy estate as his diocese's "patrimony."

J. Peter Grace The well-known industrial magnate, chairman of W. R. Grace & Company and lay champion of Catholic charities. Grace was the Trappists' business mentor and Leo's close friend until he and the monk began fighting over control of Sarita's foundation.

Bishop Rene Gracida The present bishop of Corpus Christi and current president of the Kenedy Memorial Foundation. One of Leo's supporters has accused Gracida of being "the Antichrist."

Roderick Norton (Brother Leo) Christopher Joseph Gregory Jack and Lotus Gregory's handsome and charismatic son, who "breathed God," according to Abbot Futterer. In the 1950s, Leo became Sarita's adviser and traveling companion. He encouraged the devout ranch widow's long-held desire to place the bulk of her millions in a foundation. The monk has fought ever since to gain control of the fortune.

Dom Columban Hawkins Leo's onetime novice master at the monastery in Rhode Island and later abbot of Our Lady of Guadalupe, in Oregon, where Leo barely escaped a sheriff's posse.

William Joyce Brother Leo's first attorney, who helped the monk prepare his eighty-one-page broadside against J. Peter Grace. Representing Leo, says Joyce, was "like chasing a drop of mercury across a tabletop."

Dom Thomas Keating Father Edmund Futterer's successor as Leo's abbot. Keating feared both scandal and financial ruin for the Trappists unless a deal was negotiated by which the charges against Leo would be dropped. He finally exiled the monk and then dismissed him from the order.

Elena Kenedy Starchy widow of Sarita's alcoholic brother, Johnny, and also resident at La Parra.

Bob Kleberg, Jr. Master of the giant King Ranch and lifelong friend of Sarita and Johnny Kenedy. Like his sister Henrietta Armstrong, Kleberg approved of Brother Leo's influence on Sarita. Both swore to depositions on the monk's behalf.

Archbishop John Krol The "apostolic visitator" appointed by Pope John XXIII to attempt a settlement to the lawsuit filed against Leo and J. Peter Grace. Years later, Krol told Grace he believed Leo to be "a crook."

Judge C. Woodrow Laughlin A.k.a. El Burro. Judge Laughlin understood the art of accommodation. As long as Jake Floyd's political faction was in control of Jim Wells County, it also had control of Laughlin's court.

Lee Lytton, Jr. Mrs. East's cousin Stella's son and the first person to accuse Brother Leo and Peter Grace of unduly influencing Sarita. "If there's a hero in this story," says Amie Rodnick, "it's Judge Lytton."

Jim Mattox The most recent of seven Texas state attorneys general to become involved in the Kenedy Foundation litigation.

Lawrence McKay J. Peter Grace's New York attorney, who oversaw the revision of Sarita's will and the establishment of her foundation.

Frank Nesbitt The determined attorney for the rambunctious Turcotte brothers. Nesbitt spent sixteen years trying to have both Mrs. East's new will and her foundation thrown out as the products of undue influence.

Kenneth Oden Jake Floyd's protégé and successor as attorney for the Alice National Bank. Oden was also Lee Lytton's attorney. Alleged conflicts of interests ultimately drove him from the case.

Father Patrick Peyton A Holy Cross priest and head of the Family Rosary Crusade. Brother Leo's attempts to keep Peyton off the foundation board prompted some of his later battles with Peter Grace.

Amie Rodnick The young Texas assistant attorney general who opened the official investigation of Kenneth Oden and the Alice National Bank.

Francis Cardinal Spellman J. Peter Grace's close ally inside the church. According to Grace, Spellman, too, distrusted Brother Leo.

Bobby, Jack, Joe, L.E., Jr., and Pat Turcotte Sarita's cousin Louis Edgar Turcotte's sons. They fought all the other litigants, and each other.

Archbishop Egidio Vagnozzi The "apostolic delegate" in Washington, D.C., who suspected that Leo's relationship with Sarita had been "meretricious."

Francis Verstraeten, Sr. One of the many prominent and well-to-do Argentine aristocrats to whom Brother Leo introduced Mrs. East on her four excursions to South America in 1959 and 1960. Verstraeten later defended the monk's behavior against his many accusers, only to join them as his severest detractor.

William Wright Chief lawyer for the "Mexican heirs." Wright filed the second lawsuit against Leo and Grace, alleging on behalf of his clients that their undue influence over Mrs. East was confined to the inclusion of a single clause of her new will.

THE KENEDYS

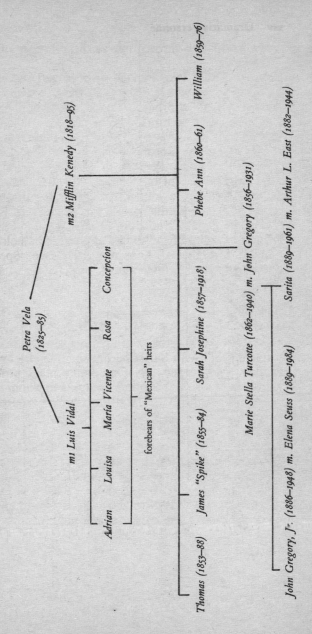

Petra Vela (1825–85)

m1 Luis Vidal   m2 Mifflin Kenedy (1818–95)

Adrian   Louisa   Maria Vicente   Rosa   Concepcíon

forebears of "Mexican" heirs

Thomas (1853–88)   James "Spike" (1855–84)   Sarah Josephine (1857–1918)   Phebe Ann (1860–61)   William (1859–76)

Marie Stella Turcotte (1862–1940) m. John Gregory (1856–1931)

John Gregory, Jr. (1886–1948) m. Elena Seuss (1889–1984)   Sarita (1889–1961) m. Arthur L. East (1882–1944)

TURCOTTES AND LYTTONS

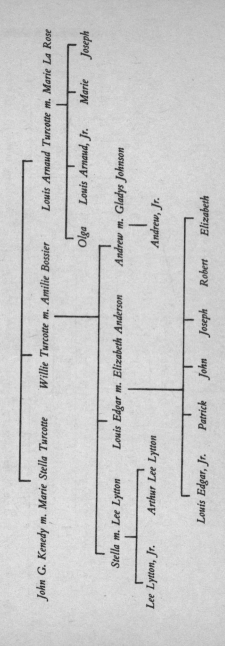

KINGS, KLEBERGS, AND EASTS

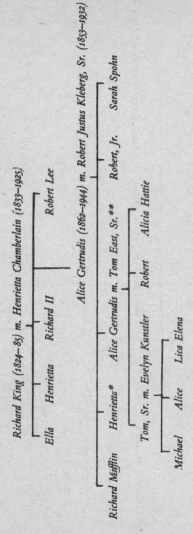

Richard King (1824–85) m. Henrietta Chamberlain (1833–1925)

  Ella Henrietta Richard II Robert Lee

Alice Gertrudis (1862–1944) m. Robert Justus Kleberg, Sr. (1853–1932)

  Richard Mifflin Henrietta* Alice Gertrudis m. Tom East, Sr.** Robert, Jr. Sarah Spohn

  Tom, Sr. m. Evelyn Kunstler Robert Alicia Hattie

  Michael Alice Lica Elena

*Married John Larkin and then Major Tom Armstrong, no children

**There were six East boys: Tom, Arthur, John, Allen, Mike, and Ed, "Lady" Florence's husband.

✛ ✛ ✛

Prologue

The limestone dust hung thick over the old desert during the drought of the early 1950s. By day it bleached the south Texas sky a bone white and at dusk transformed the sun into a blood-red balloon on the horizon. On these eerie crimson evenings, when the gloomy Headquarters house at La Parra felt most like a tomb, Sarita Kenedy East would put on her black-lace mantilla, genuflect before her bedroom altar, and then slowly make her splay-gaited way up into the gun tower atop the Headquarters, where she sat alone, surveying her endlessly flat, 400,000-acre domain.

The servants reported that the widow often remained in the tower well past dark, sipping her tumblers of scotch and sometimes boozily yodeling the exuberant country-and-western dance tunes of her youth. But most of the time—and this was what touched and saddened the ranch's vaqueros and their families—La Parra's barren *patrona* made no sound at all. From their doorsteps they watched her silhouette until she was lost to them in the later hours of milky moonglow, still sitting silently, searching the far limit of the featureless terrain.

Sarita Kenedy East of Sarita, Kenedy County, south Texas, was the granddaughter of one of the authentic giants of southwestern history, the nineteenth-century

Rio Grande steamboater Captain Mifflin Kenedy, who established La Parra in the parched wilderness of the Wild Horse Desert after helping his young friend Richard King found the mammoth King Ranch next door. The old captain was an empire builder, but his dreams of a Kenedy dynasty died in the family's third generation.

Six decades after Captain Kenedy's death his granddaughter, once a high-spirited woman, had withdrawn from the world. She was driven to her evening vigils by an inner void and by her lonesomeness. Looking out toward the nearby Gulf of Mexico, Sarita pondered the ranch graveyard, where in 1932 she had buried her father, John Gregory Kenedy, known in his day as Don Gregorio; next to him her mother, the former Marie Stella Turcotte of New Orleans, who died in 1940; then her husband of thirty-four years, Arthur L. East, a heart attack victim at the age of sixty-one in 1944; and her adored brother, Johnny, who drank himself to death in 1948, four years before the drought struck. She had arranged them in a tidy row, with a space reserved next to Johnny for his starchy widow, Elena, and another measured rectangle between her mother and Arthur, where Sarita would be interred.

The Mexican cowboys, who believed in ghosts, speculated among themselves that Mrs. East communed with her dead family on her nights in the gun tower. But Sarita, whose faith led her to trust that her parents and husband and brother were gone to heaven, mourned in the dark for what never had been, a next generation of Kenedys to carry on the family legacy, La Parra. She was the last of the line, preoccupied by her own inevitable demise and surrounded in her grief by collateral relatives who, according to Sarita's bitter metaphor, had begun eyeing her with the undisguised greed of carrion eaters waiting for a sick heifer to expire.

The Roman Catholic church also took a vital interest in the ultimate disposition of the Kenedy fortune, as well as in Mrs. East's considerable annual charity. Her church, in the person of the plump and excitable Mariano Garriga, bishop of Corpus Christi, was staked to a handsome annual income from her largess, and it had been generously provided for in her will drawn up just after Johnny's death. Garriga, a likable elderly prelate of ordinary attainments, regarded the Kenedy family money as his "patrimony," as he called it, and was fiercely territorial. His special concern was the parade of Catholic fund-raisers that Mrs. East's bounty attracted from all over the United States. Garriga closely monitored their visits to La Parra, insisting that they funnel themselves through his Corpus Christi chancery to state their business and make their obeisances before he allowed them to travel on to the remote ranch.

Sarita and her sister-in-law Elena welcomed them all; the Norbertine fathers, the Sisters of Purity (and of Mercy), Father Keller, founder of the Christophers movement, the Franciscans, the Jesuits, and representatives of a hundred other Catholic organizations, from the Negro Apostolate of the Divine Savior to the Marquette League of Catholic Indian Missions, including Father Flanagan's famous Boys Town, in Nebraska. Altogether, Mrs. East distributed from $40,000 to $100,000 a year to the Catholic church and its causes.

She would have given away perhaps twice as much, and could have donated a great deal more in the following years, had it not been for the wily determination of her attorney and chief financial adviser, Jacob S. Floyd, he of the narrow-set eyes and mirthless grin, known locally as El Vibora Seca, the Dry Snake, for his serpentine aspect. Jake Floyd never seemed to sweat and, as John Mullen, a south Texas lawyer who knew him well, remembers, "Jake bit like a snake, struck back like a rattler."

Sarita was admired as an able rancher, Don Gregorio's equal, it was said. She was manifestly better qualified to manage La Parra than was her feckless brother, Johnny, who spent the major portion of his adult years lost in a whiskey fog. Mrs. East's competence, however, did not extend to the complexities of financial, legal, and tax affairs, which she entrusted with her complete confidence to Jake Floyd's care.

Floyd interpreted his mandate broadly. Disapproving of Mrs. East's charitable munificence, for example, the lawyer, a Baptist, contained it by persuading his client that to donate more than 30 percent of her adjusted gross annual income was a punishable federal offense. More sinister were the plans he was developing for the future.

Sarita didn't realize it, but the grand prize in her estate was not her land or her cattle. It was oil—vast, hidden lakes of it sealed in the ancient seabed beneath La Parra and beneath a satellite ranch she owned seventy miles due west in Jim Hogg County near the town of Hebbronville. In the early 1950s her oil fields were just beginning to be systemically exploited. Mrs. East did her best to ignore the development and might have forbidden it altogether had it not been for the encouragement she received from her good friend Bob Kleberg, Jr., Richard King's grandson and master of the King Ranch.

Sarita did not understand the oil business and abominated it, preferring any day to see cows and calves in her pastures rather than oil rigs and stacks of rusted pipe casing. She rarely asked Jake Floyd about the drilling's progress, except to complain of its unsightliness, and therefore was easily maintained in ignorance of her true worth. In the beginning, Floyd himself couldn't guess the full extent of Mrs. East's holdings. But he knew their potential was enormous, perhaps $50 million or more.

The attorney's paramount aim in what he considered a benevolent deception (Jack Floyd would have been startled to be accused of unscrupulousness) was to prevent Sarita in her advancing years from misspending her oil royalties. Floyd was one of the executors of her will, which he had also drawn up, and his idea of prudent estate planning was for the oil money to flow quietly and undiluted, over time, into the alleged safekeeping of the Alice National Bank in Jim Wells County, another of his clients.

Jake Floyd did not fear interference in his scheming from Bishop Garriga, who was alert only to excessive greed among his fellow churchmen. Nor was the attorney concerned about Sarita's relatives; none of them, with the exception of her nephew, Tom East, Jr., was nearly so nimble-minded as Floyd. What kept El Vibora Seca on his guard, however, was the threat he instinctively sensed might come from afar, some predator with tricks and wiles of his own. Floyd was prepared to fight a lion but was surprised—and Jake Floyd did not like surprises—when his rival appeared instead in the guise of a lamb.

Brother Leo Gregory first materialized at La Parra at the sharpest moment of Sarita's despair, a grim winter's morning in 1948 as she and Johnny's widow, Elena, were kneeling amid the flowers they'd set out over Johnny's fresh grave. Just turned fifty-nine, clad in her shapeless widow's black, her auburn hair streaked with gray, Mrs. East raised her bright green eyes to the young monk and remarked to herself with pleasure—as she later told Elena—that their visitor was wearing a clerical collar.

He was thirty-one, a slender six feet tall and boyish, with an intriguing gaze, those vivid *gray eyes,* and a sulky set to his lower lip. Even the odd cant of his left eye in its socket, a souvenir of a boyhood accident, enhanced the charm of his expression.

Mrs. East registered two further impressions that day. Years of silence in the monastery had rounded, slowed, and softened the monk's speech, which fell on her hearing in soothing rhythms. Just as reassuring to her were his incongruously broad, thick-fingered hands, muscled and coarsened by manual labor. Sarita approved of a man with calluses.

She also instantly trusted any Catholic cleric and especially this one, about the right age to be her son, who spoke of God with such enveloping intimacy. Neither at this first encounter nor ever in their later adventures together did the widow doubt the purity of the monk's intentions or suspect that his passion for drawing thirsty hearts closer to God could be a cynical ruse employed to separate her from her senses, and her fortune.

That would be left to the lawyers and princes of the church to dispute. The truth, as Brother Leo revealed it to Sarita Kenedy East, was mystical, a vision to which she willingly yielded up a long-dormant spirit. It was a love story. The monk would call it their "special relationship."

ONE

✝ ✝ ✝

Child Leo

Well before sunset each sultry summer's eve during World War II, Brother Leo Gregory and the rest of the weary monks at Our Lady of the Valley Monastery in Cumberland, Rhode Island, closed their liturgical day with the canonical office of compline. The choir intoned a hymn and three psalms in sepulchral church Latin; then it raised a paean to Our Lady, Salve Regina. Chanting together in the soft light and shadows of the granite-block, neo-Gothic abbey that they had built themselves, the monks sent a resonance pulsing out into the cosmos to please and glorify their mystical Object.

It was the final holy devotion of an exhausting, seventeen-hour daily regimen begun in the dark of night with the community's first ritual, vigils, then continued through the seven succeeding canonical offices—lauds, prime, terce, sext, none, vespers, and compline. The vegetarian monks performed heavy farm labor as well, plus meditation, individual prayer, and, on Fridays, The Discipline, self-flagellation, which helped promote humility.

The last meal of the day in summer usually was a bland late-afternoon supper of unseasoned applesauce or stewed fruit and whole-wheat bread slices consumed in silence in the refectory. Then with the six-thirty celebration of compline ended, the hooded brothers and fathers shuffled off to their separate, stuffy dormitory cells, where they lay supine on straw pallets in their habits and potato-sack underclothes and, in the gathering dusk, impassively bore their nightly affliction, the insistent, beckoning rhythms of "I Got It Bad, and That Ain't Good."

"Beer Barrel Polka" was another of the regulars on the 1940s hit parade routinely to waft over the monastery wall and into the upstairs dormitories from a nearby roadhouse on Diamond Hill Road, an outpost of encroaching modern society that soon also spawned the Lonsdale midget-auto race track, within clear earshot of the distressed monks. Mingled with the shouts of the race-track crowd and the booming voice of the announcer, the captive, sweating monks could hear "Oh, Johnny" or any of the other wartime standards, from "How Are Things in Glocca Morra?" to "Doin' What Comes Natur'lly." It was in the brothers' dormitory one night that Leo first heard "Deep in the Heart of Texas."

The monks at Our Lady of the Valley were Trappists, formally known as Cistercians of the Strict Observance, so-called because of the community's adherence to the ancient monastic Rule of St. Benedict, as revived in the seventeenth century by the French abbot Armand Jean de Rancé, of La Trappe. St. Benedict compiled his detailed, seventy-three-chapter guide to correct cenobitic life at the end of the Roman era and in it laid out specific instructions covering every facet of communal asceticism, from diet to deportment.

"During all seasons of the year," he advised in chapter 22, "let two cooked dishes of food suffice for the brethren." And in chapter 40: "Let all except the weak and sick abstain from eating the flesh of four-footed animals."

"An Abbot," reads chapter 2, "is considered as representing the person of Christ." And the monks, states chapter 5, "live not according to their own will, nor follow their own desires, but, abiding in monasteries, walk according to the command and the direction of another and will to have an Abbot over them."

St. Benedict was decidedly illiberal on the question of individual freedoms. "Let no one presume to give or receive anything without leave of the Abbot," he directed in chapter 33, "nor to have as his own absolutely anything. It is not permitted to monks to have even their bodies or wills at their own disposal." Likewise, according to chapter 29, "If any brother, who through his own fault leaves or is expelled from the monastery, wishes to return, he shall first promise to amend the fault on account of which he left."

The jukebox serenades, which often lasted past midnight, were an intolerable distraction for those who would live by the saint's authoritative Rule. Beginning in 1945, the harmony at Our Lady of the Valley was further disrupted by a sharp rise in new members, also called vocations, among returning war veterans.

Behind this rush then began a second wave of would-be cenobites, men who had read the monk Thomas Merton's 1948 autobiography, *The Seven Storey Mountain*. One of this century's most famous and influential Catholic texts, Merton's book inspired hundreds of readers to follow him into the Trappists. The population of monks at Merton's monastery, Our Lady of Gethsemani, in Kentucky, began to overflow, as did the community at Cumberland. Our Lady of the Valley, which could reasonably accommodate perhaps 80 monks, and had sustained a stable population of between 50 and 60 members for forty years, mushroomed into a dangerously overcrowded community of 140 by late 1948.

The monastery was ruled by the imposing Dom (for

"Lord") Edmund Futterer, a forty-two-year-old former Passionist father elected abbot in 1945. Although an authoritarian abbot who rigidly enforced the rule of silence, Futterer was also a large and gregarious man, "a real teddy bear," in the words of Bill Roberts, an ex-monk who lived in the community as Brother Luke. "He just was a big, affectionate person," says Roberts, "who wanted to express his affection for everyone."

He thought of the brothers and the fathers at Cumberland as his family or, more precisely, his sons. Often the abbot addressed a monk as "Child," as in "Child Leo." They were his charges, and as their numbers grew, Dom Futterer recognized an urgent necessity not only to relocate the Rhode Island abbey but also to establish new daughter houses to shelter his burgeoning family. Eager as he was to do so, however, Abbot Futterer could count but $30,000 in the monastery exchequer, funds the Trappists had taken forty years to amass, with scant prospect that the community's only regular source of income, sale of its orchard and dairy products, would significantly swell that total anytime soon.

His second problem was to identify a competent abbey representative to scout potential daughter house locations, negotiate their acquisition, raise the money needed to buy them, and then oversee their construction. Futterer surveyed the monks at Our Lady of the Valley for the type of personable, intelligent, dedicated, and resourceful character capable of undertaking such an assignment and beheld the poorest possible range of candidates—a group self-selected to spurn all worldly contact, men who hardly ever spoke and certainly never about real estate, finance, and construction. After decades in the monastery, many of the older monks were so refined in their contemplative simplicity that even negotiating a train ticket, let alone a million-dollar building project, might overtax them.

Then there was Brother Leo.

Father Edmund, who was Brother Leo's confessor, made his choice by intuition. He knew the monk was untrained and inexperienced in any of the obvious skill the mission required; Leo lacked a college degree and had never held a job of any sort. But the abbot had unabashed affection for the young monk, who, along with Brother Blaise Drayton, a onetime interior decorator, was part of a small circle of Futterer's favorites within the monastery. "My best memory of Brother Leo is of his very warm, spiritual relationship with Dom Futterer," says Father Gilbert Moreau, a Marine Corps veteran who entered Our Lady of the Valley after World War II. "When they were together it was different than when I was with the abbot. He was intimidating to me then, because of his great holiness and forcefulness. With Brother Leo and with Brother Blaise, too, they might touch one another with almost a light that shined."

Brother Leo—Roderick Norton Gregory—was esteemed as an exemplary monk from the moment he entered Our Lady of the Valley, in February of 1938. He was born in Oakland, California, on August 10, 1917, the second of two sons in the household of Jackson Gregory, a hard-drinking and prolific writer of Western pulp fiction, and the former Lotus Adelia McGlashan, who in 1910, at age eighteen, had eloped with the twenty-seven-year-old Gregory, formerly her high school teacher in the Sierra Nevada hamlet of Truckee, California, not far from Lake Tahoe.

Both Rod's parents came from singular families. His grandmother Amelia Hartnell Gregory, a strict Catholic who spoke only Spanish, was the daughter of the pioneer California educator William E. P. Hartnell and Teresa de la Guerra y Noriega, descended from the colonial commander of the Spanish presidio at Santa Barbara. Amelia Hartnell's husband, Durell Stokes Gregory, a native Virginian, became a successful California real estate lawyer, politician, and, later, prominent judge. Their daughter (Rod's aunt) Susan Myra Gregory developed into a poet of some note and was a professional colleague of the novelist John Steinbeck, who dedicated his first great success, *Tortilla Flat,* to Susan Gregory.

Rod's maternal grandfather Charles Fayette McGlashan was a stern Scot with a restless intelligence, which led him to alternate and often parallel careers as an inventor and teacher, astronomer, lawyer, politician, newspaper editor, museum operator, and lepidopterist (a butterfly and a moth he discovered are named for him). McGlashan also wrote *A History of the Donner Party,* a valuable piece of historical research for which he personally interviewed many members of the infamous pioneer band that, to survive the winter of 1846–47 while stranded in the Sierras near Truckee, resorted to cannibalism.

Charles McGlashan and his wife, Leonora, were Protestants, but both were tempted by the occult and came to share in their later years a belief in mystic revelation. Nona McGlashan, Rod Gregory's cousin and her grandfather McGlashan's biographer, recounts in her book *Give Me a Mountain Meadow* that one year before Mrs. McGlashan died, in 1934, the old woman dreamed she was on a stage before a vast audience expecting her to give a guitar performance. Leonora was frightened. "Then," as she recalled the dream to Nona, "a beautiful young man came up to me and said, 'Never mind, just go through the motions on the stage and I will play the music.' Afterward, I ran behind the scenes to find the young man and thank him. 'Who are you? Tell me your name?' I begged him. He turned and looked at me full in the eyes. And he said, 'My name is Jesus Christ.' ''

Leonora's daughter Lotus, a physically stunning woman also strongly attracted to mysticism, had since her girlhood struggled with a recurring and powerful urge to leave the world and live only for God. She tried to do just that a year before her elopement with Jackson Gregory, taking herself to the door of a Catholic rectory, where she sought admission as a nun. She was refused, in part because Lotus was not yet a Catholic. But she made it a condition of her subsequent marriage to Jackson that if, when their children were grown, the need came over her again he would allow his wife to leave him for God.

Because their second son was a physically frail child (much less assertive, he says, than his dominating older brother, Jackson, Jr.) and afflicted with a stammer that other children mocked, his "mumsey" kept Rod at home through grammar school and saw to his early education herself. Lotus created a snug cocoon for her boy, delighting him with fairy tales and inculcating in him her deeply spiritual brand of Christianity. "We're all God's children, and no harm can come to us," was the first prayer she taught him. According to his aunt Victoria, little Rod was "just a dear, charming, lovable child. A bright, intelligent boy." She adds, "He loved to fantasize. Stories and little things. He loved stories, you know. I used to make up stories for him and he'd make them up for me."

By his teens he revealed a keen mind for mathematics, and although Rod was guarded, discouraging personal intimacy, he matured into an affable and agile conversationalist. After he and Lotus converted to Catholicism in 1934 (which Rod agreed to do, at the time, only to please his mumsey), Lotus Gregory did quit her marriage and left Jackson to his typewriter and liquor bottles. She moved to southern California, where she subsisted in poverty in the manner of a medieval anchoress, working as an unpaid volunteer in a Catholic-sponsored ghetto day-care facility.

Rod, meanwhile, began drifting from college to college and traveling extensively around the world. "I felt," he says of those years, "I could do anything I wanted to do. Mother's boys usually feel that way, according to Sigmund Freud, who was also a mother's boy. But the problem was, looking around, I couldn't see anything that really attracted me. I was a nomad looking for something and I couldn't find it."

He was brought deeper into his adopted faith by a monsignor he met during a brief stay at the Colorado School of Mines and by a misdiagnosis of bone cancer in his leg. He was told, at age eighteen, that he almost certainly would die in six months—"a thought-provoking situation, without a doubt," as the monk describes it.

At times Brother Leo has traced his decision to become a Trappist to Charles Boyer's dramatic performance as a monk opposite the temptress played by Marlene Dietrich in the overripe 1936 film epic *The Garden of Allah*. But his cousin Nona cautions, "Remember, all the McGlashans and all the Gregorys like to make up a good story. I always took what Rod said as tongue in cheek."

Whatever the source of his restlessness, Rod Gregory's questing ended at Our Lady of the Valley, where he gladly forswore his freedom. The postulant monk was soon admired for his selfless submissiveness, a religious virtue regarded as essential to sanctification among the Trappists. "In his early years," says Father Raphael Simon, a medical doctor and psychiatrist who joined the monastery in 1940, "Brother Leo was extremely generous. The Rule of St. Benedict is a rule to overcome independence of judgment and independence of will by submission, and he accepted that fully, worked generously in submission to his superior.''

The power of the monk's spirituality did not escape Father Raphael's notice, either. "He had a really deep faith in Catholicism,'' says the priest. "I remember when he had this stomach ulcer and was being confined to a very hard cot. It must have been quite painful. I came into his room and there were tears in his eyes, and it was evident that he was meditating on Christ, compassionating Christ in His sufferings.''

In the adjoining infirmary room, Father Raphael goes on, Abbot Futterer's predecessor, Father John O'Connor, lay with terminal cancer. Despite Brother Leo's own discomfort, he constantly jumped up to see what he could do to help the old monk, who died in Leo's arms. This was in 1945, two years after Brother Leo took his final vows of poverty, chastity, obedience, stability, and "conversion of manners'' as a Trappist lay brother.

All postulants were given the choice of two vocations when they entered Our Lady of the Valley. Rod Gregory could have selected the calling of the "choir religious,'' those monks who had taken holy orders or were working toward their ordination into the priesthood. Being priests as well as monks, these fathers were qualified to celebrate mass and to administer the sacraments of the Roman Catholic church, including baptism, matrimony, and penance, or confession. Choir monks wore white habits with black scapulars.

The alternative Rod chose was to become one of the monastery drones, a brown-robed lay brother. Since the earliest days of the Cistercians lay brothers had been brought into monasteries essentially as pious laborers. Some were intelligent and well educated. But the majority were illiterate serfs whose toils freed the educated fathers to pay fuller attention to their holy offices, prayer, and contemplation. Lay brothers ate and slept apart from the choir monks and stood in silence during the canonical offices, usually at their workplaces somewhere on the monastery grounds, where they would reverently pray sequences of Pater Nosters, Ave Marias, and Gloria Patris. The intricacies of chanting the hymns and psalms were considered beyond them.

By the twentieth century these hierarchical distinctions between fathers and brothers had blurred; although their life was less exalted than that of the fathers, the lay brethren at Our Lady of the Valley weren't shunned or considered inferior spiritual beings. Certainly not Brother Leo.

"He was very impressive," says Father Thomas Aquinas Keating, "a kind of role model that greatly appealed to me." Keating came to Cumberland—over his family's strong objections—fresh from Yale and Fordham universities as a twenty-year-old retreatant in 1943. He first encountered Brother Leo as his guestmaster. Keating observed the monk's perfect peace of mind and his special charity toward the poor, especially Cumberland's drunks and bums, whom Leo often sheltered, fed, and counseled in the guesthouse. He remembers remarking on Leo's abundant virtues to Dom Edmund. The abbot smiled and told the young retreatant, "Brother Leo is a lay brother. If you're thinking of that vocation, I can assure you it leads to God. Brother Leo *breathes* God!" Father Keating, who twenty-three years later dismissed the monk from the Trappists, remarks, "I think that *was* an accurate description of him."

Brother Leo today questions the validity of that and all the other glowing assessments of his attributes as a monk; he says his chief apparent virtue, his humility, was in truth a "natural" virtue, a neurotic symptom of self-doubt. "All of us play games to arrest our insecurities," he explains. "And I can see that one of the fundamental games that I played—which probably lay behind my being so attracted to the humble life of the lay brother—was the role of playing second fiddle. I played it well, and I played it peacefully. I grew up in a relationship with my brother, who is five years older than I, and I certainly played second fiddle there. [It was] a very serious spiritual defect that I carried right along with me into the monastery . . . that was hidden from everybody and hidden from me.''

In the early years there was but a single instance when Brother Leo's behavior belied his meek contentedness. One day in the cow barns, his novice master Father Columban Hawkins advised the monk to take a livelier interest in the manure he was shoveling. Leo surprised Father Hawkins by replying, sharply, that he was working fast enough, thank you, and that if any greater exertion was expected of him he'd be pleased to pack and leave. The moment of mild willfulness was not repeated, and everyone, including Brother Leo, agrees that he probably would have lived out his days in serene anonymity had he been left to himself, a simple lay brother eager to please his superiors and secure in his humble calling.

His journey toward a decidedly different fate began in 1946 with an inspection tour of nearly all Trappist monasteries throughout Europe and as far away as Palestine. Father Edmund and Leo rated them for their good and bad points and then returned to the United States with a list of criteria they would follow in the search for ideal monastery locations.

They reckoned that in order to meet the Rule's requirement for self-sufficiency, each daughter house, or foundation, would have to be able to generate at least $40,000 a year from its farm enterprises. Brother Leo's first job was to find quality agricultural lands in good climates with reliable growing seasons.

Second, prospective sites had to be reasonably accessible, not too remote and yet secluded enough to assure privacy and quiet. If the experience at Cumberland was not be repeated, Leo would have to gauge as best he could how much Trappist-controlled acreage would be necessary to prevent a shopping mall or drive-in from sprouting on the monks' near horizon.

He and the abbot further agreed to make a location's physical beauty a high priority. Leo was to look for rivers and hills and restful expanses of meadow. Once he found and acquired these pastoral lands, Dom Edmund and Brother Blaise dreamed of spending the money Leo raised to construct splendid monastic edifices that would last for centuries.

Happy as Leo was to accept any demands his abbot put on him, he did not look forward to rejoining the world; he had left Our Lady of the Valley only rarely since 1938, never overnight, and felt any separation from the monastery to be a hardship. Nevertheless, from 1946 onward he was on the road about half the time.

Customarily, he wore a clerical collar and dark street clothes. By all accounts he was boon company and smoothly urbane when he visited contributors and wouldn't refuse a cut of meat or cocktails at their tables. Yet he wore his clothes until they were threadbare—Leo once split the seam on an old pair of trousers—and if his food and lodging weren't free, he spent the least amount possible on a room and consumed cold meats from cans. He appeared comfortable in any situation but was also impervious, or so it seemed, to the temptations of secular life.

"I think what stood out the most," says his fellow monk, Bill Roberts, "was that he was an amazing, almost dual personality. His total devotion was to the contemplative life when he was in the monastery. He would spend *all* his free moments in the chapel and be just the most regular, quiet, unassuming monk you could ever imagine." When he returned from an expedition, agrees Father Keating, "he would disappear into the community. It was easy for him to come back."

Outside the monastery, however, Leo was a different person. Dom Edmund soon realized to his great satisfaction that the monk possessed a potent genius for persuading very rich Catholics to support an ambitious expansion program for an order of exotic ascetics of whom most of the wealthy donors had had no previous knowledge.

"He obviously could handle himself with the bigshots with the greatest of ease and the greatest effectiveness," says Bill Roberts, who as Brother Luke later served as Dom Edmund's personal secretary. "As a money raiser Brother Leo was unbelievable. Absolutely unbelievable."

The business tycoon John Raskob gave money to the Trappists, as did Joseph Kennedy, the father of President John F. Kennedy. Henry Ford II gave money and a new tractor to Our Lady of the Valley. Yet within this golden ring of deep-pocketed benefactors, all fond admirers of Brother Leo, none was more generous with his time and resources than the scion and recently anointed master of another famous Catholic family fortune, J. Peter Grace.

TWO

✦ ✦ ✦

The Autocrat

Monk and magnate first met in the summer of 1946 at the Grace family house in Northeast Harbor, Maine. The year before, at age thirty-two, Peter Grace had succeeded his physically incapacitated father as president of W. R. Grace & Company, the family enterprise his grandfather (and onetime New York City mayor) William Russell Grace established in the nineteenth century as outfitters to sail freighters in the Peruvian seabird guano trade. The company grew aggressively under W.R.'s son, Joseph Peter Grace, and by the 1940s was a formidable industrial conglomerate, with interests ranging from sugar and rubber plantations in South America to shipping, manufacture, and banking.

Young Peter came to the presidency of W. R. Grace with a well-earned reputation for inconsequentiality. As an undergraduate at Yale, where he finished near the bottom of the class of 1936, his consuming interests had been polo, yachting, fast cars, and debutantes. As a Grace company trainee starting out in the mailroom, he was best known for his pranks, such as the obscene limerick Peter composed and transmitted over the corporate teletype. According to those who know of the episode, he was obliged to apologize in person to the Western Union operator his doggerel had offended.

He was resented by Grace senior executives who had been passed over for the presidency, and disliked by the board of directors, which came within a single vote of ousting him. His selection also provoked hostility within the Grace family. Michael Grace, his brother, registered his dissatisfaction by suing Peter, again and again. Over the next forty years, Michael Grace would file thirty-eight separate civil actions against his brother.

Besides the professional and personal choler he has aroused, Peter Grace's habits of mind and speech have sometimes damaged his public image, too. He once told an audience in Dallas that "all" of the Puerto Ricans living in New York City were federal food stamp recipients. His corporate publicist called this gaffe an "oratorical mistake," for which Grace apologized. Another notable lapse came in early 1989 when Grace addressed a black-tie dinner at the Waldorf-Astoria in New York. With John Cardinal O'Connor and President Reagan on hand for the affair, Grace rose to share his views on abortion. "Everybody who's for abortion was at one time themselves a feces," Grace declaimed, according to the *New York Daily News*. "And that includes all of you out there. You were once a feces. So we thank you, Mr. President, and now dinner will be served."

But J. Peter Grace has been intelligent, tenacious, and durable enough to overcome both his enemies and his own shortcomings. He has persevered as chief executive at W. R. Grace into the late 1980s, a record for longevity among American CEOs. He is short and stocky, blunt and emphatic, nearly bald and hard of hearing in his seventies, with a gravelly voice peculiarly accented by an occasional lisp. A crusty corporate autocrat, head of a $5 billion concern, he watches the bottom line and nothing else. "I don't reflect on anything," he says. "I'm so damn busy I hardly ever reflect. How much money can I make reflecting?"

Making money occupies Peter Grace to the exclusion of everything outside his business, except for his family, his commitment to public service (Grace has served on several presidential commissions over the years), and his commitment to Catholic fund-raising. Long a tireless champion of Catholic causes, he has been rewarded for his work with the church's highest honors, including knighthoods of Malta and the Holy Sepulchre. All the Irish Catholic Graces have always given substantially to promote the faith, which was reason enough for Brother Leo to seek them out as soon as he began building monasteries in 1946.

"We just thought that Brother Leo was terrific," Grace remembers. "He had tremendous personality. He was a very, very creative person, an imaginative person, a person who could influence people to do things they never would have thought of doing."

Including J. Peter Grace?

"Including me, absolutely. I mean, he *sold* me. He was a very powerful personality."

In no time the monk was a frequent and welcome guest at Northeast Harbor, as well as at the Grace family estate on Long Island and its New York City residence. He was a favorite with the Grace children and Peter's young wife, Margie, and so charmed their German-born cook, Anna, a Lutheran, that she converted to Catholicism under Leo's spiritual tutelage.

According to Peter Grace, Anna idolized the monk, who understood such doting devotion. Leo's mother adored him, too.

"How I love you for *all* the love you shower on me," Mrs. Gregory wrote her son in a letter typical of their extraordinarily emotive, and voluminous, correspondence. "It makes life so very sweet and full. *You* are my only *attachment*—I have often thought how good God was to *let me have you,* as all else which I love was given to Him."

Leo reciprocated and nourished his ardent mother's "attachment," assuming a lord-like command of her religious life, which was her only life. "She considered him her spiritual director," explains his cousin Nona, herself a former nun of the Catholic Sisters of Social Service. "And she obeyed him. If he said don't worry about something, it was the voice of God. She really obeyed him in every way."

In the monastery Rod Gregory had accepted the name Leo, but he really wished to be called Christopher—"Christ bearer"—one of his confirmation names when he became a Catholic, in 1934. Therefore, when he went into the world, he adopted the name as his own. Peter and Margie Grace later named a son for the monk, calling him Christopher. Not until 1988, says Peter Grace, did he know that Leo's real name was Roderick.

There apparently were no other outright inventions among the few details of his personal life that "Christopher" Gregory shared with Peter and Margie Grace. He told them that he had traveled extensively as a youth, usually alone, and that he had once shipped aboard a freighter to South America as a deckhand. The Graces also knew that the monk's father had been a popular novelist whose forty-odd titles, many of which were made into Hollywood two-reelers, included *The Short Cut, The Joyous Trouble Maker, Man to Man,* and *I Must Ride Alone.* By 1940 riding alone was exactly what Jackson Gregory was doing. He died three years later.

The Graces did get to know Leo's mumsey. "Oh my God, she was beautiful!" Peter Grace recalls. "A saint. Saint-like. My wife, Margie, liked her very much. Mumsey was sort of airy-fairy, you know. I never talked to her at any length.''

Peter Grace, who likewise had never met a Trappist before Brother Leo, became acquainted, through the monk, with a hidden world he hardly guessed existed. He was uniformly impressed by the humility and holiness of Dom Futterer and the other monks at Our Lady of the Valley. But what to make of them, and how to respond to their needs, was another matter. ''They don't *do* anything,'' Grace says of the Cistercians of the Strict Observance. ''They're just up there praying. You have to have a tremendous amount of faith to think that means anything.''

It required a conversation with the much-admired Maryknoll missionary bishop Raymond A. Lane to reveal to Peter Grace the payback in prayer. He asked Bishop Lane what tangible good the contemplatives accomplished and was firmly apprised, he says, that the power of the Trappists' prayers was the very foundation of God's work.

''Here,'' says Grace, ''was the head of the most active missionary order of the church telling me that he was useless unless he had these powerhouses of prayer behind him. That was very influential to me.''

Captivated as well by Christopher Gregory's personality, Grace enthusiastically embraced the Trappist cause. He introduced Brother Leo to other potential contributors and acted as the order's business adviser, putting at their disposal his company's extensive resources, including lawyers and accountants. Given the maze of legal work and contract vetting necessary in the several phases of locating and building the new monasteries, Leo was grateful for the assistance and—at first—was careful to heed Peter Grace's authoritative word on business issues.

Above all, says the monk, he tried to shun attention for his own contribution to the program. ''The monks [at Cumberland] never knew what I was doing,'' he says. ''When I found a good site I'd call the abbot out and he would sometimes come with one or two men. They'd come out and see the thing, and they'd go back without hardly any mention of my name. The abbot was happy that I didn't mind that position, because it protected him. He would've been criticized by members of the community, and even fellow abbots, for the role he allowed me to play—being out of the monastery so much. But I was happy not to be given any of the applause. I didn't want it.

''I built Peter Grace up with that image. I sort of allowed Mr. Grace's name to be the name that would be put forward as the source of all this money, whereas he only supplied—himself—a very, very small amount. It came from a lot of other pockets, and a lot of pockets of people he didn't even know. [Once again,] on a natural level that could be called sort of a humility. Well, it's a game. It's a game I played that kept me out of the limelight.''

In fact, monks such as Father Richard Gans, today one of Leo's closest friends among the Trappists, do remember that the community was generally aware of Leo's importance.''They were aware of the fact that all of the foundations depended upon him as far as getting the finances, finding the places, et cetera,'' says Gans. ''And working with Dom Edmund in that sense.''

All the monks knew of Leo's role, agrees John Cody, another former member of the Trappists. ''As they say in business, he was the power behind the throne. In a monastery, you know, you have the abbot and various others under him; the prior, the subprior. But Brother Leo, he was the abbot's right-hand man.''

However the credit should be divided, Leo's partnership with Grace yielded spectacular results. By 1948 the monk had found an 877-acre dairy farm at

Spencer, Massachusetts, about an hour's drive north-west from Cumberland, which perfectly suited the Trappists as a new location for their mother house. Its purchase price was $90,000. Then he induced his rich friends to ante up the $100,000 needed to rescue a failing daughter house in New Mexico, the only new foundation he did not select himself. Leo also scouted and secured with another $100,000 the site for a convent of Trappestine nuns in Wrentham, Massachusetts. Then, while Brother Blaise Drayton was busy back at Cumberland with his plans for Spencer, Wrentham, and some desperately needed renovation at Our Lady of the Valley, the monk pressed on in a widening arc to investigate locations in Virginia, Colorado, and Texas.

THREE

✚ ✚ ✚

La Señora

Brother Leo attempted on several occasions to find the right combination of climate and geography to build a Trappist monastery in Texas. The well-to-do Texas Catholics he cultivated at Peter Grace's suggestion often urged him to inspect their lands for possible sites and indicated their eagerness to fund a new foundation if he thought a location was suitable. Unfortunately, if the monk found a spot with water and arable soil, it was too remote or too hot or lacked physical beauty. Never could he identify an area that met all his criteria. The Texans nevertheless became reliable donors; the monk later recalled that he did not once fail to come home with a check after a fund-raising trip to the state.

Among the earliest of his benefactors was Judge James R. Dougherty, a wealthy Beeville rancher and lawyer, whom Leo met in 1946. Two years later, after visiting the judge in Beeville, about fifty miles northwest of Corpus Christi, the monk roamed farther south, to the coastal plain of south Texas, the region known as the Wild Horse Desert to Captain Mifflin Kenedy and other nineteenth-century pioneers and as the Desert of the Dead to the Mexicans, who were glad to sell their ancient land-grant holdings in the godforsaken region to the gringos.

The cavalry officer Phil Sheridan, who crossed the Wild Horse in 1847 in General Zachary Taylor's Mexican War command, is said to have compared the land unfavorably with hell. Sheridan, according to tradition, declared that if he owned both, he would lease out the Wild Horse Desert and live in hell.

But if the territory north of the Rio Grande and south of the Nueces (from the Spanish word for "nuts") rivers was a raw wilderness that only a lizard could love, it was nonetheless an attractive investment opportunity for entrepreneurs like Kenedy and his young partner, Richard King. The pair had grown rich on the Rio Grande hauling troops and ordnance for the U.S. Army in the 1850s, then contraband and Confederate cotton during the Civil War. Even before the conflict's close, they began to buy up huge tracts of the wasteland to the north for pennies an acre.

Their plan, apparently, was twofold. First, Kenedy and King foresaw that a rail link from Corpus Christi to the border would eventually supplant riverboats as the main shipping line in the region. It made sense to acquire the land through which the railroad would one day be built.

Second, Kenedy and King wanted to produce a commodity—beef—for the postwar markets of the Midwest and the Northeast. Their idea was to found vast cattle empires on the dry plain along the coast, and they succeeded on a vast scale. The partners worked together to build the million-acre King Ranch, and then Mifflin bought a 100,000-acre tract called Los Laureles to the northeast. He sold the property to a syndicate of Scottish investors for $1.1 million in the late 1870s and reinvested his profits in the 400,000 acres of La Parra. Established side by side, La Parra and the King Ranch were the two largest ranches in Texas, their combined size being half again that of Long Island.

Nearly a century later, Brother Leo traveled the first

paved highway into the isolated cattle kingdoms, the recently completed State Route 77. Until the 1940s the Kenedys, the Kings, and then the Klebergs had successfully fought any public access into their lands except for the railroad they had helped build. Driving south, the monk passed Kingsville in Kleberg County and then came into Kenedy County (population 500) whose only settlement and county seat, Sarita, stood along Route 77 about sixty miles southwest of Corpus Christi, and a hundred miles north of his destination, Brownsville, on the Mexican border.

Leo's companion that day was the businessman Robert Harriss, a native-born Texan who lived in New York and was then a key political backer of General Douglas MacArthur. When the road sign for Sarita came into view, Harriss explained to the monk how the tiny town (originally a corral and rail depot) was named for Mifflin Kenedy's granddaughter, Sarita Kenedy East, whose only brother, Johnny, recently had taken ill and died while on a visit to the family of his wife, Elena, in Saltillo, Mexico.

Harriss suggested that a condolence call to his friends Mrs. East and her sister-in-law would be appropriate. So the two turned left when they reached Sarita and drove straight on for six more miles past mesquite and brush and the occasional Santa Gertrudis steer, maroon boxcar-shaped brutes that now grazed where Captain Kenedy's vaqueros once wrangled half-wild longhorns. La Parra had several ranch houses, but the visitors' destination was the Headquarters, a Spanish-style fortress squatting on a gentle rise, thirty-seven feet above sea level, the highest elevation in Kenedy County.

The Headquarters faced eastward toward the old ranch water-freight depot on Baffin Bay, a shallow inlet of the Gulf of Mexico three miles distant. Leo and Bob Harriss approached from the west and pulled into a palm-lined, semicircular drive that curved by a small concrete platform topped with a brass bell salvaged from one of Mifflin Kenedy's old Rio Grande steamers. The lovingly preserved relic stood opposite the rear entrance to the Headquarters, where the callers presented themselves to Mrs. East's Mexican maid, Sara Curiel.

"La Señora East no está aqui," she informed them from behind a screen door. Then the maid gave a shy gesture, directing Leo and Harriss around the side of the big house. *"La señora está en el cementerio con la Señora Kenedy."*

As he crossed the grounds on foot, Leo would have seen Mrs. Kenedy's residence, Mifflin Kenedy's original clapboard ranch house, standing amid somber oaks and dark firs in the distance. To the monk's left were the Headquarters garages, where Sarita kept her Cadillacs and Elena her Packards.

At nearer range Leo made note of La Parra's simple, white-stucco and tile-roofed chapel. Adjacent to the chapel was the less restrained stone prayer grotto that Marie Stella Kenedy, Sarita's mother, had had built on the model of the holy shrine at Lourdes, in France. Between the outdoor grotto altar decorated with marble angels and the chapel was the fenced cemetery, where at last he saw the two black-clad widows kneeling motionless over Johnny Kenedy's grave, quietly clutching their rosaries.

Elena rose and said hello to Bob Harriss with her customary stiff formality. Sarita, by far the warmer of the two women, ended her prayer and then glanced up toward the monk, greeting him with a small, sad smile.

Catholic clergyman were seen as commonly as cowboys at La Parra. Leo, however, was an entirely novel experience for Mrs. East. She had encountered Catholic monks before, especially Franciscan and Benedictine fathers whose Texas monasteries she helped to support. But Sarita, like Peter Grace, had never met a

Trappist lay brother or any cleric who seemed to breathe God as the young Trappist did.

As her sister-in-law would retell the moment, Mrs. East remembered the hour and, according to the rules of ranch hospitality, insisted that Bob Harriss and Brother Leo stay for lunch. The fare, since it was deer season in south Texas, would have been a venison roast. Mrs. East was an avid hunter, a dead shot with pistol or rifle, and most likely had bagged the noon meal herself.

She led her guests back through her formal palm groves to the Headquarters, which her father, Don Gregorio, had begun building in 1917 (the year Leo was born) on the site of his father's steamboat-shaped ranch house. This building, now Elena's house, was dragged away, intact, by harnessed teams of hundreds of mules. Then the progressive John Gregory Kenedy engineered every state-of-the-art contraption and system available into what he envisioned would be his dream manor on the prairie.

What John Gregory Kenedy achieved was thick-walled and imposing from a distance, a great hacienda cooled in the summer by an ingenious, if primitive, air-conditioning system using water from a nearby artesian flow. A second innovation required a water tower. Kenedy embedded a grid of piping inside the Headquarters's walls and used the weight of the water in its tower to create a suction within the network. On cleaning days maids went from outlet to outlet along the pipe system, attaching to it short hoses that functioned as vacuum cleaners for each area of the house.

The tower atop the Headquarters was fitted with a Gatling gun, an effective defense against Mexican bandits, who were a threat to the ranch well into Sarita's teens. Behind a door in a corner of his first-floor office, Kenedy installed a huge safe with a trap in it opening down into the basement. Should the need arise, the family could climb through the steel box, close its heavy door, and then step downstairs to a tunnel that connected the main house with a fortified and provisioned outbuilding-bunker about a hundred yards away.

Expensive, impressive, and well built as it was, no one in the family ever felt comfortable in the new Headquarters. There was something institutional and deadening about its interior that Marie Stella Turcotte Kenedy unsuccessfully sought to mitigate with Persian rugs, Victorian settees, and Belle Epoque French figurines. The family's taste for overwrought religious oils and mounted game heads did nothing to enhance the Headquarters's livability, either. Family members felt they were inhabiting a museum or a mausoleum. And Don Gregorio's daughter, Sarita, had spent the better part of the last thirty years absorbing this melancholy.

Born September 19, 1889, in Corpus Christi, and baptized Sara Josephine Kenedy a month later, Sarita attended the Incarnate World Academy, in Corpus Christi, and various other parochial boarding schools before spending a term or two at H. Sophie Newcomb Memorial College, in New Orleans. Round-ups, hunting, fishing, and campfires, however, appealed to her more than book learning and New Orleans society, so Sarita quit college and came home to La Parra.

In 1910, at the Corpus Christi cathedral, she married Arthur L. East, one of six brothers in a Kingsville ranching and horse-trading family. Henrietta Kleberg, Richard King's granddaughter, was Sarita's maid of honor. Her marriage certificate was witnessed by her cousin Stella Turcotte and Lee Lytton of Fort Worth, Stella's future husband.

Sarita was a sturdy, vivacious young wife who might have borne Arthur the large family they expected to raise had they not both contracted undulant fever in the first years of their marriage. Sarita's brother, Johnny (who called her Sally), likewise was incapable of producing heirs; in 1913, just after his marriage to Sarita's former classmate Elena Seuss of Saltillo, Johnny was left sterile by a case of the mumps.

The sudden realization that the Kenedy line was to be extinguished in its third generation cast a permanent pall over La Parra. Don Gregorio bore it stoically, but it wasn't long thereafter that he began to fail perceptibly from the diabetes that finally killed him in 1932. By then Marie Stella Kenedy, also a diabetic, was herself reduced to a semi-invalid state by the disease, and she spent the last eight years of her life in dolorous seclusion.

During the elder Kenedys' long decline their son, Johnny, himself descended further into the antic dissolution that had been his parents' vexation since his teens. An example of his boyhood prodigality occurred when, as an undergraduate at Texas A&M, in College Station, Sarita's brother read in a magazine of the polygamy among Mormons in Utah. Mistaking a religion-based practice for promiscuity, he and a pal took a train out to Salt Lake City to sample this imagined lotus land of unfettered carnality. His father had to dispatch the Pinkertons to retrieve the young man.

With time Johnny became an episodic, not a linear, drunk, who looked forward each year with keen anticipation to his roistering summer benders with the King Ranch boss Bob Kleberg and their good friend and fellow rancher Major Tom Armstrong. The major would later marry Kleberg's sister—and Sarita's best friend—Henrietta.

During some years Johnny and his drinking buddies flew off for their carousals. One well-remembered season they took their guns to Washington, D.C., and spent an evening shooting out street lamps around Capitol Hill. More often, however, the three packed their customized ranch hunting vehicles with food and liquor and tore away across their combined acreage for weeks-long rampages. Burly and wild and covered with a heavy mat of body hair, Johnny loved to wrestle with his friends. As they went winging over the prairie, he would call for stops at stands of sharp-edged bear grass and challenge the other two to strip and grapple with him. For Kleberg and Armstrong, it was the drunker the better for these free-for-alls. Johnny Kenedy claimed that because of his thick body hair he couldn't feel the slicing, stabbing shrub leaves at all.

Sarita treated her brother's excesses with sisterly indulgence. The blood bond between these last two Kenedys was strong. It was enough for her that Johnny was happy in his way. After all, it wasn't as if he had to set an example for anyone.

Little is remembered about her husband, Arthur, a Protestant whose deathbed conversion to Catholicism, say family members, was perfunctory. "Arthur," Bob Kleberg later said of his neighbor, "wasn't really a person who particularly liked to mix. Actually, he was a very entertaining, fine fellow to be around. He had a very good sense of humor, very knowledgeable on many things, and we were great friends. But he didn't particularly like to, just say, be around people, and Sarita was just the opposite."

According to Sarita's relatives on her mother's side, the Turcottes, Mrs. East carried her husband on the La Parra payroll as an employee. Others recollect that Arthur was only an intermittent presence at the Headquarters, preferring to spend most of his time by himself at his wife's Hebbronville ranch, called San Pablo, which adjoined a property owned by his nephew Tom East, Jr.

Sarita's preoccupation was with La Parra and its management. She was particularly proud of her Santa Gertrudis cattle—a breed developed by the Klebergs. The work consumed her attention and, to an extent, crowded out her sorrows. Yet she slowly became captive to her memories and to her liquor bottles.

Sarita was typically reticent around strangers, but her shyness quickly melted away in Leo's company. The monk put her at her ease. He was tactful, Elena Kenedy would remember, and an attentive listener who seemed eagerly interested in Sarita's favorite topic of conversation—tales out of the colorful, and often violent, Kenedy family past.

As the group walked into the Headquarters, Sarita pointed out her grandfather Mifflin's dour, gimlet-eyed likeness hanging in the hallway between her formal dining room and main parlor. She retold how Captain Kenedy, a Pennsylvanian, had come to the Rio Grande in the late 1840s and, supposedly, had fallen deliriously in love with Sarita's grandmother, the aristocratic Petra Vela de Vidal, daughter of a Mexican governor and, inconveniently, married at the time to a Spanish army officer. Petra Vela had borne Lieutenant Luis Vidal five children. She rebuffed Mifflin's advances for these reasons, but Captain Kenedy, according to legend, obviated them by arranging for her husband's murder.

Mifflin installed his new wife in a house on Elizabeth Street in Brownsville, where she bore six more children, bringing the combined number of their offspring to eleven. It was the males in both sets of children who would be Mifflin Kenedy's lifelong heartache. Adrian Vidal, for example, born in 1843, joined and deserted the Confederate army during the Civil War and then led a band of marauders who terrorized the Anglo population of south Texas. Shouting, *"¡Muerte a los Americanos!"* Vidal's raiders would ride into border towns and onto remote ranches, where they killed every hated gringo they could find. These victims included a number of his stepfather's friends and business associates. Then Adrian joined the Union army, deserted again, and entered Emperor Maximilian's imperial Mexican armed forces. Once again he deserted and was put to death by a firing squad in 1865.

Another of Sarita's lunchtime yarns was the story of her rambunctious uncle James Kenedy, known as Spike. He was accused in October of 1878 of the gunshot murder of a Dodge City actress named Dora Hand, a.k.a. Fannie Keenan, who was the Dodge City mayor "Dog" Kelly's fiancée. Spike was tracked down and wounded by a celebrity posse led by Wyatt Earp and Bat Masterson. Sarita's uncle eluded the noose for this crime (thanks, probably, to Mifflin's discreet application of a bribe) but died in December of 1884, at age twenty-nine, of a fever at La Parra while under investigation for another killing.

Then there was uncle Tom, Mifflin's oldest son. In 1888, in the course of running as a candidate for sheriff of Brownsville, the thirty-four-year-old Tom Kenedy began courting Elvira Maria Esparsa, whose estranged husband, José, was a Brownsville deputy. According to contemporary sources, Tom's opponent in the sheriff's race, the incumbent Santiago Brito, inflamed the high-strung José Esparsa against Kenedy, hoping to provoke bloodshed. The ploy worked. On the night of April 15, 1888, Tom Kenedy's thirty-fifth birthday, Esparsa gunned him down from an ambush on a Brownsville pier.

Frank Yturria, a Brownsville businessman who traces his family back to the early days on the border, says the story he has always heard is that Deputy Esparsa fled into Mexico, where two of Mifflin's stepgrandsons, Frank and George Putegnat, found the deputy, killed him in a gunfight, and brought Esparsa's head back in a sack for the captain. As for Sheriff Brito, he was assassinated four years later. "To this day," explains Yturria, "no one knows exactly who ordered Brito's assassination. But the guy everyone *knew* did it was Mifflin Kenedy's *pistolero* [or gunsel], Herculano Berber."

Mifflin's granddaughter recounted such stories with raucous good humor. She was surpassingly proud of her heritage, including her Hispanic ancestry. But happy as she was to entertain her luncheon guests with anecdotes from her family's legendary past, she was also intensely curious about the monk.

She questioned Leo at length, Elena would recall, about the Trappists and about his own background. It delighted Mrs. East to learn that Leo,too, had inherited Spanish blood via his paternal grandmother—and that his grandfather Gregory had been as adamantly pro-South during the Civil War as was Captain Kenedy. Sarita set great store by lineage, and the monk's endeared him to her. Later, Leo would tell attorneys that Sarita wondered whether she and he might somehow be distantly related.

For his part, Leo naturally also dwelt in some detail on his order and his mission. Sitting near him at the luncheon table, Mrs. East closely followed his descriptions of the hidden life inside the cloister and the monks' pursuit of sanctification through prayer. Elena noticed Sarita's absorption and sensed that a synthesis of thought and emotion had been struck in her sister-in-law. The two women agreed that the monk was very charming.

Sarita pledged a thousand dollars to the Trappists after the meal and said good-bye to Brother Leo with regret that their chance encounter had been so brief. She and Elena Kenedy extracted his promise to return, but the women thought it unlikely that they would see the monk again, if ever, anytime soon. Mrs. East was partially correct in this expectation; Christopher Gregory would be seen seldom at La Parra over the next few years. But most everything else Sarita then believed about the future and her new friend the monk proved wholly mistaken.

FOUR

✛ ✛ ✛

Fire and Crash

The stresses of overpopulation weren't the only problems to confront the community of Our Lady of the Valley in the late 1940s. In December of 1946, just months after Brother Leo went out into the world, a fire devoured most of the monastery's winter food stores, leaving the monks to subsist until spring mainly on donated surplus potatoes. The community saw this reversal as God's will, but no monk among them was so prideful as to believe he could decipher the Lord's message to the Trappists, if there was one.

Then, at about 9:45 on the night of March 21, 1950, Jerome R. Speeder, forty-six, of Baltimore was nodding off in his second-floor room within Our Lady of the Valley's wooden guesthouse when he was startled awake by the smell of smoke. Speeder jumped up and ran to the stairwell, where he saw flames licking up from the first-floor pantry. Fourteen other retreatants were in the guesthouse that night, and sixty or so monks dozed above them on the third floor. Had Jerome Speeder not sounded the alarm when he did, firemen later opined, all seventy-five men might have perished.

As it was, the guests were barely able to negotiate the flaming staircase to safety, and many of the monks were forced to jump twenty feet down from their dormitory to escape the blaze, which soon engulfed the entire guesthouse. "They were caught like rats in a trap," Dom Futterer told a newspaper reporter the next day. "But somehow they did get out."

The monks fought a futile battle with the fire through the night. It was cold, with snow on the ground, and their rickety pumps gave out almost immediately. When fire companies from ten local stations responded to the alarm, they found that the monastery hydrants were dry. By eleven o'clock, the fire had spread to the granite-walled abbey church, and by morning it and the guesthouse were both in smoldering ruins. Neither structure could be saved. And though most of the rest of the abbey still stood, fire and smoke damage to Our Lady of the Valley rendered it no longer habitable as a monastery.

At first light, the members of the community gave thanks to God that not one of their number was killed, or even seriously injured, in the conflagration. This they counted as a miracle, or at least a blessing. But the fire was a devastating setback for Dom Futterer's expansion program. The Trappists carried minimal insurance on their abbey, and most of the money that Brother Leo had raised had already been spent on the new sites at Spencer, in Massachusetts, and elsewhere.

He and Peter Grace were making wonderful progress. Cumberland's first daughter house, near Pecos, New Mexico, was operating with thirty-five fathers and brothers, led there in 1948 by Columban Hawkins, Leo's former novice master. But work on the dairy farm at Spencer was just beginning, and it would take at least six months to make the cow barns there habitable.

Moreover, the tide of new vocations had continued to rise. Despite the opening of the New Mexico foundation, Cumberland's population of monks had again reached 140, and now they were all homeless. With few options available to him, Dom Futterer sent most of the men to temporary shelter at Portsmouth Priory. Rhode Island's governor at the time, John Pastore, offered the Trappists an abandoned Civilian Conservation Corps camp. The community accepted and renamed the drafty barracks Our Lady of Refuge. Before Spencer was ready to receive them that autumn, twelve of the monks developed tuberculosis.

Then the traumatized community was shaken by another near catastrophe. According to Peter Grace, it was Brother Leo's suggestion in the autumn of 1951 to rent a Lockheed Lodestar passenger plane in Hot Springs, Virginia, for an aerial tour of the Shenandoah Valley, where the monk, working with the Charlottesville real estate broker William Stevens, had identified several potential monastery sites. Grace, his wife, Margie, and three of their children came along, together with Brother Leo, two fathers from Cumberland, Dom Futterer, and Dom Gabriel Sortais from France, the Trappists' new abbot general.

Grace says that it was against his usual, better judgment to hazard his and his family's lives in a takeoff in a heavily loaded aircraft from the short mountaintop airstrip. Only with great hesitancy, he says, did he strap himself and his family into the lumbering plane, which, just as its wheels cleared the runway, was caught in a furious crosswind.

"One guy was pulling this way, and the other guy was pulling that way," Grace remembers. "The plane was bumping all over the place."

By Grace's estimate the Lodestar was skimming along at about one hundred miles an hour as they nearly smashed into a pile of oil drums. "Then we started hitting trees, see? Then he jams it up again. He was going to try to take off after hitting a tree! Finally, fortunately, we hit one big tree and we landed in a cow pasture with cows dodging cows. The plane broke in half, and I was sitting out in the sun in my chair!''

Brother Leo, the first in the group to regain his senses, scrambled back into the wreckage to rescue the Graces' youngest boy. Otherwise, all but Dom Futterer came through the crash with no permanent physical trauma. He was found still strapped in his seat, stiff and in shock.

Quickly, Leo found a bystander with a hip flask who contributed a swallow or two of spirits to Dom Edmund's recovery. Then the abbot was taken by ambulance to the hospital, where doctors found that he had sustained several broken ribs. Later, a Boston neurologist examined Futterer and concluded that he had also suffered a seizure during the plane wreck, causing some minimal brain damage. "So his judgment may have been impaired," says Father Thomas Keating. "I know I noticed a change over the years. I wouldn't exactly say a lack of judgment—more imprecision and lack of vigor. Exhaustion. He didn't sleep well, and he took a lot of sleeping pills."

✝ ✝ ✝

FIVE

The Simple Life

Dom Edmund's diminished capacities did not dim his enthusiasm for the expansion project, now made more urgent by the loss of the mother house at Cumberland, or for Brother Leo's superlative performance in his key role. The monk was a Midas. In Virginia he located and acquired a $300,000 cattle ranch on a picturesque bend of the Shenandoah River near Berryville, in the northwest portion of the state.

Today, Brother Leo looks back at his accomplishments with satisfaction. "I always enjoyed doing things," he says. "It's fun to create something. It was satisfying to locate those monasteries, to find them, to get the money for them, to set them up. I must confess that I enjoyed that work."

At the time, however, many of his fellow monks recall, Leo petitioned the abbot again and again to be relieved of his duties. "Brother Leo," says Bill Roberts, the former Brother Luke, "kept saying how eager he was to come back and forget all this stuff. I really think that most of the time he meant it. He didn't enter the monastery to do all this gallivanting. He kept insisting he was doing it just because of obedience, because his abbot told him to do it."

The duality Brother Luke speaks of in Leo's nature seems to have become more pronounced as time passed. On the one hand, he told Dom Edmund that he "loathed" being away from the monastery and asked to be brought back, permanently, as the cobbler at St. Joseph's, the new mother house at Spencer. On the other hand, his creativity as impresario of the expansion program apparently got the better of him from time to time. "Once," Father Raphael Simon, the psychiatrist, remembers, "he showed up with news of an airplane! It was crated in boxes, he said, and was ready to be shipped. The abbot said to him, 'Get rid of that immediately!' Another time, he put in a bid for a locomotive from war surplus. He had big ideas."

Abbot Futterer chose to take Leo's request to become the monastery shoemaker as an opportunity to further challenge the monk's resourcefulness. He agreed to the idea—once Leo raised the cash to complete the new abbey's construction. "You may have the job," is how Leo remembers Futterer putting it, "but it will cost you a million dollars."

The monk earned his cobbler's tools by raising not $1 million but $2 million for his abbot's building budget. Yet rather than being allowed to finally disappear again into the cloister, he was sent out in search of another site. Near Aspen, Colorado, Leo found a spectacular location for which he raised an additional $300,000. St. Benedict's at Snowmass, as it would be called, brought to four the number of new foundations the monk had started for the Cistercians by the mid-1950s. In all, he had raised about $5 million.

In retrospect, says Brother Leo, he may have succeeded *too* well. There is a restricted pool of talent in any monastery, Leo explains, capable and energetic men who keep the community running smoothly. Because these were the same monks who were sent out as pioneers to the daughter houses, strains began to show at the new mother house at Spencer, and criticisms of Dom Edmund were heard. "They weren't," he says, "criticizing the way the foundations were being run; they were criticizing what was happening to the community at home. And I can see their point. There should have been a longer interval between foundations.''

The Spencer community's dissatisfactions with the abbot's priorities would later turn into questions about his sexual orientation—a perhaps deliberate misreading by some of the monks of Dom Edmund's affectionate physicality. He did grasp his ''children'' in lengthy embraces and sometimes kissed the monks on their lips. Although he would strenuously deny that he was homosexual, overt or otherwise, the rumors and complaints to the abbot general in Rome ultimately led to Futterer's forced resignation.

Dom Edmund apparently never sensed the restiveness in his family of monks, or appreciated its causes. Instead of slowing the expansion's pace to allow time for the community to assimilate so many changes, he decided to accelerate the program with another, even more momentous, commitment.

Pope Pius XII, Eugenio Pacelli, had in the early 1950s directed his church to address its eroding influence in Latin America, home to the greatest numbers of Catholics in the world. The pope worried that the universal church was losing ground in Latin America to the spread of Marxist ideology, as well as to the competing religious doctrines of Protestantism. Every Catholic parish, diocese, and order was expected to respond to the perceived threat to the faith, which gave Dom Futterer an inspiration. There was, at the time, not a single Trappist monastery south of Mexico, and there had never been a permanent Trappist foundation on the South American continent. Father Edmund decided that Leo was just the man to correct this void.

J. Peter Grace, in fact, had first encouraged the idea in 1946. Much of the Grace corporation business still was centered in South America at that time, meaning that he could provide the Cistercians of the Strict Observance with extensive assistance, including introductions to wealthy Latin-American Roman Catholics who might be persuaded to support Trappist monasteries in their countries. At Grace's urging and in his company, Brother Leo made an initial scouting trip south of the equator early in the expansion program.

Latin America presented a formidable challenge to the monk. Although overwhelmingly Catholic, it was physically remote. Outside its main cities—which themselves were unsuitable as sites for Trappist foundations—transportation by any means except aircraft was slow. Telephone service was primitive and unreliable. The mail routinely did not go through. The political situation in most Latin-American countries was unstable. And, for Leo, there was the further disadvantage that he did not speak the local language, either Spanish or Portuguese.

The continent was also plagued with poverty, its capitals and commercial centers girded by abysmal slums. Brother Leo, as usual, moved in the best society wherever he went, but he was not blind to the grim disparity between the privileged lives of Latin aristocrats and the destitution of their less fortunate countrymen. He saw urban barrios as fertile gardens for the cultivation of godless communism and was moved by the message of the activist Catholic clergy in Latin America, who were beginning to argue for the economic as well as the spiritual salvation of the poor. They showed the monk how even a little money could do a lot of practical good, and Leo could easily envision the many things that might be done with a *lot* of money.

Building grand and expensive monasteries was not among them.

Since the start of construction at Spencer, Leo had been appalled at the costs involved and the excess, as he saw it, of Brother Blaise Drayton's tastes. "Brother Leo was a traditionalist," says Bill Roberts. "He had a conservative approach toward monastic life. Brother Blaise had an artistic flair, a *tremendous* artistic flair. He furnished Spencer with a lot of antiques and things that Brother Leo had no use for at all. Brother Leo didn't like that approach. He thought it was becoming too arty. So Brother Blaise and Brother Leo, who did admire each other, did not see eye to eye on that. They argued a lot.''

Leo readily concedes these differences with Blaise and with Dom Futterer. ''Abbot General Sortais made a very nice distinction about Spencer,'' relates the monk, ''when he said, 'Spencer has the style of simplicity, not simplicity of style.' And I don't think Dom Edmund ever saw that point. I think he was blind on that point. [There were] some very painful disagreements that he and I had from time to time over the architecture.

''I don't know how to describe Brother Blaise's taste. But it's expensive, and Dom Edmund and I nearly came to blows—don't take that literally. . . . We certainly had very serious arguments over the costs of construction.''

One of these tiffs was sparked by Leo's discovery of the abbot and Brother Blaise's plans for a guesthouse at Spencer. So bothered by the proposed structure's opulent interior was the monk that he refused to raise a nickel toward its completion. Abbot Futterer, in turn, was so hurt by Child Leo's outburst against his father that he froze the monk out of his inner circle for a time, treating Leo to a cold silence until Leo relented and agreed to provide the cash to complete the guesthouse as designed.

The disagreement was quietly papered over. But except for visits to see his mother, Lotus, who had been provided a cottage at the monastery at Margie Grace's expense, Leo did not enjoy his returns to the mother house. He harbored a principled, and personal, distaste for what his efforts had wrought.

SIX

✛ ✛ ✛

Family Matters

Sarita Kenedy East always yearned to travel. In her girlhood, she had seen a little of the United States, mostly in her parents' company, either on summer resort vacations in the West to escape the south Texas heat or with Don Gregorio and Marie Stella on their journeys to spas and sanatoriums, where the elder Kenedys chased the chimera of a diabetes cure.

Her homebody husband, Arthur, rarely accompanied Sarita on these emotionally trying expeditions and refused to consider much travel at all during their thirty-four years of marriage. Only after the death of her brother, Johnny, in 1948—and before the onset of the drought four years later—did Sarita begin to satisfy her wanderlust. She took two overseas excursions, one a pilgrimage to Rome in a tour group led by Francis Cardinal Spellman of New York, a personal acquaintance.

Back in Texas, where Sarita had to stick close to La Parra to guide the great ranch through the brutal, years-long drought, her one organizational affiliation of note was membership in the Equestrian Order of the Holy Sepulchre, an exclusive society of prominent Catholic women. Bishop Mariano Garriga arranged for the church to convey the honor on both Sarita and Elena Kenedy, just as the local bishops before him had seen to it that Mrs. East's father, mother, and brother similarly were decorated by the church for their charity. The prelates of the diocese of Corpus Christi (which then extended all the way to Brownsville, near the mouth of the Rio Grande), spared no effort to protect, preserve, and promote their Kenedy family "patrimony."

The garrulous Bishop Garriga often came to La Parra for dinner, to hunt deer or to take weekend vacations at the ranch beach house on Baffin Bay, near the water-freight landing. He was also brought down to say mass in Marie Stella's stucco chapel on important anniversaries, which usually were death commemorations. Johnny Kenedy's annual rites, held each November 26, were the most solemn of all.

Sarita's confessor, the Irish-born Father Dwan, was an Oblate of Mary Immaculate, a French order of missionary priests who arrived in south Texas in the mid-nineteenth century. Tough and incredibly resilient frontiersmen, known in their day as the "Cavalry of Christ on the Rio Grande," these itinerant padres rode horseback over the region, braving ambush murder by Comanches and bandits as they visited ranches such as La Parra to baptize, marry, and bury the faithful.

The Oblate missionaries always were warmly received by Sarita's mother, a woman of some refinement, who looked forward to the padres' visits as a chance not only for confession and mass but also for conversation, in French, about something besides cattle and the weather. Marie Stella Turcotte Kenedy generously supported the Oblates, as would Sarita, who agreed with her mother after Don Gregorio's death that the Headquarters house, plus the lands adjacent to it, should one day be donated to the order. In 1948 Mrs. East incorporated that wish into her will.

Father John F. Dwan, O.M.I., was assigned to Our Lady of Guadalupe Church in Sarita at Mrs. East's request. He was a gentle and sweet-tempered priest who lived no better than a hermit on the ranch property and was possessed of no ambition except to serve his little flock of mostly Spanish-speaking parishioners, Sarita's ranch employees. Mrs.East, these vaqueros and their families later related, endeavored time and again to provide Father Dwan with creature comforts. She gave the padre hundreds of dollars a year, money that she urged the priest to spend on himself. Usually, Father Dwan politely refused the offerings. When Sarita insisted he accept her checks, the priest did so and then endorsed them over to his Oblate superiors. Father Dwan, to Mrs. East and everyone else in Kenedy County, was the model of the truly holy padre.

Outside her church and her community, Sarita made relatively modest annual donations to a wide range of secular causes. In 1956, for example, these included the Defenders of the Furbearers ($25), the March of Dimes ($100), the National Braille Press ($10), the Red Cross ($200), and the Save-the-Redwoods League ($10).

Nothing, however, gave Mrs. East more personal pleasure than helping the poor, whose needs easily aroused her sympathies. Her friend Henrietta Kleberg Armstrong would recall traveling in Mexico with her and how the widow could never refuse the outstretched hand of a beggar. Luis Ruano, Elena Kenedy's Guatemalan-born chauffeur, remembers a typical incident that occurred one Saturday in 1956 when he drove Mrs. East into Kingsville on errands.

Sarita was approached in the Kleberg Bank parking lot by a shabby-looking cowboy, who introduced himself and asked for a job. The vaquero explained that he was broke and had a sick wife, for whose medical care he owed the local hospital $200.

Ruano sized up the cowboy as a rounder and a con

man, but Mrs. East would hear none of it. She handed the stranger $200 in cash from her purse and told him he could report for work at La Parra following mass the next day.

"We never saw him again," says Luis Ruano. "But the lady, she kept asking me once in a while, 'Have you seen him? That poor man! He needed that money.' "

Most of Sarita's nearly three hundred employees lived on the ranch, as had many of their parents and grandparents before them. All were provided their houses, medical care, and beef as part of their compensation. Every year, each vaquero was issued new leather gloves and a coat. Ammunition was free and always fresh.

Everything else the *patrona* thought her ranch employees needed, they could buy, on credit, at the ranch commissary in Sarita. None owned an automobile, nor would it have made sense to if they could afford one. The only gasoline available in Kenedy County until late in the 1960s was used to fuel ranch machinery, an effective way to restrict employee mobility, as well as to discourage public traffic through the ranch kingdoms. At election time, according to custom, the Mexicans in Kenedy County all voted the straight Democratic slate as preapproved by the ranchers and political bosses—another means of maintaining the status quo.

Legally, Mrs. East and Mrs. Kenedy were La Parra's co-owners; Sarita leased Elena's half of the ranch as she had when it was Johnny's share, inherited equally from their parents. But Sarita was La Parra's unquestioned boss, a situation that rankled Johnny's status-conscious widow, who chafed, as well, at her secondary station as Johnny's foreign-born widow, an outsider in the closed society of the Kenedys, Klebergs, and Armstrongs. Sarita had no patience with

Elena's caste envy; in fact, she exacerbated it by permitting her sister-in-law only a few-thousand-acre miniranch to operate as her own, not much more than a sandbox by south Texas standards, large enough to sustain about six hundred cattle. As a result, Elena bore Sarita a cordial enmity. She called her "bossy."

The rest of Sarita's remaining family was divided into three groups: the Turcottes, the Easts, and the relatives later known collectively as the "Mexican heirs," the scores of individuals who claimed kinship to Sarita by virtue of descent from her grandmother Petra Vela's first marriage, to Luis Vidal.

The Turcottes were all descended from Marie Stella Kenedy's two brothers, Louis Arnaud and Willie, who, with a third brother, the bachelor George, accompanied their sister from New Orleans to the wilds of south Texas. Marie Stella often conversed with her siblings (and itinerant Oblates) in French, which she later taught to both her children.

Sarita's uncle Louis Arnaud and aunt Marie had four children. Their son Joseph, later a foreman at La Parra, was a cash beneficiary in Mrs. East's will. Uncle Willie and Aunt Amilie Turcotte were the parents of Sarita's cousins Andy, Stella, and Louis Edgar, who bore an uncanny physical resemblance to his uncle—Don Gregorio.

The family records preserved in the big safe at the Headquarters make little mention of Sarita's cousin Andy Turcotte, except to indicate that he, like all the cousins, was educated at John Gregory Kenedy's expense and that he had once nearly succeeded in committing suicide. His son, Andy, Jr., became a mortician in Kingsville.

Cousin Stella Turcotte married the rancher Lee Lytton of Fort Worth and bore two sons by him, Lee, Jr., and Arthur. Lee Lytton, Sr., died in 1952. His widow then moved into the Headquarters to live with Sarita.

Stella Turcotte Lytton, according to the terms of Sarita's 1948 will, was to inherit half of her portion of La Parra, about 100,000 acres together with mineral rights.

Her mild-mannered son, Lee Lytton, Jr.—later to fire the first legal salvo against Brother Leo and the monk's alleged coconspirator, J. Peter Grace—was a lawyer, Mrs. East's personal secretary, and the elected judge of Kenedy County. Lee Lytton lived with his wife, Mary Elizabeth, and their three children, Savita, Lee III, and Molly, in the town of Sarita.

The remainder of Mrs. East's portion of La Parra, another 100,000 acres and mineral rights, was left to her cousin Louis Edgar Turcotte, Don Gregorio's favorite nephew, whom he treated like a son. As a youngster, Louis Edgar had been as responsible and trustworthy as Johnny Kenedy was incorrigible. Later he gradually assumed many of Johnny's responsibilities at the ranch. Following the don's death, in 1932, Louis Edgar became second in management authority at La Parra only to Sarita.

He and his wife, Elizabeth, raised five strapping sons—Louis Edgar, Jr., Pat, Bobby, Jack, and Joe Turcotte—boys whom Sarita regarded as her nephews. They were an unruly lot, avatars of Mrs. East's wild uncles. "They'd have what they called a family meeting," remembers Frank Nesbitt of Corpus Christi, the Turcotte boys' later attorney. "And they always had a keg of beer. Well, they'd all get drunker than a coot, and before it wound up there'd always be three or four of 'em fist-fightin' with each other.

"At a roundup one time, Jack and Louis Edgar got into it and Jack whipped the hell out of Louis Edgar. Sarita called Jack up and said, 'Look, we don't do that. Not in front of the men. If you're gonna whip your brother, you take him off someplace else.' "

All five Turcotte brothers worked for Mrs. East at

La Parra at one time or another. Jack, for example, earned $200 a month as a cowboy, plus another $90 as Kenedy County treasurer. When he came home from Korea in 1952, he told his "aunt" that he wanted to accept an army commission that would have paid him $400 a month. "Jack," he remembers Sarita's replying, " 'you need to come back to work at the ranch.' I said, 'I'm making more money in the army than you're paying Dad, and Dad is runnin' the ranch! You all just don't pay enough.' She said, 'No, you and your brothers are going to get this ranch. You all need to help build it.' "

Jack describes his aunt Sarita as "strictly the cowgirl type," who mingled easily with her ranch hands and their families and often attended their weekend barn dances, where, after a few cans of her favorite beer, Pabst, Sarita would cut an energetic Texas two-step or the Cotton-Eyed Joe. "She'd just dance up a storm," he remembers.

Elena, whose cattle Jack and his brother Joe tended, was Sarita's exact opposite. "She was strictly a lady," he says. "And she thought you had your place in society and you didn't change it."

Tradition-minded?

"I'd say serfdom," he answers. "That's the polite way of saying it. She ran roughshod over people. And listen to this. She never made a contribution unless her name was put on it. Sarita K. East never wanted her name put on anything. She didn't let them make any to-do or put her picture in the diocesan paper. She just wanted to help. But not Mrs. Kenedy."

Although Sarita in her will divided her half of La Parra between her cousins Stella and Louis Edgar—and told Louis Edgar's boys they would one day operate the ranch themselves—there was another contender for control of La Parra: Tom East, Jr.

In the East family, Sarita's closest ties were to her

brother-in-law Ed's widow, Florence, who lived in Nashville. Florence, nicknamed "Lady," was a frequent guest at La Parra and stayed at the Headquarters with Sarita and Stella. Lady East was remembered in Sarita's will with a nominal cash bequest, as was Arthur's brother Allen East, a west Texas motel operator.

The East brothers' most notable talent appears to have been their knack for marrying well. Arthur won Sarita, heiress to the second-largest ranch in Texas, while his brother Tom, Sr., wedded Alice Gertrudis Kleberg, Bob and Henrietta Kleberg's sister, who would inherit a significant share of the King Ranch.

But the Easts also had a contentious streak in them. After Mifflin's partner Richard King's widow, Henrietta, died at age ninety-two, in 1925, there ensued bitter interfamily strife over the disposition of her million-acre spread. The fight pitted her grandson Bob Kleberg, the King Ranch boss, against his sister Alice, her husband, Tom East, and others who resisted Bob Kleberg's formula for keeping most of the giant property intact.

The rivalry persisted into the next generation. Tom East, Jr., grew up determined to supplant his uncle Bob as the largest landholder in the state—the greatest of all Texas cattlemen. "There was some real hard feelings between those two families," remarks Frank Nesbitt. "Tom East and his uncle Bob sure didn't get along. They had a fistfight, knock down and drag out. They hated each other."

Tom East was a lank and laconic, archetypal Texas ranchman who spent the majority of his time on horseback. He affected a boots-and-saddle bumptiousness, but those who dealt with him knew East as a shrewd and highly intelligent cowman. He was a director of the Alice National Bank, and one of Jake Floyd's most important clients.

His appetite for land was insatiable, and East financed his leases and purchases, to a great extent, with oil revenues from the East family's San Antonio Viejo ranch, near Hebbronville and adjacent to Sarita's San Pablo spread, which also was drenched in oil. Under the terms of her 1948 will, Tom and his siblings, Robert and Alicia Hattie, were to inherit the 80,000-acre San Pablo ranch in equal shares.

East and his lawyer Mr. Floyd, of course, realized that the inheritance was potentially worth tens, if not hundreds, of millions of dollars. But Tom East's hunger was for land and cattle, not dollars, and this ambition naturally drew the rancher's attention to La Parra. Just how early Tom East first plotted to make his aunt's ranch his own is not known. But he clearly had disclosed his ultimate wishes to Jake Floyd, who lay coiled in readiness until the day when Brother Leo Gregory inadvertently provided Floyd his opportunity to strike.

SEVEN

✝ ✝ ✝

The Foundation

By 1956 it had been eight years since Brother Leo's graveside encounter with the widows Mrs. East and Mrs. Kenedy. Over that time his visits to La Parra had been infrequent and brief, and he was not always invited into the Headquarters. It was Elena Kenedy, as she later told the story, who disclosed to the monk the reason why Sarita sometimes had to refuse callers.

One evening, according to Elena, she and Brother Leo were chatting in her parlor when he happened, idly, to ask how Mrs. East was. Elena knew at the moment that Sarita was deep into her cups at the Headquarters, but she said only that her sister-in-law was not feeling well. Over her protests the monk went to see for himself how sick Sarita was. After a long interval, he returned to say good night to Mrs. Kenedy, offering no comment on what he had encountered at the big house.

Not long thereafter the Trappist lay brother began acting as an informal lay therapist to Mrs. East, coaxing her toward moderation, he would later say, by means of the twelve-point Alcoholics Anonymous program he had studied and used to good effect in counseling the drunks he brought to the old guesthouse at Our Lady of the Valley in Rhode Island.

These sessions, Elena observed, afforded Sarita not

just the benefit of Brother Leo's highly sympathetic guidance. Mrs. East basked in the glow of his undivided attention. Until then the monk had spent much more time with Mrs. Kenedy.

There was, in truth, no one else with whom Sarita could comfortably unburden herself, except for "Lady" Florence East, whom she saw irregularly. Mrs. East revealed to Leo her morbid conviction that she didn't have long to live. Reportedly, she had recently been hospitalized for depression. This was not a subject on which Father Dwan or Bishop Garriga knew how to offer soothing reassurances, or one that Sarita cared to take up with her family.

She also explained to the monk that although she cherished La Parra, her life there now oppressed her. She worried about the ranch's future, knowing the vicissitudes of the cattle business and the possibility that her heirs might have to sell off parts of the ranch in order to keep it going. This was why she had talked privately to her neighbors (and Johnny's old drinking companions) Bob Kleberg and Tom Armstrong about the possibility of establishing a tax-exempt foundation—to be named in her parents' honor—to sustain her charities and protect the ranch once she died. Both Kleberg and Armstrong endorsed the idea. But for reasons Sarita could not fathom, her attorney, Mr. Floyd, was temporizing.

Brother Leo absorbed the older woman's frustrations and confusion and advised her to consult Mary for help and solace. Grateful for what seemed to her to be his disinterested compassion, Sarita responded materially with a check for $10,000, her first substantial donation to the Trappists. Elena Kenedy, according to the widows' usual practice, matched the gift with a $10,000 contribution of her own. The monk humbly accepted the checks—earmarked for work at St. Benedict's Monastery in Colorado—and then vanished for another long hiatus, as he resumed his mission to Latin America.

Despite the language barrier, Brother Leo delighted in his every return to South America, especially to regions of Argentina and Chile were the land reminded him of his native northern California. Nothing assuaged his abhorrence of the plight of the urban Latin-American poor. But pressing on with his characteristic brio, Leo visited every country in South America and inspected at least a thousand potential monastery sites before arriving in March of 1958 at the offices of Dr. Cosme Beccar-Varella, a highly successful attorney in Buenos Aires whose many U.S. corporate clients included W. R. Grace & Company. Beccar-Varella also represented a number of prominent Argentine families, among them the wealthy Don Pablo and Doña Carmen Acosta, childless Catholics entering their old age and owners of a vast and fertile *estancia* on the grassy pampas about 150 miles south of Buenos Aires, near the provincial town of Azul.

Like their south Texas counterparts, Argentine cattle ranchers were rangeland autarchs; they formed another closed culture of the few presiding over their estates in medieval grandeur. To sell land except under the direst need was unthinkable; so rare were real estate transactions that it was difficult even to establish a fair market value for prime pampas countryside.

On the other hand, the patrician Don and Doña Acosta, growing old with no direct heirs, had indicated through Beccar-Varella that they were amenable to the idea of a community of simple monks on their land. What was more appropriate to an essentially feudal landscape than the signature medieval institution—a monastery? It would be a holy gesture to settle the brethren in rustic solitude where they could tend their cattle and crops and pray and chant in their cloister on the hill. An abbey would rise. And one day Don Pablo and Doña Carmen might rest together beneath it in a founders' crypt, just as Peter and Margie Grace hoped to do at the new mother house at Spencer.

Dr. Beccar-Varella arranged an afternoon tea conversation between Brother Leo and Doña Carmen. The chat resulted in a mutually attractive agreement to build a Trappist foundation at Estancia Acosta. The monk indulged himself in a moment of unmonk-like pride for having achieved this coup—the first permanent Trappist daughter house on the South American continent. What spoiled the triumph for him was Dom Edmund's decision to erect another elaborate structure at Estancia Acosta, this time a one-third-scale replica of the Massachusetts mother house that would cost $300,000 to complete.

Whether because he was annoyed with Dom Edmund and Brother Blaise's monumental tastes or because the monk really did want to disappear back into the cloister, he had recently threatened to leave Spencer for a Cistercian house in France. According to notes of an interview Dom Edmund later granted the lawyer Kenneth Oden of Jake Floyd's Alice, Texas, law firm, this work became "so loathsome" to Brother Leo that he said he couldn't do it any more.

> The Abbot (Dom Futterer) told Leo to go to [Dom Eugene Boylan, an Irish-born abbot Leo admired] and open his heart and talk with him and abide by [his] decision. . . . The Abbot says that after this long talk . . . Leo came back looking absolutely radiant and that [Dom Boylan] told Leo that the Abbot was ordering or directing Leo to do these things because it was the Abbot's responsibility, and this ties in with the vow of obedience which Leo took. . . . The Abbot then says that Leo put his heart in his work and that in the abbey itself Brother Leo was more dedicated than ever.

In the autumn of 1958, after his visit with Doña Carmen Acosta, Leo journeyed again to Texas to see Sarita and to accept another $5,000 donation from her. He found her restive as ever, painfully unhappy at La Parra and still perplexed at Jake Floyd's interminable delays in establishing her foundation. The project had grown more urgent to her as she approached her seventieth birthday. According to ranch employees, Sarita was also drinking more than ever.

But Leo, as always, had a tonic effect on Mrs. East's mood. Sarita suggested that they take a short excursion together so that she could show him her San Pablo ranch, where she was thinking of building a new ranch house.

Settled in the back seat of her black Cadillac with her driver, Chano Longoria, at the wheel, they motored north on Route 77 to the little town of Riveria (between Sarita and Kingsville) and then headed west on Texas State 285 to the outskirts of Hebbronville, where they turned south and drove on three-quarters of a mile to the front gate at San Pablo.

Mrs. East was customarily close-mouthed about details of her finances. Brother Leo assumed from what little she told him—derived from what little Mr. Floyd allowed Mrs. East to understand—that she was moderately well-to-do, that for all her land the Kenedy estate was nevertheless worth no more than $5 million.

What the monk beheld at San Pablo that day unveiled to him an entirely different picture, the one Jake Floyd had been so careful to conceal. As Leo and Sarita drove onto the ranch, he saw rows of oil rigs and signs everywhere of a major exploratory—and production—effort. After talking with the oil company geologist at the ranch, the monk made a few rudimentary calculations in his head and concluded, conservatively, that his elderly companion was worth at least ten times more than she realized. Leo had stumbled onto the Dry Snake's secret.

He grasped the magnitude of his discovery quickly but, contrary to his usual impulsiveness, adopted a deliberate attitude toward it. Rather than suddenly trying to enlighten Sarita to the obvious extent of her fortune, he saved his news for J. Peter Grace. There was now a very definite need for Mrs. East to get her stalled foundation started.

✝ ✝ ✝

EIGHT

Brother Leo's Agenda

There were those whose skepticism made them immune to Christopher Gregory's magnetism. "He was always talking about the grace of God and the holy saints," says Francis Verstraeten, Jr., a Buenos Aires stockbroker, now forty-four, who remembers the monk from his teen years when Leo was a frequent guest in the Verstraeten house. "It's true! He had a very special way with hypnotism, or whatever. Especially with women. He did it to men also, but if you knew him it was, 'Don't bullshit me! That's enough.'"

Another keen student of the monk's career, a Grace company executive, remembers Leo's familiar presence at corporate headquarters, on Hanover Square, in lower Manhattan. "He was," says this former employee, "an extremely handsome, clean-cut charismatic young man who wore immaculate clerical outfits. I always remember that because I had an uncle who became a Trappist monk. So I was interested in Brother Leo for that reason.

"Many of us believed that he was not connected with the church at all; that he was in some ways a phoney, that he was a fund-raiser. Until I heard later about the scandal and so forth, I thought that Brother Leo was probably a guy who'd been hired by the Trappist order, someone who was in some way connected with the church who was allowed, or had chosen, to wear an outfit in which he appeared to be a brother. I always assumed that he was not a brother, that he was a bit of a charlatan.''

As for Leo's relationship with J. Peter Grace, ''We thought of him as being an engaging rogue. And we all knew that he could get Peter to do anything that he wanted. Peter was a very unreasonable person most of the time, and insensitive to other people's feelings. But Brother Leo didn't seem to be the least bit concerned about what Peter thought. Brother Leo had his own agenda.''

Peter Grace, who is proudly impervious to subtlety, applied a blunt logic to Leo's behavior as he saw it. ''I am not,'' Grace explains, ''a suspicious person. He prayed all the time. If you saw him in church, he was absolutely lost in prayer. He never noticed anything. And in the monastery, he prayed all the time. He did that for years. I mean, that doesn't sound like someone that wants to get much out of life, making shoes and praying all the time. Why the hell would he do that? That's a complete waste of time if you're a phoney.''

Grace also claims that he does not recollect the occasion or substance of Leo's first mention to him of Sarita's wealth or of her wish to establish a foundation. According to their later correspondence, however, the monk advised him of his discovery in 1958. Grace, at that time, was too busy on a lumber deal to offer his assistance. Therefore, Leo deferred direct action and concentrated on shaping Sarita's thinking in other important areas.

On November 4, 1958, he wrote to her of his progress at Estancia Acosta:

My dear Sarita—may God's peace and grace fill your heart!

* * *

This is just a line to let you know that nine of our monks from Spencer, Massachusetts have come down here to Argentina and are moved into a little wooden house that we've built to shelter them until we can get part of the permanent Monastery built.

Your generous help will enable us to start on this first Monastery building in the next few weeks. We hope to have this first wing completed by the end of the Argentine summer, if we can finance it.

Brother Leo repeated his thanks, assured Sarita she was being "kept in [their] prayers in a very special way," and mentioned his hopes that her health was good.

"Life here below on earth is so short," he went on,

and that wonderful Eternity that His love has prepared for us is so so very long! We were made for Eternity, and this short life is just to prepare us for that wonderful Life that He has in store for those who love Him and Trust Him and try to do His dear Will!

May He pour out His strong grace in sweet abundance upon you, Sarita, and fill you with the best of His gifts of grace and peace and joy and life!

with all His love,
Brother M. Leo, O.C.S.O.

The monk's appearances at La Parra, now more commonplace, nevertheless escaped the notice of most of Mrs. East's relatives, who were thoroughly accustomed to visits from traveling Catholic clergy and paid little attention to Sarita's collared callers. When the trouble later began, many of the Turcottes had no recollection of him at all. The ranch employees, however, quickly sorted the Trappist from the rest of the usual retinue. And several conceived a dislike for him.

"Really," says Luis Ruano, Elena's driver, "everybody at the ranch, not just me, thought this guy was too somber, not like the bishop or Father Dwan. I can't judge him for what he was doing. He was the guy they sent out, you know. But he didn't talk to you much. Just say, 'Hi,' and that was it. He wouldn't establish no conversation with you at all. And you know Texans are not used to that. I think most of the people took it for rudeness. Many people took it like this: 'You're not my class.' That's what I got from what they said."

Brother Leo was not consciously dismissive toward Sarita's ranch employees; indeed, he was apt in most cases to take special notice of a poor man or a peasant. He was oblivious to ranch workers' hurt feelings as he was heedless of the mockery he provoked among some Grace company officials. When focused on an objective, says Father Raphael Simon, the monk ignored just about everything but his goal. "Brother Leo," he explains, "was a man who didn't like red tape, who liked to get where he was going fast. And he didn't take into consideration everything that prudence requires."

The monk visited Sarita at La Parra again in the spring of 1959. She received another progress report on the new monastery at Estancia Acosta on the Argentine pampas, as well as Brother Leo's description of a breathtaking site he had found in high meadowland across the Andes Mountains from Argentina in Chile, not far from the Chilean capital, Santiago. With the south Texas drought now broken, Mrs. East was quick to consider his idea that she might want to see for herself what her money was helping to build for the Trappists in far-off South America.

Sarita never had traveled alone, and for this prospective tour she considered companions from within her family. Elena, who also had contributed to the Argentine monastery program, was an obvious choice, as was her sister-in-law Lady East of Nashville. Cousin Stella Turcotte Lytton, now a resident at the Headquarters, was another candidate, although Stella disliked long trips.

On his flight back to Spencer, Leo scribbled Sarita a note on Delta Airlines stationery, datelined ''en route NYC. April 7th.''

My dear Sarita—may God's grace and peace fill you!

It was *good* to see you again. You are kept very deep in our thoughts and prayers, that God may pour out upon you an abundance of His best gifts.

(Leo's letters were all highly iterative.)

Here is a little book on *Confidence* that I told you I would send you. Hope you enjoy it.

The greatest and most important lesson that this life here on earth can teach us is a two-fold one: *First,* that we are poor needy sinners, and of ourselves capable only of falling. This is a bitter truth, and takes a long time to learn. The *Second* truth is a very sweet and consoling one, and this is that God's love for us is a Love of Pure Mercy and endless patience and tenderness. He knows our weaknesses & temptations, and His love and tender pity for our suffering is infinite.

So, let your heart grow and expand in a firm Trust in God's power and mercy. He wants us to humbly acknowledge our falls; *Then* He wants us to turn away from ourself [*sic*] towards Him, and make an *act* of sincere Trust in His love for us, and in His desire to help us and to have mercy upon us. The measure of our confidence determines the measure of His mercy that He can pour into our hearts!

He loves you, Sarita! Believe in His love!

Our gratitude to you for your interest in our new monasteries is *very* great. God will reward you!

Hope that you & Elena and Lady East will be able to visit us next month. How good it would be if you could come down to Chile and Argentina.

God love you!
Brother Leo

PS I will write again next week about the land.

It turned out that Mrs. East was not ready to commit herself, just yet, to the South American expedition; Leo returned to La Parra three more times that summer before she finally made up her mind. But the delay was not without its compensations. That summer she made two $25,000 donations to the Trappists, fully half the amount she usually gave to all church causes in a whole year. Both checks, filled out only two days apart in late June, were drawn on the Alice National Bank.

NINE

✝ ✝ ✝

South America

Stealth was Jake Floyd's forte. "He was like a chess player," says his fellow attorney Frank Nesbitt, who practiced law with and against El Vibora Seca over many years before becoming entangled himself, as the Turcotte brothers' counsel, in the later warfare over the Kenedy millions. "What he was movin' over here you didn't see the results of over there until four or five moves later. Jake was *that* good, he sure was."

J. Peter Grace ruefully concurs. "He was a brilliant man, absolutely," says the industrialist. "He was as smart as anybody I've ever met."

And Jake Floyd was ruthless.

Such attributes made it not unreasonable for Sarita East to place herself in naïve dependence upon Floyd's business judgment. The ranchers Sarita knew and respected, including her nephew Tom East and his uncle Bob Kleberg, spoke highly of Floyd's acumen in advancing, or protecting, their interests. Jake Floyd knew how to fix things, and if his practices were often sharp—he was said to have accepted legal retainers from the very drilling companies with whom he negotiated oil deals on Sarita's behalf—he nevertheless delivered; the oil men who developed Mrs. East's fields complained with some apparent justification that Floyd had snookered them into onerously high royalties.

Furthermore, Floyd, like Brother Leo, did not covet Mrs. East's millions for himself, coincidental traits that made both these later adversaries' motives difficult for the uninitiated to discern.

Leo invoked a higher authority, while Jake Floyd's currency was temporal, political power, specifically Democratic political power, which he wielded out of his tidily kept law office in the town of Alice, seat of Jim Wells County and home of the Alice National Bank.

Floyd was a political boss, an able practitioner in the south Texas style of governance that was, and to an extent remains, brutal and corrupt. Jim Wells* County, for example, was where the boss George Parr in 1948 "found" the 200 votes that made the then obscure congressman Lyndon Johnson a statewide winner in the U.S. senatorial primary. Without George Parr, "Landslide Lyndon" surely would not have gone on to become president.

Parr, who coined Jake Floyd's nickname, had elbowed the attorney aside in Jim Wells County, supplanting the Floyd machine with his own to control patronage, county contracts, and the local courts. He had Floyd outgunned but never outwitted. By 1952 Jake had collected enough information on several Parr associates' involvement in a gambling and prostitution operation to threaten the Parr machine's continued dominance. Some one or more of these men responded by putting a contract out on Floyd's life.

The killer was stationed in Floyd's garage, poised to shoot the attorney as he emerged from his house. Instead, it was Floyd's son, Buddy, who stepped

---

*Named for the attorney James B. Wells, Jr. (1850–1923), the acknowledged progenitor of south Texas boss rule. Among Wells's most prominent clients and allies were Richard King and Mifflin Kenedy, as well as Sarita's father, Don Gregorio.

through the door toward his father's green Ford coupe and into the *pistolero*'s fusillade.

His son's murder obsessed Jake Floyd for the balance of his days. But once he finally broke George Parr's hold on Jim Wells County politics, Floyd did not allow his unsuccessful pursuit of Buddy's slayer to interfere with the conduct of important business on other fronts. One was the close surveillance he maintained on the Kenedy family estate.

Sarita's first two sizable checks to Brother Leo, one for $10,000 in 1956 and another for $5,000 in 1958, had not alarmed Jake Floyd unduly. In the summer of 1959, however, as he sat at his desk, his pearl gray Stetson resting at its customary spot on the low credenza behind him, Floyd studied Mrs. East's two $25,000 drafts carefully. Apart from its size, one check was particularly curious for the clear difference between the handwriting of the date, amount, and payee's name (the monk's script) and that of the signature, which Floyd recognized as Sarita's.

The Alice lawyer was well aware of Sarita and Leo's visit to her San Pablo ranch the preceding autumn and of the monk's conversation with the site geologist. Little of potential interest escaped Jake Floyd's attention. He also had learned from his informal intelligence network that Sarita was talking to the Trappist about her foundation.

A man of Floyd's experience did not panic easily, but he did conclude that the anticipated interloper was on the scene and that the Alice National Bank's cozy custody of Sarita's oil income was at risk. The lawyer therefore put on his cooperative mien and composed a letter to his client, dated August 5, 1959, in which "the writer," as Floyd commonly referred to himself in business correspondence, proposed for the first time a substantive step toward creation of the foundation, the transfer under a deed of conveyance of two San

Pablo mineral leases into a trust, the management of which he would suggest be handled by the Alice National Bank.

Mrs. East did not answer, or ever acknowledge, her attorney's letter. The initiative, for the time being, was with Brother Leo.

On August 27 Sarita renewed her passport and then traveled with her cousin Stella to southeastern Colorado for a visit to another of her ranches, called Twin Peaks, which Mrs. East had purchased in the early 1950s. When the drought was at its worst, she shipped part of her herd to Twin Peaks for pasturage.

The monk, just returned again from South America, met Sarita and Stella Lytton in Colorado Springs and then drove them northwest across the state to Aspen and nearby Snowmass, where he showed Mrs. East St. Benedict's Monastery. There she met the cloister superior, Father Thomas Keating, and his recently opened community of twelve fathers and brothers. It was Sarita's first visit to a Trappist monastery.

She had hesitated until this moment to finally, firmly commit herself to going to South America. But after a genial reception from the monks at St. Benedict's, all of whom deeply admired Brother Leo, she called her sister-in-law Elena back at La Parra to broach the idea of the trip. Elena, a decade later, recollected her surprise at the suddenness of the invitation, but she agreed to accompany Sarita in a group that would include Lady East and Elena's brother, Paul Seuss, of San Antonio. Leo, by virtue of his long association with Peter Grace, was able to tap the travel department at W. R. Grace for just-so luxury steamship accommodations for the foursome—Sarita was nervous in airplanes—and came up with staterooms aboard the liner SS *Brazil,* leaving New York harbor on October 2, 1959.

The 5,550-mile ocean voyage south through the Caribbean, down the east coast of South America, and past the equator to Buenos Aires took twelve days, with brief stops at Miami, San Juan, Puerto Rico, Rio de Janeiro, and São Paulo. Sarita enjoyed the trip, as her collection of shipboard snapshots attested. These included several blurry photos of the ritual crossing-of-the-equator party aboard the *Brazil*.

Mrs. East's command of geography was not strong. She had some difficulty adjusting to the novelty of newly leafed shade trees and spring flowers in Buenos Aires's many parks when the countryside back home was a dusty, burned brown. Argentina's immensity impressed her, too. Four times the size of Texas and shaped like a huge, 2,300-mile long leg of beef, Argentina has climates that vary from the bleakness of subantarctic Patagonia, on the Straits of Magellan, in the extreme south, to the rainy maritime zone around Buenos Aires and, farther north, the steamy Chaco jungles stretching into Paraguay.

Buenos Aires itself bore a superficial resemblance to Paris (which Sarita had not seen) with its wide boulevards, cafés, distinct neighborhoods, ornate architecture, and low skyline dictated by the threat of earthquakes. Unlike the majority of Latin American metropolises, BA, as its English-speaking residents called it, had a minimal Indian population; the Spanish conquistadors and early settlers killed off most of Argentina's indigenous peoples. There also were very few blacks. Again unlike most other Latin American countries, Argentina had never had much of a plantation economy and, therefore, no market for slave traders.

The majority of BA's citizens—*portenos,* as they called themselves—were of European descent. Forty percent of the city was ethnic Italian, with substantial numbers of English, Irish, and Germans, too. It was said of typical *portenos* that they were Italians who spoke Spanish and thought they were English.

Brother Leo met Sarita's party at the dock in Buenos Aires's La Boca district, the oldest in the city, and shepherded the four to their suites at the venerable Plaza Hotel, on San Martin Plaza, the center of BA's toniest neighborhood. Once they were settled, he introduced the *norteamericanos* to the closest of his many friends in the Argentine capital, Francis and Rachel Verstraeten, upper-crust Argentines from old families who resided with their large and growing brood of children in a grand stone mansion on Maipu Street, not far from the Plaza. Leo had told the Verstraetens of Sarita's tour; according to Francis, the monk described the widow as "a rich Texan who is going to finance the monasteries" and said he'd be grateful if the Verstraetens "would be as nice as possible to her."

His friends were pleased to oblige him. "We both were then very fond of Brother Leo," says Francis, now in his early seventies. "He was quick-witted, good company, and seemed very sincere. At that time, I was a strong Catholic. I deeply believed in the church. What he was doing, building monasteries, was good work to me. I didn't know what his setup was, and I tried not to ask questions. Generally, I give someone the benefit of the doubt."

Verstraeten genuinely liked Sarita Kenedy East. "She had nice eyes," he recalls, "very beautiful and big eyes, sort of sparkly. She was very shy, talked very little except about her ranch and Santa Gertrudis cattle, and always dressed in dark, dark, dark clothing, like women in the provinces here dress. She didn't care at all about her appearance.

"Sarita was also homely and very rustic with big hands; not at all feminine. She aimed her backside when she sat down. At the same time, however, I found her a very charming female. She had something which went past all that and made her an interesting woman."

With the Verstraetens' help, Leo saw to it that Mrs. East and her companions were introduced into BA society, many of whose members at first thought that she was the monk's mother. "She met everyone who was interesting," says Verstraeten, "estate owners, bankers, industrialists, all of whom were from excellent economic positions and from our best families. They received her warmly as one of their own.

"I also noticed that at luncheons and suppers with alcohol her shyness disappeared. She was a bit astonished to see that so many ladies of our society managed various languages and had wide knowledge on general topics. Sarita spoke typically Texan English and a little Mexican Spanish. She was only interested in simple, rudimentary things."

Sarita was not much for the *portenos'* nightlife. She did not sample Buenos Aires's famous tango parlors or acquire the locals' fondness for a midnight stroll or for a late-hour cup of espresso and political conversation in a *confiteria.*

She did visit the city's noted steak houses, where reputedly the best beef in the world is served. Argentina barbecue, *parrilla,* surprised her—partly because almost every part of the steer is consumed and partly because charred or well-done beef, the way she was used to eating it, is anathema to the Argentine palate.

Verstraeten remembers that Mrs. East preferred evenings spent at the house on Maipu or in the restaurant at the Plaza. "In fact," he says, "she enjoyed it more at the Plaza because there she could take a few snorters and jump into bed. It was simpler than taking a cab to go home."

Nor was Sarita ever happier than when the attentive Brother Leo was at her side. "He was very kind, always trying to work her into the conversation," says Verstraeten. "Always trying to make her look her best. And she was obviously in love with him."

Lady East made little impression on Verstraeten during the group's two-week stay in Buenos Aires. Nor did Elena Kenedy's brother. "Paul Seuss," he says, "was a dud, a very boring fellow." Elena, whenever he saw her, was remote and cool. "It wasn't very subtle with her," Verstraeten remembers. "She saw what everybody else saw and didn't like it. That was obvious. There was an undercurrent between her and Sarita."

Mrs. East's favorites among her new Argentine acquaintances were Arturo ("Chito") Boote and his wife, Teresa. Chito Boote was a personable aristocrat with what Francis Verstraeten describes as a serious drinking habit. "To Chito," he says, "the hour of the whiskeys was sacred." Sarita could appreciate that attitude, just as she enjoyed Boote's good humor and informality.

He had inherited a portion of a family-owned office-supply company and was a sometime diplomat and appointed official in the post-Peronist democratic government of the Argentine president Arturo Frondizi. But Chito Boote's main occupation appears to have been the unofficial exercise of influence; he was a trader in favors.

Alfredo Bracht, an Argentine business associate of Peter Grace, had steered Brother Leo to Boote when the Trappists encountered Argentina's prohibitively high import duties on tools and machinery for the new monastery at Estancia Acosta. It would have cost the order as much as $100,000 to bring in their electrical generator and other gear if Boote had not interceded with his friend President Frondizi, who waived the fees by special permit. Brother Leo also encouraged Chito Boote to cultivate his friendship with Sarita, one reason the Bootes went along with Mrs. East's party on their scheduled visit to meet Doña Carmen Acosta and inspect the new monastery site at Estancia Acosta.

The countryside was Sarita's element, and it was at its lushest at the start of the Argentine spring season. She discovered that the pampas were every bit as flat as her south Texas ranchland, but more fertile, clement, and well watered. The broad plains were crowded with fat cows of several breeds, half hidden by the tallest, richest grass Sarita had ever seen. She took it all in from her window with a practiced and approving eye, instinctively envisioning her own herds of massive Santa Gertrudis cattle growing sleek on the verdant expanses all around her.

Once the party passed through the town of Azul, it drove up into a somewhat hillier terrain of serene vistas dotted by eucalyptus glades and stands of towering, dark-green cypresses. On one side of a gentle valley stood the brick-and-stone hacienda Acosta, a graceful structure surrounded by woods atop a sloping meadow. From her big windows Doña Carmen could look down and across the valley to the partially completed monastery. Don Pablo had died that spring of a heart attack; his remains now rested temporarily at the Recoleta necropolis in Buenos Aires, where the don would be stored until the Acostas' crypt was ready to receive him.

Sarita was taken by the beauty of the place, and despite a twisted ankle (which aggravated an old bone break), she ranged over Estancia Acosta everywhere with her camera. She recognized its familiar feudal ambience and the lonely life of another widowed *patrona.* However, Doña Carmen's isolated fiefdom was complete in its medieval anachronism. It had a monastery populated with monks who treated Carmen Acosta with a warm and loving deference. They even relaxed for her the strict rule against females within the monastic enclosure. One of Sarita's first inspirations after the visit was that La Parra, too, could be home to a

Trappist community, a notion Leo would have to discourage, politely.

After a brief return to BA, the next major stop on
the tour was Chile, where Sarita was to look over the
land Brother Leo had found the preceding spring.
Elena, who couldn't tolerate high altitudes, flew over
the Andes with her brother Paul and waited for Mrs.
East and the others at the Hotel Carrera in Santiago,
owned by another friend of Leo's. Sarita hired a car
and driver to take her, Lady East, and the monk west
to see Bob Kleberg's recently begun Argentine cattle
operation, Rancho Carmen, then northwest to the pic-
turesque adobe town of Mendoza, the capital of Argentina's wine-producing region, about a hundred
miles from the Chilean border.

They rested overnight in Mendoza and then boarded
a train for the eye-catching trip up into the Andes.
From an elevation of about 2,000 feet the railroad
climbed upward more than a mile to a frigid pass in
the Andes between Aconcagua to the north, the highest mountain (22,831 feet) in the Western Hemisphere,
and Tupungato to the south, the third-highest (22,310
feet) peak. Up and over the rugged Andes and then
down into Santiago, Sarita kept her camera clicking
all the way.

In Chile, Elena decided to skip the forty-five-minute
drive west from Santiago to Las Condes, the alpine
tract Leo had identified as ideal for a possible monastery. But Sarita, eager to assess the site, was rewarded with a lovely panorama of a tranquil slope
above a little valley dominated by snow-capped mountains in the distance and well suited to support a monastic community in solitude.

Las Condes was, however, not far as the crow flies
from Santiago, which was sprawling rapidly in the
property's direction. Someday, Leo worried, the land
would be overrun by civilization, just as Our Lady of

the Valley had been. The monk had solicited an opinion on the matter from his friend Manuel Larrain, the bishop of Talca, in Chile. Providentially, Larrain convinced Leo that Las Condes was too choice a parcel for him not to acquire if he could.

After a week's stay in Santiago it was time for the next leg of the trip, an excursion south by rail to Chile's scenic Lakes District, where, ostensibly, Sarita and the monk were to look over another potential monastery site. Once again, Elena and her brother Paul stayed behind.

On the way south into the rainy region in the western Andean foothills, Sarita, Lady East, and Leo stopped in the town of Talca to visit Bishop Larrain, then vice-president of the Episcopal Conference of Latin-American Bishops (CELAM), one of the more active, although hardly radical, church organizations then focusing on the plight of the poor in Latin America. Sarita had not seen much human hardship in relatively prosperous Argentina, but in Santiago, according to Leo, she had been deeply disturbed by the wretchedness and misery of its slums. Again according to Leo, Mrs. East spoke privately of her cares and concerns about the Latin-American poor with Bishop Larrain, a dedicated expert on the problem.

From Talca the party continued south for a three-day stay at a country hotel in the shores of romantic Lake Villarrica, in the center of the Lakes District, also known as the Switzerland of South America. After so much travel it was a chance for Sarita to catch her breath, and for her and Leo to converse away from Elena's reproving eye.

It was at Lake Villarrica, according to Leo's later testimony to the Turcottes' attorney, Frank Nesbitt, that Mrs. East made unprompted mention of her foundation. The monk, under oath, characterized his role in the conversation as passively helpful; he volunteered nothing to Nesbitt of his discovery of the drilling activity at Sarita's San Pablo ranch in 1958 or of his earlier discussions of Sarita's foundation with J. Peter Grace.

"I believe," the monk offered instead, "that I told her that, if she wished, I [was] sure that I could arrange for an appointment between her and Mr. Grace."

TEN

✛ ✛ ✛

Gold in These Hills

The believability of Brother Leo's testimony hinged in large degree on the credulousness of his listeners, many of whom suspected he was a compulsive fabulist. "He was *somethin'!*" Frank Nesbitt remembers of his confrontation with the monk. "Leo was a character. I *liked* him. I wouldn't have trusted him as far as across the street, but I liked him."

The Fort Worth lawyer Joe Day, another of Leo's later interrogators, also admired the monk's way with words. "It was bullshit *forever,*" says Day. "It's just incredible how that fella wrapped people around his thumb."

The suspected dissembling that so tickled Leo's legal questioners had never been a problem inside the monastery, where his fellow monks regarded Leo's word as reliable, or at least the truth as the lay brother saw it. "Brother has a vivid imagination," says one. "And what he intuits happened he can take as a fact."

His recall sometimes was selective, a trait that Father Raphael believes is linked to Leo's relentless optimism, his inability to accept a reversal of fortune. "He used me as a go-between with the abbot when he had differences with him," Father Raphael explains. "And there was a situation where he felt he was being treated unfairly. So I said, 'Okay, I'll call a meeting of the Spencer officers and discuss it with them.'

"Well, the treasurer, Brother Alan Hudon, said he wouldn't attend. He said, 'This matter was already decided.' But Leo treated it as if it were still open. That was characteristic of him."

Sarita East seems never to have doubted the monk's reliability. In fact, she placed extraordinary trust in him. Under normal circumstances, the widow would not have sought the financial counsel of a total stranger, even one so prominent as J. Peter Grace.

She said nothing of her Lake Villarrica decision to do so to her sister-in-law Elena, nor did she mention her upcoming appointment with Grace in a November 7, 1959, letter from Chile to her cousin Stella's son Lee Lytton, Jr., back in Sarita. "I do not have much time for writing, as we are constantly on the go," Mrs. East informed Lytton in her looping, barely legible hand. The letter briefly apprised Judge Lytton of a change of plans in which Elena and Paul Scuss would be returning to La Parra via New Orleans on November 25 (just in time for Johnny's anniversary service the next day), and it told him that Sarita and Lady East were taking a separate ship through the Panama Canal to New York, where Lytton could reach her at the Barbizon Plaza Hotel. She promised to be home for the start of hunting season.

Her Grace Line steamer, the *Santa Isabella*, docked in New York on December 2. Once more, Leo was there to greet the women and to help navigate their mounds of luggage and gifts through customs. The next night, a chilly one, he drove with Sarita and Lady East to a dinner party in their honor at Peter Grace's country estate house, a three-story Georgian manor set among 235 forested acres in Manhasset, on Long Island.

Before dinner Grace and Leo separated Sarita from

her sister-in-law for a private guided tour of the rolling, beautifully landscaped property. The three bundled into Grace's station wagon. "Well now, Sarita," Peter Grace would remember the monk saying from the front seat as they pulled down the estate's gently curving drive, "I have mentioned to Peter here that you were interested in getting some advice, and here we are . . ."

Under oath, Brother Leo was able to recall nothing of the station wagon tour. Grace, however, in his later deposition related that Sarita, on the strength of their brief acquaintance, agreed to have all her pertinent income data forwarded to him for his analysis. Moreover, according to Grace, Mrs. East's two-month excursion seems to have fundamentally altered her ambitions for her foundation. He recollected that she said nothing about the protection of La Parra but that "she said she was particularly interested in helping Latin America. She had seen tremendous need down there. She had talked to a number of bishops and she would like to be able to do more for the church, particularly at this time in Latin America."

The next morning, Mrs. East and Leo took a cab down from the Barbizon Plaza to her favorite New York store, the old Abercrombie & Fitch sporting-goods emporium on Madison Avenue. Sarita led the monk past the duck decoys and the down jackets upstairs to the gun department and there instructed him to select a weapon; Leo was going to go deer hunting. He chose from the display cabinets a gleaming Winchester .308—a good deer rifle—and also accepted from Sarita a second gift, a .357 magnum handgun with a tooled leather holster. That afternoon Sarita and Leo put Lady East on a flight for Nashville and then caught the train at Grand Central Station for Houston.

The following week, Leo became the first known solemnly professed Cistercian of the Strict Observance ever to shoot a deer in Texas. Mrs. East didn't fare as well on the hunt at San Pablo. Whether because of poor eyesight (which Sarita tried to hide) or because, as her driver Chano Longoria later reported, Mrs. East had too freely helped herself to the scotch that afternoon, the target she took for a buck turned out to be a cactus.

Sarita's second disappointment came with the monk's diplomatic explanation why the hot summers and scarcity of irrigation water in Kenedy County made her lands unsuitable to support a monastic farming community. It was better, she came to understand, for her to support the Trappists' expansion program in South America.

Meanwhile, back in New York, J. Peter Grace had received Mrs. East's financial records. The documents, according to his recollection, set off bells and whistles in his mind. As he recreated the scene for Frank Nesbitt, he looked over the numbers and then exclaimed, "Well, wait a minute! If you do this, this, this—*Yes!* You could do that! And then BING! BING! you know? And say, hey, this looks like some gold in these hills!"

Grace's conclusion? "I could see this thing developing now. This looks like this woman can double, quadruple, what she has been giving to the church, which she wants to increase, and live better or the same."

The industrialist's preliminary review almost exactly confirmed Brother Leo's earlier estimate of Sarita's overall worth, although it took Grace's accountants several days to piece together the picture that Leo had toted up in his head in a matter of minutes. She was worth, the numbers showed, about ten times the three to five million dollars that Jake Floyd had led his client to believe she was worth. "Floyd kept her nice and ignorant, didn't he?'' Grace says today.

So, for the time being, did he and Brother Leo. Now they, together with Jake Floyd and, presumably, Tom East knew the true value of the Kenedy estate. But the time apparently was not propitious for anyone to inform the widow herself.

On December 29 Grace flew south from New York to La Parra to meet with Mrs. East and outline for her the foundation tax angles under which she could safely increase her charitable giving. Present for the four-hour meeting were Sarita, Leo, Grace, and Mrs. East's second cousin Father Henry Tiblier, a Jesuit priest whom she favored with regular donations to his parochial school in Laredo. Elena Kenedy attended a part of the discussion. But Jake Floyd was not notified of the gathering. Sarita, whose conscience was troubled for having had to turn to J. Peter Grace for assistance, hoped somehow to spare her attorney's feelings regarding what she feared he would take as an insult to his professional competence.

Mrs. East was also mindful of her bishop, Mariano Garriga. Now that her proposed foundation had developed a Catholic, charitable orientation—and despite Peter Grace's testimony that her prime objective was helping the church and the poor in Latin America—Sarita evidently saw Garriga as an attractive candidate to help run it. According to Father Tiblier's handwritten notes of the December 29 meeting, the only surviving record of the gathering, Mrs. East explicitly mentioned Garriga among ''the persons who will be the ones to determine how the income of the foundation will be allocated among the beneficiaries she will have named.'' Subsequently, Bishop Garriga later testified, Sarita personally informed him that she was about to set up a foundation and that she anticipated being able to increase substantially her yearly giving to the diocese of Corpus Christi.

On Wednesday, January 6, 1960, Brother Leo escorted Mrs. East by air back to New York from Texas; Sarita was overcoming her fear of flying. The next morning, Peter Grace introduced her to his Pine Street attorney, Lawrence McKay, of Cahill, Gordon, Reindel & Ohl. On Friday, Sarita and Leo met with McKay and his associate Paul H. Fox for two hours in her room at the Barbizon Plaza. Mrs. East produced for the lawyers a copy of her 1948 will, as well as its single codicil, dated 1950.

The foundation, as conceived for her by the attorneys, would feature a two-tier executive hierarchy. There would be members, who decided how the foundation's charity was to be spent, and then directors, whose responsibility would be to carry out the members' orders. Sarita instructed McKay and Fox, as Fox's notes reflect, that she wished the directors of her new foundation to be herself, her cousin Louis Edgar Turcotte, and her cousin Stella's son Judge Lee Lytton. Then, apparently as soon as she had made this decision, Sarita changed her mind. Lee Lytton's name was struck from Fox's draft and was replaced by Jake Floyd's. There was no mention in Fox's notes about prospective members—those who would wield actual decision-making authority. These presumably still included Bishop Garriga.

On Saturday, January 9, Sarita and Leo returned to Texas, where she was scheduled for a routine physical examination in San Antonio. The following Wednesday, Peter Grace's chief accountant, Thomas Doyle, took fifty dollars of his boss's money to open an unusual checking account for Mrs. East at the Grace National Bank. Her name did not appear on the checks, and instructions were given that all statements and canceled drafts be sent *not* to Sarita at La Parra but to her in care of Doyle at his home address in New York City. A power of attorney giving Leo full access to the funds in the account also was drawn up.

That afternoon, January 13, the lawyers McKay and Fox flew to Houston and checked into the Shamrock Hotel. Brother Leo and Sarita arrived in Houston from San Antonio that evening and took rooms at the Rice Hotel, where the next morning Fox hand-delivered to her drafts of a new will, plus her foundation's charter and articles of incorporation. Paul Fox later testified that on Sarita's "instructions" Louis Edgar Turcotte's name did not appear among the designated directors. He had been replaced by Brother Leo.

✛ ✛ ✛

ELEVEN

If You Love Me . . .

One of the functions of Mrs. East's semisecret checking account at the Grace National Bank (part of Leo's "financial laboratory," in Brother Alan Hudson's wry phrase) became clear on January 15 in Houston: Sarita had decided to buy the Chilean property—Las Condes—for the Trappists, a $305,000 donation. She made out two checks to herself, one for $150,000 and another for $155,000, and then gave them to Leo. Unlike her two $25,000 checks of the preceding summer, these checks were drawn not on her Alice National Bank account but on two separate accounts she maintained in Houston banks. Jake Floyd would not immediately see the enormous expenditure, and all that Sarita's local accountant would receive would be the canceled Houston bank checks with Grace Bank endorsements on their reverse sides. There would be no other hint of where the money had gone.

Sarita was scheduled to sign the final foundation and will documents in Houston on the twenty-second. On Friday the fifteenth, after she wrote out the two checks, Leo flew to New York with them. He deposited the money in Sarita's new Grace Bank account on Monday the eighteenth. Then, under his power of attorney—which conferred on Leo complete control of the account—he transferred the funds again to his "Brother

Leo'' account, one of several he maintained at the Grace Bank.

There was no reason for the monk to ''wash'' Sarita's funds, as he later described the operation, with such haste. It was a risk, after he had been the widow's nearly constant companion for three months, to leave her alone in Texas with only seven days left before she was scheduled to sign her new will and foundation papers.

The monk had not yet caught on—nor would he for some months to come—to Jake Floyd's craftiness. ''He underestimated Jake,'' says Frank Nesbitt. ''I think he thought he had control over Mrs. East to the point where it was, 'Forget it, Jake.' That wasn't smart.''

On January 15, at Sarita's direction, the lawyers Fox and McKay met with Floyd in Houston and showed him the documents they had prepared. Floyd, Fox's later memo of the session reported, ''said that Mrs. East had been considering taking such steps for five or more years and had consulted him in a cursory way about such steps from time to time. He said that he was pleased to hear that Mrs. East had finally decided to go forward with the program.''

Floyd had a very different story for Sarita. After his meeting with the New York lawyers, he told her that he thought potential tax problems might arise with the foundation and also conveyed his disappointment that Mrs. East had taken such a step without first consulting him. Their conversation put Sarita in a dither.

A luncheon at La Parra with Bishop Garriga was even more distressing to her. Elena Kenedy, who did not disguise her own skepticism at what her sister-in-law proposed to do, would remember the bishop's railing at Sarita for abandoning him and his diocese in favor of the Trappists. Reddening at any mention of Leo (whom he had met but once, several years earlier), Garriga was not mollified by Mrs. East's repeated assurances that the Catholics of south Texas were first in her heart and that she hoped the bishop would play an important role in the management of the foundation. Garriga's outburst both hurt and angered Sarita, Elena later said, and was ill considered in view of Mrs. East's obvious trust in, and attachment to, Brother Leo.

On January 19 Leo was back at La Parra, where he personally handed Sarita a two-page, single-spaced typewritten letter. "Christ," the letter read,

> told us that loving God means to do His Will. "If you love Me, you will do My Will even as I love my Father and always seek to do those things that give Him pleasure." Loving God means to try—all day long, and in all that we do—to please Him by doing the duties of our state of life, for His Sake, and by accepting all that His Will sends into our daily lives, with trust and love. Loving God means to do His Will for love of Him and to accept His Will also for love of Him.

Two paragraphs later, Leo repackaged and repeated his letter's basic message of duty and submission:

> God's Providence oversees all that happens here on earth. Nothing can happen unless he allows it to happen, and he only allows it to happen provided he can foresee how—if we accept His Will with love & trust—He can bring good out of it for us. If he allows pain or suffering to come to us, no matter through what secondary means, He wants us to accept this little cross as coming from Him. If we refuse to accept what His Providence sends into our lives with love and with trust, then His Will is unable to work our sanctification within our souls. If someone hurts us, our faith must show us that God has allowed this for our eternal

good. We must accept His Will for love of Him. "If you love Me, you will do My Will."

There is no evidence that Mrs. East wavered in the slightest when she returned to Houston with Leo to finalize the momentous decision to tear up her will and then divert the bulk of her estate into her foundation. It had been just seven weeks since she had met J. Peter Grace, who flew to Houston with his lawyer, Larry McKay, for the signing.

Unlike Leo, who had interpreted Jake Floyd's warnings to Sarita as the reasonable response of an honest country lawyer trying to protect his client's interests, Peter Grace had little trouble discerning Floyd's anger in Houston on January 22. "He hated my guts, I could tell," Grace remembers. And the animosity was mutual: "As soon as I saw him I looked upon him as a real maneuverer. I could tell by looking at him."

How?

"His eyes, face, presence. He didn't look honest. He looked like a real manipulator. Dishonest. Wouldn't believe a word he said. He was extremely clever."

Floyd was clever enough to gauge the power of affection Sarita held for Brother Leo and sufficiently shrewd to refrain from attacking Brother Leo personally. He made no overt attempt to dissuade Mrs. East from signing her new will or the foundation papers that day. Jake just smiled his dry smile, coolly acquiescing in the creation of the foundation he had already laid plans to steal away.

Sarita's rewritten will contained unpleasant news for just about all her major heirs. The big losers, first of all, were the Oblates of Mary Immaculate. The south Texas missionary congregation, close to the Kenedy family for eighty years, would still inherit the Headquarters house plus 10,000 acres surrounding it, but it lost all its mineral rights.

Stella Turcotte Lytton and her brother Louis Edgar Turcotte no longer coinherited Sarita's half of La Parra. Instead, they would split the surface rights to her San Pablo ranch, formerly bequeathed, complete with mineral rights, to Tom East, Jr., his brother, Robert, and their sister, Alicia Hattie. These three were dropped from the will altogether.

There were many detailed provisions regarding Sarita's personal staff. Her maid, Sara Curiel, was given $3,000 and a lifetime annuity of $1,200 a year. Her chauffeur, Chano Longoria, also received $3,000, plus $1,800 a year for life.

Sarita specifically remembered several of her more distant relatives among her grandmother Petra Vela's numerous descendants by her first marriage, to the slain Luis Vidal. Mrs. East maintained close and cordial relations with this wing of the family and made individual bequests to them in amounts as high as $25,000, including the $10,000 and $3,600 annuity she left to "Miss Irene" Putegnat of Brownsville, whose uncles, according to legend, had avenged Tom Kenedy's murder at Captain Mifflin Kenedy's order. Miss Irene came often to La Parra and was one of the usual participants in the females-only weekend benders Mrs. East occasionally hosted for "the gals" at the Headquarters.

The new will, like the old, forgave a long list of personal debts. Under "Notes Receivable" the various forgivenesses came to an aggregate $538,427.21. These included three notes totaling $25,000 that Sarita held from her brother-in-law Allen B. East. Judge Lee Lytton was forgiven $60,000. Andy Turcotte, the mortician, was excused close to $45,000. The largest note, for $100,000, was from the Mercy Hospital in Laredo.

A second schedule, designated "Accounts Receivable," listed dozens of trivial sums owed to the ranch commissary by Sarita's vaqueros and their families. Arnulfo Fonseca, for example, was forgiven his $15.00 arrears. Miguel Valles's debt of $4.10 on the ranch account books was likewise erased.

Sarita had provided her new attorneys with these names and sums from her records. Their precision, to the penny, reflected how meticulously the books were kept at La Parra. Yet under "Accounts Receivable" in the new will there was an alphabetical gap between Pedro Guevara ($13.00) and Manuel Garcia Torres ($42.58). It appears that the page listing employees with surnames beginning with *H* through *S* was dropped, or overlooked, altogether.

Still, enough care was taken in writing the new will that no one was plunged into penury. Tom East, Jr., for example, was an oil multimillionaire in his own right; he hardly cared about the loss of royalty income—huge as it undoubtedly would be—that he and his siblings were to suffer by their exclusion from the San Pablo property. The rancher would be much more passionately interested to hear from his lawyer and ally, Jake Floyd, that Stella Lytton and Louis Edgar Turcotte no longer were going to inherit their 200,000 acres of La Parra. Whoever controlled the Kenedy foundation would now control this land.

And there were generous compensations for some of those whose expectations had been hurt the worst. Bishop Garriga lost 13,000 acres of La Parra (including mineral rights), but the Corpus Christi diocese already had been granted a San Pablo royalty assignment worth about $200,000 a year in income. Stella Lytton and Louis Edgar Turcotte also retained fractional royalty assignments from which they would realize handsomely, albeit not on the scale they had once envisioned.

Yet, for all the generosity that survived revisions of her 1948 will, Mrs. East's major assets—half of La Parra and the majority of the mineral rights beneath both it and her San Pablo ranch—fell under Clause 26 of her 1960 will, the so-called residual clause in the document. These properties and everything else not specifically mentioned elsewhere in the will (or otherwise disposed of in Sarita's lifetime), read Clause 26, "I give, devise, bequeath and appoint to The John G. and Marie Stella Kenedy Memorial Foundation."

Thus, in the three and a half months since Sarita had stepped aboard the SS *Brazil* in New York and sailed south to Argentina, her foundation idea had become reality. It was, as she had always wanted, named in honor of her parents.

But no provision was made for the future protection of La Parra, an original concern, except for one equivocal admonition in Clause 26: "It is my earnest wish and desire that said Foundation continue to hold and operate my ranch properties located in Kenedy County unless it clearly appears to be impracticable and not in the best interest of said Foundation to do so." Nor was the foundation any longer to be managed by a panel of prelates, including Bishop Garriga, as Father Tiblier's notes of the December 29 meeting indicated Sarita wished. Instead, Mrs. East was persuaded, for the time being, that she alone should be a member, with Garriga relegated to a codicil that named him her successor in case of her sudden death.

Leo has ever since insisted it was *his* idea to name the bishop in the codicil—proof, says the monk, that he had no self-interest in the establishment of the foundation. Peter Grace recollects that Jake Floyd suggested the one-page amendment. Whichever version is accurate, however, the point is moot. Attorneys on hand from the Houston firm of Baker, Botts (the local tax and foundation experts recruited for their expertise by Larry McKay) indicated that they could not guarantee that a codicil to a will was legally effective, in Texas, to pass on membership in a foundation. As it turned out, most lawyers later agreed with Baker, Botts (and Jake Floyd) that it wasn't. If Mrs. East believed at the time that Bishop Garriga was then her legal successor as sole foundation member, she was mistaken.

Brother Leo thought that the signing itself had gone wonderfully and told Peter Grace as much in a note scribbled to his friend en route back to South America. *"Thanks very much,"* Leo wrote, "for the excellent job you and Larry did in Houston."

There were two ways in which the Kenedy Memorial Foundation could be funded. The charity could stand as an empty corporate shell until Sarita's death and then, as an entity, inherit the bulk of her estate via Clause 26. In the alternative, Mrs. East could begin to transfer her income-producing oil leases under irrevocable so-called inter vivos gifts, which would allow the foundation to begin functioning at once as a charity *and* would protect these sums from any subsequent attack on her will. Even if the will was someday challenged (a reasonable fear, given the drastic redistribution of the Kenedy estate) and thrown out of court, any assets transferred by Sarita into her foundation while she was alive and in good health would remain in the charity. It was this course, the immediate and direct transfer of oil leases as inter vivos gifts to the Kenedy Memorial Foundation, that Brother Leo urged on Sarita.

Jake Floyd, too, was prepared to begin filling the foundation treasury, but not before the attorney made certain adjustments of his own. On January 26, four days after the foundation was established, and with

Brother Leo about 4,600 miles away in Argentina, Floyd welcomed Sarita to his Alice law office, where they were to clean up a few legal details.

One was to empower the Alice National Bank to act as official depository for foundation assets. But Floyd was not yet through. He again raised the reliable specter of the IRS, deliberately disconcerting Sarita with the news that the federal government would not rule on the Kenedy foundation's tax-exempt status until it had been in operation for a year. In view of this and of the ironclad nature of inter vivos lease transfers, he soberly advised caution in assigning assets to the foundation and counseled getting a second opinion.

In New York, Peter Grace countered Floyd's warnings with an offer to Mrs. East of his own Serra Fund, which he explained to her had already been granted its tax exemption and was available right away as a vehicle for Sarita's charitable bounty.

Floyd's answer to this proposal was blunt, and misleading. Although Grace offered Sarita full control of the fund, Jake asked what guarantees there were that the easterner Peter Grace would honor this commitment in the future.

The latest confusion unsettled Sarita again. She feared the tax man as much as she loved her church, and she heard nothing in Floyd's arguments that roused her suspicions. Unsure of what to do, Sarita turned to Leo with her worries in a telephone call to Buenos Aires on January 27.

The monk by now was intimate enough with Mrs. East to address her as "Carissime" ("Dearest One") the same term of endearment he and Lotus used with each other in their correspondence. "Carissime," he wrote Sarita the day after their telephone conversation,

I was disappointed to hear that Mr. Floyd is still so reluctant to let you go ahead on your Foundation. As

Peter said, unless you have a strong Faith, and regard your obligation to the Church, the whole Foundation idea loses much of its appeal. Mr. Floyd evidently doesn't feel that much is lost to the Church by your yearly Charity being kept at around $100,000, instead of being able to push this up to three or four times that amount.

My suggestion is to continue to work with Mr. Floyd a bit more, and then you should make up your own decision, doing what you feel Our Lord wants you to do.

Later readers of this note, which like the rest of Leo's correspondence to Sarita ended up as evidence in court, have remarked with interest that the monk made no reference in it to the poor of Latin America, or of anywhere else. He confined his observations on Mrs. East's intents exclusively to her churchly "obligation."

If you feel God wants you to go ahead with this Foundation and that Mr. Floyd doesn't know how to cooperate, or that he doesn't want to, then perhaps the easiest way is to simply tell Peter to go ahead and set the thing in motion, and afterwards tell Mr. Floyd what you have done, while asking him—for a fee—to please act as manager of the assets.

Peter and his lawyers are certain that you can go ahead with the Foundation (both Serra and Kenedy) as soon as you want to. They do this type of work continually. If Mr. Floyd wants to delay for 2 to 3 to 4 years before putting this into action, at the expense of half a million dollars or more that you could have given to the Church, you are in no wise obliged to go along with him.

May God and Our Lady help you, Sarita! It is difficult work, and yet it is one that can give God much

glory and give you a great deal of satisfaction. Try to
view this whole affair from God's viewpoint (through
Faith) and then ask Him to strengthen you to do what
you feel He wants you to do!

All goes well here. Plan to be in Santiago at the
Carrera Hotel, Tuesday night, February 2nd. Will call
you around Thursday.

Sara Curiel, many years later, was able to re-create,
in pantomime, her mistress's gestures as Sarita read
the letter from Leo. The maid indicated that Mrs. East
scanned it slowly, several times, biting her lower lip
and once in a while gazing up from her desk with a
distracted air. At last Mrs. East smiled to herself at
Leo's closure, "your beadsman," an archaic term for
a personal rosarist that the monk had found in a vol-
ume of Shakespeare. He signed many of his personal
letters, to men and women, "your beadsman." Then
Sarita tucked the note into her desk drawer with all
the rest of the letters she received from the monk.

She had decided by the time the letter arrived at La
Parra to follow Jake Floyd's advice, notwithstanding
Leo's suggestions to the contrary. On February 3,
1960, Mrs. East summoned Chano Longoria to fetch
her Cadillac for a drive to San Antonio. There, Floyd
had arranged a meeting for Sarita with a Washington,
D.C., tax lawyer, Charles Burton, who was to conduct
a personal review with Sarita of both her new will and
her foundation.

Burton would remember arriving in San Antonio
from Washington on the evening of the third, and
checking into the St. Anthony Hotel, where Jake Floyd
provided him with a general briefing that night. As
Burton later testified, Floyd informally described his
client, her wealth, and her background and mildly offended Burton when he warned him not to disparage
Mexicans in Sarita's presence. "He specifically men-

tioned that her grandmother was a Mexican lady,'' Burton recalled under oath, ''and therefore I should be careful not to say anything anti-Latin, which of course I wouldn't have done anyway.''

The business conference, with Floyd in attendance, began with breakfast at eight and lasted until about four in the afternoon. According to Burton's later deposition, Sarita clearly explained her wishes. ''She said that strangely enough she didn't have any direct relatives as such. That there were cousins and other collateral relatives and that the ones she wanted to receive a part of her estate she was specifically mentioning in her will. But the other people were just kind of sitting on the fence like vultures waiting to grab her estate when she died, and she just didn't wish them to get it.''

The ''vultures'' were not identified by name.

As for the balance of her estate, Burton testified, ''she wished to have the property devoted to church uses. She mentioned specifically that she wanted a good deal of her property to be used in the area in which she lived, in the Corpus Christi area generally, and also she had some special interest in some work in South America. I believe it was specifically mentioned—Chile—that she wanted to make sure it was set up so that if it went to the foundation the trustees would have the right to use some of this money outside the United States. And there was specific mention of, I think, two activities in South America, but I only remember Chile as the one that sticks with me.''

Burton also took notes of the meeting, which he ordered typed upon his return to Washington. ''It was agreed,'' he wrote within hours of talking to Sarita, ''it was not advisable for Mrs. East to be the sole Member of the Foundation. As a consequence, it was agreed that Mr. Jacob Floyd would be a Member with Mrs. East, together with a local judge [Lee Lytton,

Jr.] who is highly regarded by Mrs. East and who is friendly to her. In addition, the By-Laws will be amended to provide that if any of the Members die, the surviving Members will elect a successor. However, the successor must be approved by the Archbishop [*sic*] in Corpus Christi.''

The only direct mention of Brother Leo in Burton's notes came in the final paragraph, where the monk was described as ''a Brother of some Catholic Order.'' Noting that Leo was, at that time, a codirector of the foundation with Sarita and Jake Floyd, Burton reported ''as soon as it can be done in a diplomatic way, Brother Leo will be called to resign.''

TWELVE
✛ ✛ ✛
Dreams Fulfilled

Sarita spent a fitful February 1960 at La Parra waiting for Leo to return from Argentina. After her meeting with Jake Floyd and Charles Burton, she was happy to be able to tell the monk by telephone of Floyd's sudden tractability, how he was busy putting together the first inter vivos oil lease gift to the Kenedy Memorial Foundation for her signature. Floyd also had prepared for Sarita's signature a second codicil to her will, an addition that spelled out in greater detail some of the terms of the will proper. But Mrs. East did not tell Leo the price of peace with Jake Floyd; her lawyer and Lee Lytton now were comembers of the foundation, a voting majority.

Her health was another source of disquiet. Sarita suffered from a range of age-related infirmities, from glaucoma to painful bouts of rheumatism. Yet while she had no concrete reason to suspect that she suffered from any more life-threatening diseases, she was preternaturally certain that she did not have long to live.

In December, after her return from Latin America, her throat had begun to bother her. At her January checkup in San Antonio, the doctors had advised bed rest and prescribed antibiotics for the condition. But by February the soreness had still not subsided, and she was having difficulty swallowing.

February's weather at the ranch mirrored Mrs. East's restless mood. The mercury bobbed back and forth between the thirties and the eighties in abrupt cycles of wind and sun and damp cloudy days. Sarita, as Elena would remember, was by turns tense and aloof and then excitedly voluble for no apparent reason. Finally, one morning late in the month she suddenly, and without explanation, disappeared from the ranch and was gone until sunset.

Elena and Stella Lytton were standing near the rear of the Headquarters that day when they saw the last glint of sunlight sparkling from the Cadillac's big windshield a quarter of a mile away. As Chano Longoria wheeled the black car to a stop, they walked toward it, curious to learn where Mrs. East had been. Four steps from the rear door they stopped and gaped in amazement to see Sarita clambering out in a knee-length peasant dress of dark blue, covered in a pattern of bright yellow flowers. Then they noticed her hair. It had been cut, coiffed, and sprayed, unusual enough for Sarita, but it had also been dyed a vibrant auburn, more or less her true hair color but positively *loud,* or so Elena thought to herself, against Sarita's blue-and-yellow dress.

"Well, Sarita!" Stella Lytton finally managed to blurt. "Aren't *you* something!"

Stella Lytton's forced gaiety did not dispel the awkwardness of the moment, made more acute by Sarita's announcement that her new dress, hairdo, and the "few little things" she'd purchased that day were all in preparation for another trip to South America, to begin within a week, and this time without a family escort. Mrs. East was to fly south alone with the monk. Although Sarita in all likelihood had livened her wardrobe not to please Leo (to whom fashion was an alien concept) but rather in response to the clothes consciousness she'd encountered among the Verstraetens and their friends in Buenos Aires, Elena and Stella suspected that the reverse was true. Before she went to bed that night, Mrs. Kenedy called both Bishop Garriga and Jake Floyd with the news.

Floyd was unruffled. Leo returned from South America sometime in the third week of February and together with Sarita on the twenty-sixth visited Floyd's Alice law office for the signing of the first inter vivos deed transfer. There was no mention made in the monk's presence of the new foundation membership alignment, nor did he ask to see any of the foundation records. Ignorant of the true state of affairs, Leo was satisfied by Floyd's easy geniality that all was moving smoothly, according to God's will.

From Alice, Chano Longoria drove Mrs. East and the monk north to San Antonio, where she wanted her troublesome throat examined again before she left the country. At the San Pablo Clinic, not far from the ruins of the Alamo, in downtown San Antonio, doctors discovered some small bumps on Sarita's thyroid. They saw no immediate cause for alarm but did warn Mrs. East of the possible need for surgery should the condition persist. She was cautioned not to exert herself, and to moderate her drinking.

Their next stop was Peter Grace's farm in South Carolina, where Mrs. East looked over the cattle operation and found it poorly managed. When she and Leo met Grace in Palm Beach, Florida, a few days later, she told him that as a cattleman he made a good industrialist. On March 15, 1960, after another round of clothes shopping in Palm Beach, Sarita boarded a jet for Chile with Leo.

The monk had not been idle in the weeks since the signing of the will and foundation papers. When he hit a snag in negotiations to acquire Las Condes, the Chilean monastery property, he instructed the Grace Bank in New York, by letter, to take $200,000 of Sarita's $305,000 donations from his "Brother Leo" account and to invest it in ninety-day notes at the Bank of Chile. His typed instructions to William O'Connell at the Grace Bank included the request "If possible, could you act as my agent in this matter, so that my name will not appear on the certificates of deposit?"

In a separate transaction (which wouldn't be discovered by the monks at Spencer for another year), Leo opened a new, back-channel money pipeline at the Grace Bank. Besides Sarita's covert account (which he controlled) plus his own and the official Trappist account, styled "Cistercian Abbey of Spencer, Inc.," Leo opened a second clandestine account, which he entitled "Cistercian Abbey of Spencer, Incorporated," where he would be able to park, or transfer, money with complete secrecy.

He had also been working on a third initiative that very adroitly addressed several issues at once. Leo proposed to Sarita during February that she consider buying about eight hundred acres of Estancia Acosta from Doña Carmen Acosta for $200,000. According to the plan as Leo outlined it in a letter to J. Peter Grace, Sarita would build a cottage on the property and run a small herd of Santa Gertrudis cattle there, adjacent to the new monastery. She would in this way "share" the monastery with Doña Carmen, a consolation for not having the monks establish themselves at La Parra.

The eight hundred acres—a track separate from the land the Acostas had already given the Trappists— would be held by an Argentine foundation and pass directly to Trappist control at Sarita's death. And her $200,000 purchase price would be Doña Carmen's donation to the Trappists for their abbey building fund. In effect, Leo had devised a way to double a $200,000 contribution to his order.

On March 15, the monk flew with Sarita as far as

Santiago, Chile, and then temporarily placed her in the willing care of the Bootes, Chito and Teresa. While Leo was seeing to his various projects in both Chile and Argentina, the Bootes escorted Sarita southeast and over the Andes into the Argentine lake district and the resort town of Bariloche, on Lake Nahuel Huapí. In the winter (that is, August) Bariloche is a ski center. In March, an autumn month, Bariloche and the surrounding region are famous for their fishing, probably Sarita's favorite sport. She caught several large lake trout on her visit to Bariloche and seemed to Teresa Boote to enjoy the outdoor life there much more than she did hotel living in Santiago or even in Buenos Aires. Mrs. East was more open with her new friends, as well, much franker in her doting regard for Brother Leo, and willing to confide her desire to adopt him as her son. Francis Verstraeten, Jr., then a teenager, came down to Bariloche from Buenos Aires for part of Sarita's stay there and heard the same rhapsodizing over the monk. "Leo was God to her," he recalls. "That is a fact. If he told her to jump out a window, she would."

April 4, 1960, found Sarita at Estancia Acosta, where she and Doña Carmen Acosta ratified the purchase and fund-transfer arrangement as Brother Leo had laid it out, by letter, to both of them. Mrs. East selected a shady spot for her cottage to be built on and asked Francis Verstraeten, Sr., to manage construction of the three-bedroom structure. She foresaw the house as simple—a single story with decorative grillwork featuring the laurel-leaf design of her grandfather Mifflin's original, Los Laureles, cattle brand. According to her emerging plan, Sarita hoped to spend as much as half her time at Estancia Acosta in the coming years.

The small community of monks at Estancia Acosta, led by Father Owen Hoey, were as fond of Sarita as of

Doña Carmen, perhaps more so, because of Mrs. East's motherly warmth toward them. "She was just a sweet, lovely person," remembers John Cody, a member of the first community at Estancia Acosta. "You'd want your mother to be just like her. And she seemed very, very pleased that she was part of this happening in South America. She thought it was wonderful to have a couple groups of contemplative monks in a foreign land that heretofore hadn't had any monks, you know.

"I knew she was a very wealthy woman and that she had no children and, somehow or another, Brother Leo had gotten her interested in South America. And, you know, he helped her. He weaned her off that bottle. She was hittin' that ol' jug pretty heavily. And he weaned her off that. And he certainly got her enthused in a way that did something for her because she certainly was happy to be down there in South America and she felt what she was doing was good."

Sarita, once again traveling with the Bootes, spent Easter 1960 in the Presidential Suite of the posh Colonial Hotel at Mar del Plata, the seaside resort and gambling mecca called "the Monte Carlo of Argentina." While relaxing at the ocean, Mrs. East received an unexpected visitor, Jake Floyd's law associate Carmel Davis, who flew down from Texas with a second inter vivos deed transfer for Sarita to sign. The unsuspecting Brother Leo did not question why Floyd would go to such lengths to have the document executed so swiftly, especially since Sarita was due back in the States in a couple weeks. He didn't know, of course, that at that moment Jake Floyd was funding his own foundation.

Following Easter at Mar del Plata, Mrs. East flew north to Buenos Aires and then set off on yet another side trip, a flight in Francis Verstraeten's private plane to a rural region directly north of Buenos Aires called Entre Ríos. Verstraeten had established a business venture at Entre Ríos (in which Sarita was a minority stockholder), a pilot paper-processing plant.

But aside from looking in on her investment, the objective of this excursion was for Mrs. East to evaluate Entre Ríos as a possible site for a model Santa Gertrudis cattle-breeding operation. Although Santa Gertrudis cattle were developed in a breeding program at the King Ranch, Sarita was just as proud of the animals as was Bob Kleberg. She liked the idea of starting a ranch at Entre Ríos—which Sarita would call Los Laureles—and also delighted in the notion that once the ranch was self-sufficient, it could become another Trappist monastery.

Leo had free-lanced this idea, apparently discussing it with no one except Francis Verstraeten (and swearing him to keep it a secret, even from Peter Grace). As the monk envisioned Los Laureles, a simple and utilitarian cloister would be erected there and ready for habitation before Dom Edmund or Brother Blaise or anyone else at Spencer knew of its existence.

THIRTEEN

✦ ✦ ✦

Dom Edmund's Blessing

By May of 1960 the undeclared warfare between Leo and Jake Floyd for command of Mrs. East's millions had become so thoroughly tangled that no one, least of all Sarita, had any clear notion of what was actually happening or what to expect next.

And the serious skirmishing had not yet begun.

The monk flew back from Argentina to the United States with Mrs. East on May 7 and collected from her, on May 9 in Houston, two more checks, for a total of $100,000. By May 12 Leo was back in Buenos Aires, where he received a cable from John O'Connell at the Grace Bank. "TEXAS CHECKS CLEARED," wired O'Connell. "ONE HUNDRED THOUSAND DEPOSITED IN YOUR PERSONAL ACCOUNT AS OF TODAY AFTER WASHING THROUGH OTHER ACCOUNT. AWAITING WORD FROM BANCO DE CHILE CONCERNING NINETY DAY CERTIFICATES."

"Now that's quite a picture, isn't it?" the attorney Frank Nesbitt asks with a smile. "Leo was havin' more fun takin' those funds and depositing them here and there and makin' some interest when he could."

The $200,000 February investment at the Banco de Chile (money earmarked for purchase of Las Condes, in Chile) netted Brother Leo about $3,500. Then, in late May, when the negotiations were complete, he wrote Sarita the good news. "Sent you a cable this morning," read the monk's letter, "to tell you that the Chilean property is finally ours, thanks to your tremendous charity and to God!"

As it happened, Dom Edmund Futterer also was in Buenos Aires in mid-May, on what would prove to be his last trip to South America as abbot. The Dom's failing health, now complicated by prostrate problems and atherosclerosis, had for some time affected his mental acuity. But his major problem was the simmering discontent at Spencer. The monks at the mother house in Massachusetts were more unhappy than ever over the upset and dislocations in their lives caused by the expansion program. Their complaints were being heard outside the cloister walls and would lead, before long, to an official investigation into Futterer's behavior, ordered by Abbot General Sortais in Rome.

The abbot himself remained unaware of, or indifferent to, his peril. To be sure, he was fully occupied with his expansion program, and he was overjoyed at Sarita's massive contributions to it. "Be assured," he wrote to her from Argentina on May 14, 1960, "that I have told Brother Leo that he has my wholehearted permission and blessing to help you in this foundation in any way that is necessary."

It is possible that Sarita had recently asked Futterer about Leo's continuing involvement with her foundation, hoping to secure his aid in the months ahead. Or, as she mentioned to others, Sarita may have suggested to the abbot that Leo's extended stays outside the monastery were endangering his vocation. Either concern, if expressed, would explain why Abbot Futterer felt the need to reassure Sarita.

Brother Leo, however, today insists that his help to Sarita was, in effect, bought and paid for the preceding December when she, in an exchange of letters with

Dom Edmund, agreed to pay for the Trappists' Latin-American expansion in return for Leo's help in establishing her foundation. Thus, according to Leo's story, his association with the widow from late 1959 onward was both a contractual obligation and a duty, in obedience to his abbot's orders. The $305,000 she gave the Trappists in January, the monk says, was a first payment donated under this explicit, written understanding.

Unfortunately for Leo (and for his credibility), the correspondence he insists spelled out this arrangement cannot be found, leaving the balance of Futterer's May 14, 1960, letter to Sarita as the only contemporaneous discussion of how and why the abbot assigned the monk to work with the widow. "Ordinarily, of course," he explained to her,

> I would not have the right to give such a permission to one of the monks of my community, no matter how great a work for the Church it might be. But in this case, where it has not only been a question of a tremendous work for the Church in general (and that it certainly is going to be in a most wonderful way!), but where intimately linked with the overall good to the Church is the great good that is resulting for our own Order, for this hidden vital member of the Mystical Body of Christ—I can give this permission to Brother Leo in perfect peace that it is what God wants—that it is a wonderful, integral part of Brother Leo's vocation. How true it is that in a great work that God wills and blesses *everyone* concerned receives deep blessings from God through it all. The relationship which God has created between you, Sarita and us—represented to such a great extent in this connection by Brother Leo—is a fine example of this, isn't it? That is why you must not hesitate to call on Brother Leo when it is necessary and helpful to you.

Futterer mentioned in his letter that he, along with Brother Leo and Brother Luke Roberts, his secretary, was coming north later in the month and that he hoped he could pay a call at La Parra. "My dear Father Abbot," Sarita wrote him back.

Thank you for your very kind letter. They are always a source of renewal, strength and consolation to me. I am so happy to know you, Brother Leo and Brother Luke are planning on stopping in Texas on your way back home. The time you have selected is perfectly convenient with me. I will be in New Orleans attending a young cousin's wedding, [but I] expect to return May 29th.

You are very generous in offering to have given [*sic*] Brother Leo permission and blessing to help me with my Foundation. It is due to his help and encouragement that a good start has been made on it.

According to his successor, Dom Thomas Keating, Father Edmund would not have placed such warm benedictions on Leo's relationship with Sarita had he then known of the clandestine "Incorporated" account at the Grace Bank or of the shadow monastery the monk hoped to build at Entre Ríos, in Argentina.

Also in the dark was Bishop Mariano Garriga in Corpus Christi. Garriga, at this point, did not know of the codicil naming him Mrs. East's successor as head of the Kenedy Memorial Foundation, or of her instructions in February to Jake Floyd that the bishop was to be given a veto over any other successor members, a directive that Floyd in any case had neglected to honor. He was supposed to incorporate the condition into the foundation's bylaws, but didn't.

What Bishop Garriga did know, or believed he knew, was that he and his diocese were Mrs. East's uppermost charitable concerns, that the Catholic church of south Texas, and Corpus Christi specifically, continued to enjoy a primacy in her affections. This mattered more to the bishop even than the amount he received from Mrs. East—it was a question of pride—and so he reacted violently in late May when it appeared to Garriga that his preeminence was being challenged anew.

The episode began with Mrs. East's luncheon date at Garriga's diocesan manse, on Corpus Christi Bay, a comfortable residence built, in part, with Kenedy money. The topic was the Jesuit seminary then about to be completed in Corpus Christi and the $15,000 Garriga needed to furnish the structure. Sarita told him that she would be pleased to underwrite the total sum but that her donation would have to wait until the start of the next tax year.

The delay in funding didn't bother Bishop Garriga. What sent him into another paroxysm of anger—his first since the January luncheon at La Parra—was the news (courtesy of Elena Kenedy) that Dom Edmund Futterer, Brother Luke Roberts, and Brother Leo had arrived from South America and were, at the very hour of the bishop's luncheon appointment with Mrs. East, taking their ease at her San Pablo ranch. Garriga didn't have to know that, while denying him the $15,000, Mrs. East had just handed another $150,000 to Dom Edmund (bringing her donations, for 1960, to $750,000) to be enraged at the Cistercians' unannounced presence in his territory. It was the old bond of loyalty between priest and parishioner that he felt had been violated. Impetuous as ever, Garriga communicated his anger in a telephone call to the ranch. It was an ill-considered move.

His second tirade of 1960 was fresh in Sarita's mind on Wednesday, the first of June, when Leo once again escorted her north to New York for another dinner meeting at the Grace estate on Long Island. Leo's object was for Mrs. East to begin to fine-tune the future course of her foundation by considering alternatives to Bishop Garriga as her successors.

The monk did not foresee a direct management role for himself. His broader purpose was to shape the foundation's destiny and so, in keeping with his, and her, care for the plight of the poor in Latin America, Leo urged Sarita to name activist clergy to her foundation, men such as Bishop Manuel Larrain of Talca, with whom she had by then had several conversations in Chile, or other members of CELAM, the Episcopal Conference of Latin-American Bishops. Also present at dinner on June 2 was the bulky Father Patrick Peyton, a six-three, 250-pound Holy Cross priest and head of the "Family Rosary Crusade."

J. Peter Grace deeply admired Peyton, fifty-one, and his crusades, huge rallies the priest held all over the world in which hundreds of thousands of the faithful were exhorted to daily repetitions of their rosaries to promote family unity. Grace saw Peyton's crusades as a potent antidote to the spread of the common enemy, communism, especially in Latin America, and had encouraged Sarita to support the priest. She had already met Peyton on several occasions and had attended one of his rallies in Chile. Mrs. East, too, admired, the priest's work.

Grace's own commitment to Peyton was absolute. The Holy Cross crusader was as frequently seen at the W. R. Grace executive offices in Manhattan as was Leo, and he was accorded the same respect and courtesy that the monk enjoyed. "We all thought of Peyton as sweet and simpleminded," says the same former Grace official who recalled Leo as a rogue. "Peyton was not at all astute, completely different from Leo, and he was very spiritual."

On one occasion, says this executive, Father Peyton meekly walked in on a senior management conference. He asked the startled Grace company officers for their prayers that his upcoming crusade go well. Grace himself, who was leading the meeting, halted all discussions. The CEO dropped to his knees, as did the rest of executives in the room; then they all prayed for Father Peyton's good fortune.

Peyton reportedly said very little on the night of June 2. It was a balmy late-spring evening, clement enough to allow for an outdoor stroll after dinner. Father Peyton confined himself to quietly murmuring his rosary as Sarita, Leo, and Peter Grace spoke.

According to Grace's later version of the conversation, it was apparent that Mrs. East was not yet prepared to accept Brother Leo's CELAM candidates to run her foundation. Rather, she asked him what he would do. Grace answered that he hoped to have a foundation of his own, funded at about $16 million, by the close of his life. He then added that he believed each age produced people with "providential ideas" for spreading the faith, and these were the types of persons Grace hoped would manage his foundation. Two such men of the present time, he went on, were Leo and Father Peyton.

The monk was surprised at his friend's comments and suggestions, but Leo did not demur when Sarita accepted Grace's arguments. After a moment's reflection, she asked if all three of her companions there on the lawn would consider accepting the responsibility of managing the Kenedy foundation in the event of her death.

Two days later in Manhattan, Lawrence McKay drew up codicil three, which ousted Bishop Garriga and installed the new membership triumvirate as Mrs. East's successors.

Sarita also directed that a fourth codicil, incorporating other changes in her will, be executed at the same time. In it Mrs. East placed the "request" that

10 percent of the Kenedy Memorial Foundation's net annual income be earmarked for the diocese of Corpus Christi. She also left her cousins Stella Lytton and Louis Edgar Turcotte each an additional $25,000 a year for life, from the oil revenues at San Pablo. For the Oblate Congregation, she reinstated 10 percent of the lost royalties under its 10,000 acres at La Parra.

Mrs. East also looked ahead to the future management of her ranches and mineral properties. She requested the future members of her foundation to appoint the Alice National Bank and the Frost National Bank in San Antonio to oversee her lands and added, "I have deep respect for the ability of the present managers and sub-managers of my ranching operations [meaning, for the most part, the Turcotte family]. Accordingly, I request the foregoing banks to give preference to the present managers and sub-managers and their children for appointment to the jobs which they or their parents now hold. . . ."

With these codicils written and signed, Lawrence McKay was told that he could present Mrs. East with a final bill for his legal work. Cahill, Gordon, Reindel & Ohl's invoice for $12,874.96 was first submitted to Leo. "Itemize it a bit," the monk wrote back to McKay, "so she can better see how much work you've done."

The statement was mailed on June 7, the same day Sarita's sore throat was reexamined by her physicians in San Antonio. The lumps on her thyroid had persisted, grown more distinct, and they now worried the doctors at the San Pablo clinic. A thyroidectomy was indicated, and Mrs. East with trepidation prepared to go under the knife at Hermann Hospital in Houston on June 16.

She was told that the lumps might be cancerous and that the procedure required a general anesthetic, two

factors that put Sarita in mind of her mortality. Such
thoughts now necessarily involved her fledgling foundation, which is probably why, on June 9 in Houston,
she at last disclosed to a flabbergasted Leo that since
February Jake Floyd and Lee Lytton had been her
foundation comembers. Sarita also told the monk that
she believed the Floyd and Lytton memberships were
only a tax-avoidance expediency, that the two Texans
were only paper presences on the foundation, with no
real function in its management. This was when Leo
put Mrs. East on the telephone to Lawrence McKay in
New York. McKay asked Sarita what arrangement she
preferred. Mrs. East answered that she wanted, at least
for the time being, to run the foundation by herself as
sole member.

McKay then went into action. He composed a letter
and had it pouched, overnight, to Sarita in Houston.
The two-page correspondence, which McKay knew was
to be forwarded to Floyd and Lytton, firmly emphasized that it was Mrs. East's "intent" to run the John
G. and Marie Stella Kenedy Memorial Foundation by
herself during her lifetime. McKay referred to this "intent" in connection with her first codicil, naming
Bishop Garriga as her successor member, but the lawyer said nothing in the letter of the recently signed third
codicil that ousted Garriga and replaced him with Leo,
Peter Grace, and Father Peyton. No one in Texas was
to know that Sarita, on the eve of major surgery at the
age of seventy, had entrusted the bulk of her family
fortune to the monk, the magnate, and the priest.

With McKay's typed letter in hand, Leo then drafted
notes to Floyd and Lytton that Sarita copied almost
verbatim in her own hand on Rice Hotel stationery.
"Dear Mr. Floyd," read the first one.

As you can see from the enclosed letter, I spoke with
Mr. McKay about the extra members we ap-

pointed last February. Since Mr. McKay and his Houston lawyers [Baker, Botts] assure me that I can remain the sole Member for life, I would prefer—since I am putting so much of my assets into the foundation—to retain this priviledge [*sic*]. Would please sign the enclosed form, and mail it to me here at the New Hermann Hospital where I'll be for the next ten days or so. I have a little growth in my throat which the doctors want to remove. They assure me that I'll be back in the saddle by the 25th.

I am writing Lee along these lines, since I am anxious to retain my priviledge [*sic*] ⌐f being the sole member of my parents' Foundation. Thank you for your kindness and cooperation which you have always shown me.

Sincerely, your friend, Sarita K. East.

A postscript at the bottom of the letter apparently was Sarita's afterthought. "I am sure you will understand my position," she wrote, "especially since I did not clearly understand the consequences of the resolution that I signed in February, raising the number of Members to three."

Larry McKay in New York warned Brother Leo at this juncture, as he had before, that he continued to doubt that Sarita could transfer membership by codicil and that he recommended that codicil three, naming Leo, Grace, and Peyton as successor members be replaced with a resolution, or corporate act, such as the one Jake Floyd used to name himself and Lee Lytton as members. Leo, impatient with that kind of legal detail, ignored McKay's advice. Instead, he mailed Sarita's handwritten notes and resignation forms to Floyd and Lytton, and considered their threat extinguished when the signed papers came back on the fifteenth.

The next question was how to profit from his time in Houston during the days of Sarita's postoperative convalescence. Once before, when Mrs. East was undergoing tests in San Antonio, the monk had had some dental work done. Now it was decided that he should do something about his chronic, aching feet. On June 15, both the widow and her beadsman checked into Hermann Hospital—she to have her thyroid removed and he to receive a bunionectomy.

Lois Randolph, chief nurse to Mrs. East's surgeons, Drs. George W. Waldron and Hampton Robinson, thought Leo and Sarita a peculiar twosome from the moment he arrived with her in the surgeons' treatment room. "Most people," Nurse Randolph later told Frank Nesbitt in her deposition, "don't bring a priest into the treatment room." The nurse decided, as had others, that the younger man (Leo was now in his early forties) in the clerical collar must be Mrs. East's son.

Both patients withstood their surgery well. A biopsy report found that Sarita's lumps were "benign follicular adenomas"; no cancer was detected. Brother Leo's only difficulty was significant postoperative pain from his bunionectomy, soreness that immobilized the monk for a few days.

But even from his bed Brother Leo was Sarita's solicitous companion, at one point summoning Nurse Randolph to his room to ask if perhaps Mrs. East could have her usual cocktails during her stay. Dr. Waldron approved the request.

Lois Randolph also related another episode that to her seemed to capture the essence of the curious relationship between the monk and the widow. "I remember traipsing down the hall and going into his room," the nurse told Nesbitt. "It was a corner room, and we are not very polite in the medical profession. I just hit the door and walked in at the same time. When I did, Mrs. East was sitting in a chair right by the bed. Brother Leo had his head elevated and was in bed. Whether [their hands] were touching or not, I don't know.''

Sarita had a drink in her hand and was leaning close to Leo. ''I was embarrassed,'' Randolph continued, ''because I felt like that I had interrupted something. I blushed and said, 'Excuse me,' and started backing up.

''And she said, 'Oh, no,' or something like that. I don't remember what I said, but I got out of there.''

Frank Nesbitt pressed the nurse on why the tender moment she had witnessed in Leo's room unnerved her so.

''Well,'' she answered, ''there was just . . . I don't know. It was just something about the way she was looking at him, and everything, that embarrassed me.''

''Would you describe the way she was looking at him?'' the lawyer asked.

''Fatuous. Sort of fawning. Have you ever seen a mother with a child that was hovering over him when they were sick? Well, that was the impression that I got. And it was enough that it, that it bothered me. It embarrassed me.''

FOURTEEN

✛ ✛ ✛

A Grand Tour

Brother Leo maintains he still did not distrust Jake Floyd, even after discovery of the Floyd and Lytton memberships, which, had they stood, would have revested complete control of the Kenedy fortune with Sarita's family and the Alice National Bank. He reports, however, that Sarita had lost patience with her lawyer and might have fired Floyd that summer had the monk not talked her out of it.

On July 1, 1960, a week after her discharge from Hermann Hospital, Mrs. East wrote Leo another $100,000 check. On the third they were at St. Joseph's Abbey at Spencer, where Sarita met Lotus Gregory as well as most of the monks. "She looked upon us as sort of her boys, in a way," remembers Father Richard Gans. "It was really delightful, you know, when she came up to Spencer and told her stories of Texas and whatnot.

"She was a kind of grandmother, very kind, but she was a firm lady."

In what way?

"Well, just the stories she told about shooting rattlesnakes and whatnot in Texas, you know? You don't connect that with a grandmother who's piddling away in the house all the time."

Father Gans was to be among the first group of

monks to pioneer the monastery at Las Condes, in Chile, that September. "Dom Edmund," he says, "would confide certain things in those of us who were going to Latin America. When Sarita came to visit—I forget if it was before or after she spoke to us—Dom Edmund said to me, 'You know, I've given Child Leo permission to work with Sarita East. She's got this thing where she wants to set up a foundation to help out the poor of Latin America. And it's such a good cause I think it's worthwhile [for me to give] Brother Leo's services to her for what she's doing for us. She's doing a tremendous good for us, and she's doing a tremendous good giving her fortune to Latin America.' "

On July 5 Brother Leo and Sarita flew together to Buenos Aires. It was now nearly the dead of winter in Argentina, chilly and damp in Buenos Aires, the least appealing season of the year. Because of the poor weather and her recent surgery, Sarita curtailed her schedule, spending most of her time with the Verstraetens at long lunches and then dinners and "snorters" in her room at the Plaza.

Francis Verstraeten, Sr., had by now partially completed Mrs. East's cottage near the new monastery at Estancia Acosta, and her cattle-breeding station cum concealed monastery, Los Laureles, was under construction at Entre Ríos. Verstraeten, who had accepted responsibility for overseeing this work, too, remembers Leo pressuring him to complete the building as quickly as possible. Verstraeten had been given $15,000 to get started in May. On this trip, according to his personal records, Sarita provided a quarter of a million more dollars for the Entre Ríos project.

Mrs. East stayed nearly seven weeks on this, her third trip to Argentina; all told, she had spent more than half her time and in excess of a million dollars in Latin America since first embarking for Buenos Aires aboard the SS *Brazil* with Elena, Paul Seuss, and Lady East in October of 1959.

On her third return trip home to the States, the accommodating and companionable Bootes, Chito and Teresa, were her invited travel mates. From Buenos Aires the trio journeyed up to the Chaco and thunderous cataracts at Iguaqua Falls, on the Argentine-Brazilian border, and flew on to the Brazilian Atlantic coast port city of São Paulo.

They then visited the Brazilian interior and the country's futuristic new capital, Brasília. Thence northward, by air, to the Caribbean and stops at Trinidad, Barbados, and, finally, Puerto Rico. Chito Boote would remember, under oath, that Sarita took photographs everywhere they went and stopped to admire every religious statue and edifice they encountered. Chito's wife, Teresa, shared Mrs. East's passion for cathedrals, shrines, and altars. Her husband, a recent convert to Catholicism, did not. "I wasn't so enthusiastic," he acknowledged in his testimony.

Brother Leo, recently returned from a trip to Europe with Peter Grace, joined the party in Puerto Rico and accompanied them north to the Grace family summer house at Northeast Harbor, on the coast of Maine. The purpose of the trip, as Chito Boote understood it, "was so Peter Grace could advise her on some of her affairs." But the Argentine's primary recollection was of the Graces and their many children splashing in the chilly ocean. "They were bathing in water about ten degrees above zero," Chito Boote recounted in amazement. "And they didn't seem to feel the cold. They are what I would call Eskimos. I don't know where they got so tough."

Mrs. East, in the past eleven months, had covered more than sixty thousand miles by boat, train, car, and airplane on her various travels with Leo. She had also moved in and out of two dozen hotels in seven states and seven foreign countries. Now she packed for New York from Maine and then was briefly reentrusted to the Bootes' care for the next stop on her tour, New Orleans. Brother Leo caught up with the party in the first week of September 1960, in Houston, where Sarita's throat was reexamined. All test results were negative.

She was eager for Chito and Teresa Boote to see La Parra; Mrs. East had looked forward to showing off her ranch and to treating the Argentines to some Texas-style hospitality. But she decided to delay her return home for a few days in order for Peter Grace and Brother Leo to arrange a special, private meeting for her in Houston with an oil expert, William Sherry of Tulsa.

Until this time Sarita had remained ignorant of her true worth. Peter Grace, in his later testimony, would describe how Mrs. East had been awakened to the immense amount of good she could accomplish with her foundation *in her lifetime*, but the problem had been to find someone she trusted to evaluate her oil and gas holdings and to confirm to her that she could afford to do more because she was very rich, and getting richer.

The solution came by chance to Peter Grace while he was at a luncheon at Notre Dame University. Across the room, he spied Bill Sherry, a petroleum engineer known to him and to Mrs. East; Sherry, a Catholic, had officiated at Mrs. East's 1949 induction into the Equestrian Order of the Holy Sepulchre.

"I grabbed him as soon as lunch was over," Grace wrote to Leo in early September, "and got him into a corner to explain the situation and ask him whether or not he'd be willing to help out here as a favor to the Catholic Church." Sherry quickly agreed to be of assistance, and arrangements were made for him to meet with Mrs. East in her Houston hotel room.

As Bill Sherry would remember his interview with

Sarita at the Shamrock, she explained to him how "she was dismayed over the fact that she wanted to put this money in South America and the local people, even the bishop, were so disconsolate over her plans that she was so enthused about."

Sarita told the oil engineer where to find the necessary records in order for him to conduct a review of her holdings, but she warned him to be discreet. "She told me," Sherry testified, "that she wanted this report made and delivered to her. Any communication I had was to be with her personally, and any time I had occasion to write her to make it personal and confidential."

According to Sherry, when he asked Mrs. East if anyone in the towns of Sarita or Alice was aware that she wanted this review and evaluation made, "she very knowingly smiled and said no."

Sarita passed the balance of the month entertaining the Bootes at La Parra. The Argentines didn't make much of an impression on her nephews, the Turcotte boys. "I thought they were both weirder than three-dollar bills," says Jack Turcotte. "Strange people."

Mrs. East fussed over the poor health of her dog, Tuffy. Chito Boote got drunk and shot three wild turkeys out of season. But the only untoward incident during their stay at the ranch came when Sarita asked Bishop Garriga to baptize the newly converted Chito as a Catholic. "She was proud of thinking I would be confirmed in Corpus Christi," Boote later testified. But Garriga refused to officiate. "Bishop Garriga was very, very nasty about it," explained Boote. "He told her among other things he wouldn't baptize one of her drunken friends. That drunken friend was myself."

Brother Leo reappeared at La Parra in late September as Sarita was about to decide on a retirement insurance plan for her employees. Her office manager, Walter O. Bourgeois (related to her through the Turcottes), who had been working on the program for some time, remembered in his testimony that the monk "just appeared in the office at Sarita," where Leo examined the facts and figures, as Bourgeois had assembled them. Then the office manager was called to a conference at the Headquarters.

"Brother Leo," Bourgeois would remember of the gathering, "found everything in shape, and all the figures, but he wanted it all dropped." The monk's explanation, according to Sarita's office manager, was "that he had a man who handled insurance to take care of it."

Sarita, Leo, and Walter Bourgeois enjoyed a cocktail together during the discussion, in which Mrs. East said little.

"In other words," Frank Nesbitt asked Bourgeois, "he did most of the talking with reference to the insurance plan?"

"I'd say he did most of it."

"Did you ever get an insurance plan?"

"No, sir."

FIFTEEN

A Diagnosis

Dom Edmund Futterer was a confused and often dispirited abbot in the autumn of 1960. He continued to have trouble sleeping and was afflicted with memory lapses. He faced prostate surgery later that fall. And the official investigation into his conduct, led by Dom James Fox of the monastery at Gethsemane, in Kentucky, had begun. Although the allegations of homosexuality were denied and were not supported by the evidence, it was clear how Dom Fox would have to decide. Father Edmund was in the waning days of his abbacy, and his leave-taking from the community would be wrenching for many of his "children." "I loved Dom Edmund Futterer very deeply," says John Cody. "He was just a great man of God, in my estimation, and he suffered an awful lot when the shit hit the fan."

"His electroencephalogram," says Father Mark Delery, a medical doctor who joined the Trappists in 1954 and who served as Futterer's physician, "was grossly abnormal. Dr. John Sullivan at Tufts University made a diagnosis of mild cellular atrophy; the brain cells were damaged. So there was memory loss and, basically, bad judgment. For example, when he knew he might be relieved of his duties he took me aside and said, 'I've been thinking about sending you to Argentina. Do you want to go?' Now, going to Argentina was something for which you prepared yourself for at least six months to a year.

"Then he said, 'I'm going down there and be in charge.'

"That type of thing, you see? Poor judgment."

Added to Dom Edmund's mental burdens was the disclosure, sometime late in the summer of 1960, of the project at Entre Ríos, Sarita's proposed Argentine cattle-breeding station and proto-monastery. The abbot did not as yet know of the secret accounts at the Grace Bank, and it is unclear how Dom Edmund learned of Los Laureles. But his response to it was clear. On October 8 a confidential "MEMORANDUM re THE FINANCING OF SPENCER'S EXPANSION PROGRAM" was drawn up and signed by the abbot, by his secretary, Brother Luke, and by Brother Leo. The document outlined in specific detail how Leo henceforth was to comport himself, what he could and could not promise Mrs. East, and exactly how her money was to be handled.

On Los Laureles, for example, if a monastery was to be built there, permission would have to come from Rome. Sarita could be "encouraged" to hope that someday a monastery might be built on the property, but "it is clearly understood that this hope and encouragement is not, and can not be, a commitment binding St. Joseph's Abbey, nor may this information be given to others without specific permission of Reverend Father."

Futterer agreed "in principle" that Leo could go on seeing Sarita but restricted their time together to one month out of the year, for the remainder of her life, at Estancia Acosta. If the monastery at Los Laureles became a reality, Father Edmund noted in the memo, Leo might visit with her there, as well.

The memo directed further that in the future all donations "will be turned over to the Controller [Brother Alan] who, in Reverend Father's name, alone budgets and spends them." Futterer, who had by this time discovered that Leo was a director of Sarita's foundation, now gave his direct permission for the monk "or some other representative of the Abbey whom Reverend Father might choose" to become an officer of the Kenedy Memorial Foundation. However, the memo explicitly stated that service to the Kenedy Foundation could be permitted because of the anticipated help the order would receive from the foundation over the coming years. Abbot Futterer, according to Father Raphael Simon, felt that Brother Leo's vocation would be best aided if he was put back into the shoe shop at Spencer (where the telephone would be ripped out to enforce Leo's isolation) and if another monk, agreeable to Leo and to Peter Grace, was appointed liaison between the monk and the industrialist with regard to foundation matters.

For the time being, however, Brother Leo was allowed to rejoin Sarita in Houston, where she was nervously awaiting the results of yet another battery of diagnostic exams. While in Colorado with the Bootes, she had begun to complain of chest and back pains. The discomfort worsened so quickly that she telephoned one of her surgeons, Dr. Hampton Robinson, in Houston. Upon hearing of Sarita's symptoms, Robinson advised her to come down at her earliest convenience, which was the next day.

She was examined on October 5 and 6 in Houston by the internist Dr. James A. Greene. The doctor told Mrs. East that she had developed osteoporosis, discovered some evidence of diverticulosis, and opined that her pain perhaps derived from a recent chest infection—his antiquarian term for the condition was "rheumatism of the chest."

Dr. Greene gave Sarita dicalcium phosphate for the

osteoporosis, suggested she cut fats from her diet and consume more vegetable protein, and advised aspirin and heat packs for her pain, which he predicted would gradually subside. Greene further recommended that she reduce her active travel schedule and that she stop drinking altogether for at least two months.

Despite the favorable prognosis, however, Sarita's pain did not go away. "She got about," Chito Boote recalled in his deposition, "but was all the time complaining of her sore back." Yet Mrs. East would not cancel another planned trip to Argentina. And whether from long habit or for their analgesic effect, she did not give up her daily tumblers of scotch.

Two weeks later, on October 22, 1960, Sarita and Brother Leo gathered with J. Peter Grace at the Park Lane Hotel in New York City to hear William Sherry's secret evaluation of her mineral holdings. Sherry gave the group his conservative guess that the recoverable oil and gas deposits were worth about $36 million. Sarita, Sherry would recall in his deposition, was "exuberant" at the news.

The petroleum engineer's positive report, however, did nothing to mitigate Sarita's physical suffering. Peter Grace noticed how stiffly she was holding herself. Francis Verstraeten was disturbed by her appearance, too. Sarita looked haggard to him when she arrived with Brother Leo in Buenos Aires on Halloween night, and she made little attempt to conceal her agony.

Verstraeten was accustomed to Mrs. East's nagging ill health; on her previous trip, in August, her glaucoma had worsened suddenly and Verstraeten had to arrange for an emergency consultation for her with a Buenos Aires eye doctor. Now he suspected a deeper problem and privately voiced his concerns to Brother Leo.

"I told him I thought we should have a doctor look at her," he remembers. "Leo told me she had just been to one in the States and that he'd given her a clean bill of health. He also said Sarita didn't like doctors and would not go to one if she could help it."

On November 4 the monk wrote Jake Floyd from South America. Above his close, "Most cordially yours in Christ," Leo attended to several business details of the type his abbot now strongly preferred the monk to avoid. He told Floyd, for example, of a $5,000 donation Mrs. East wished to make to a Catholic mission to the poor in British Honduras (now Belize). The monk also had a direct query for the lawyer: "Mrs. East asked me to ask you to estimate the income to the Foundation for the year 1961." In his letter to Floyd, Leo described his ailing benefactress as "well and happy."

On November 9 the monk typed "just a quick line" to the accountant Tom Doyle at W. R. Grace & Company in New York, informing the executive (who had opened Sarita's account at the Grace Bank), "We urgently need an estimate of Mrs. East's cash in banks at the end of the year, and how much surplus cash you feel she has."

On the tenth he informed Jake Floyd, again by letter, "Mrs. East's health is good." The same day, Leo disclosed in a letter to Lawrence McKay that Sarita wanted to make a $150,000 loan to her Argentine foundation (which held title to the land at Entre Ríos, as well as her acreage at Estancia Acosta). "Write out a codicil to her last will," the monk instructed McKay, "wherein she forgives after death both interest and re-payment to this loan." Toward the end of the letter, Brother Leo inquired, "Does Jake need a note from her to hurry him up on the transfer of the minerals?"

Meanwhile, a worried Francis Verstraeten had watched Sarita's pain consume her. In view of her supposed aversion to physicians, he didn't try to persuade her to see one. Instead, he contacted Dr. Leon Soldati, an eminent Argentine cardiologist then married to one of Rachel Verstraeten's sisters. With some reluctance, Dr. Soldati agreed to assess Mrs. East's health surreptitiously.

Verstraeten arranged for the doctor to be introduced to Sarita at a dinner. Midway through the meal in the Plaza Hotel dining room, as Verstraeten tells the story, Soldati dropped the ruse and told her that her evident physical discomfort demanded immediate medical attention. According to Verstraeten's memory and handwritten diaries of the time, Dr. Soldati examined Mrs. East that night in her room at the hotel. The next day, November 17, the cardiologist checked her into the Catholic Little Company of Mary Hospital, in Buenos Aires. No one in her family was notified of the hospitalization.

Leo did wire Dr. Hampton Robinson in Houston on the morning of the eighteenth: "SARITA'S CHEST PAIN HAS CONTINUED SINCE LEAVING TEXAS. BUENOS AIRES DOCTORS NOW DIAGNOSE PLEURAL EFFUSION FROM XRAYS TAKEN YESTERDAY. PLEASE CABLE ME. . . . YOUR LAST EXAMINATION OF CHEST AREA LEFT SIDE, ALSO LAB RESULTS OF SEDIMENTATION RATE AND BLOOD CELL COUNT. REGARDS. BROTHER LEO.''

If the monk, as he later testified, had not noticed anything wrong with Sarita until her hospitalization, Dr. Soldati's grave suspicions now spurred him into action. Over the next week Leo closed her Grace Bank account and transferred its remaining balance, $61,000, into his "Brother Leo" account. Sarita had not written a single check of her own against the moneys in this secret account. Brother Leo personally had "washed" every dollar in, and out, of the account.

On November 24, Thanksgiving Day 1960, Dr. Soldati confirmed what he had guessed from Mrs. East's first X ray. "DEFINITE DIAGNOSIS," Brother Leo cabled Dr. Robinson. "THORACIC METASTATIC CARCINOMA."

Sarita was riddled with cancer.

There was no question about Soldati's diagnosis or about his fatal prognosis: Mrs. East had only a short time to live. But instead of arranging for her to return to south Texas to die, Brother Leo cabled J. Peter Grace in New York, requesting him to find a cancer specialist to fly to Argentina. Mrs. East was not going to believe she was dying of cancer unless the diagnosis was confirmed by a U.S. physician. On December 1, 1960, Dr. John Pool of Memorial Center (now Memorial Sloan-Kettering) in Manhattan came to Sarita's bedside at the Little Company of Mary Hospital and told her that she was fatally stricken.

Leo still had not informed Mrs. East's relatives of her mortal illness, although, as it turned out, they already knew. On November 26, Dr. Hampton Robinson had telephoned Stella Lytton with news of Dr. Soldati's Thanksgiving Day cancer diagnosis. At Stella's urging, Robinson telegraphed back to Brother Leo in Buenos Aires that Sarita should receive "further medical management" in the United States.

There was no further communication from Argentina to south Texas. Elena Kenedy tried to telephone the Bootes. According to her, when she finally got through, Chito Boote would tell her nothing. Not until December 6 did Sarita's family finally reach J. Peter Grace in New York, who informed them that Mrs. East had been admitted to the Francis Cardinal Spellman wing of St. Vincent's Hospital in New York City.

Three days earlier, Brother Leo and the Verstraetens had placed Sarita aboard a Panagra flight in a special hospital berth for the fourteen-hour flight from Buenos Aires to New York. Dr. Pool accompanied Mrs. East on the airplane and administered the synthetic narcotic Demerol to her at least three times during the trip. Six hours before landing at Idlewild, he gave her 400 milligrams of the tranquilizer Equanil. "This woman," the doctor noted on Sarita's chart at her first destination, Memorial Center, "is *miserable.*" The emphasis on *miserable* was his.

Memorial Center offered the most advanced cancer treatment in the world, but Sarita's condition was well beyond any realistic hopes of medical science. The crowded facility also had no private rooms available. And Sarita wished to be in a Catholic institution. Therefore, two days after her arrival—and at her insistence—she was transferred by stretcher to St. Vincent's on West Eleventh Street, where the tumor-shrinking X-ray therapy Dr. Soldati had begun in Argentina was continued.

Hormone treatments were tried, as well. Both measures were essentially palliative. The pain, which had spread to Sarita' neck and abdomen, was at first manageable with these therapies and with drugs. Much more difficult to control were her cold sweats, nausea, retching, and a worsening shortness of breath from the fluid filling her lungs.

Mrs. East's torments, apparent from her hospital charts, were nonetheless intermittent. Late nights and early mornings were the worst times. In the afternoons, she appeared to stabilize and was generally alert. This was the Sarita recollected by her many visitors over the next several weeks, people who usually saw her sometime soon after 2:00 P.M.

Most of her callers later recollected Brother Leo as a nearly constant presence at the hospital, discreet and unoffending around her many friends and family members. People like Bob Kleberg of the King Ranch and the Armstrongs, Major Tom and Henrietta, had been introduced to Leo both in Argentina and in Texas, and

they liked him. Henrietta Armstrong, especially, believed the monk had been a positive influence on Sarita. These friends were now pleased that Mrs. East
had the monk at her side.

But Leo is remembered quite differently by the hospital staff. Reportedly he provided them with a list of
suitable visitors for Sarita, and the staff was expected
to inform him of all callers. One nun, who declines to
be identified, today complains of the monk's dismissive attitude toward her—much as Mrs. East's employees at La Parra resented what they took to be Leo's
hauteur. This nun also recalls Brother Leo's aggressive
interference with her duties, and how he presumed the
authority of a doctor.

Elena Kenedy, who together with her brother Paul
Seuss and Stella Turcotte Lytton arrived in New York
on December 8, saw her sister-in-law every day. Their
conversations in Sarita's room usually drifted into
reminiscences and ranch topics. Sarita, who read a
south Texas newspaper in her bed each day, expected
updates from Elena on how her cattle were doing and
all the news of her vaqueros and their families. She
often asked about her dog Tuffy, too. It was decided
not to tell her that Tuffy had died.

She was most adamant, according to Elena, on
where she wished to spend her remaining time, and it
was not in a New York City hospital. The president of
Humble Oil had offered Sarita a company plane, rigged
with a berth, to return her to Texas. And the Spohn
Hospital in Corpus Christi (where Sarita was born)
assured the Kenedy family that as much could be done
for her in Texas as in New York. Contingent upon the
effectiveness of her daily X-ray therapy in inhibiting
the cancer's progress, it was provisionally agreed that
she would fly home to Texas on January 1.

Elena's once-warm regard for Brother Leo had ev-
anesced the preceding June when she learned from

Jake Floyd of his and Lee Lytton's forced resignations from the Kenedy Memorial Foundation. "Greedy" was her term for the monk thereafter. But Mrs. Kenedy was careful not to mention her irritations to Sarita, either about the resignations or to complain that the monk had spirited Mrs. East to New York, without showing the family even the minimal courtesy of personally informing them that she was dangerously ill.

It was Sarita, according to Elena's testimony, who raised the sensitive issue of her foundation. One afternoon toward Christmastime, Mrs. Kenedy remembered, she found her sister-in-law upset. The source of the disquiet, said Elena, was a note that Sarita then handed to her to read. It was dated December 17 and postmarked Rome.

"My dear Mrs. East," began the typewritten message from Eugene Cardinal Tisserant, a French cleric Sarita had never met. "It has come to our attention that you in your kindness and goodness have set up the Kenedy Memorial Foundation for the principal purpose of helping the needs of the Catholic Church in the Latin American area."

Tisserant's source for this news, says Peter Grace, was Father Patrick Peyton.

"The purpose of this letter," the cardinal continued, "is to express our thanks and appreciation for your generosity and for your perceptivity in taking a personal responsibility which has the highest priority in the work of the Catholic Church today." Three paragraphs later Tisserant closed, "May God bless you with his choicest graces. Respectfully yours in Christ, Eugene Card. Tisserant."

Elena Kenedy put down the letter and looked at Sarita, who was ashen with pained surprise. "Elena," she said, "that is a mistake and should be corrected. You know I would not treat Texas like that."

✛ ✛ ✛

SIXTEEN

Deathbed Decision

Cardinal Spellman telephoned Elena at La Parra on December 28 to tell her Sarita would not be coming home after all. The cancer had spread throughout her spine, he explained, making almost any movement unbearably painful for her. Sarita herself, said Spellman, had decided that she could not withstand the trip home. Her sister-in-law trusted that the cardinal was telling her the truth, as he knew it. But Elena no longer trusted the monk and wondered whether Sarita had made the decision or whether Leo made it for her.

Spellman, who was on friendly terms with Bishop Garriga, seems also to have been suspicious of the monk. J. Peter Grace remembers the cardinal's warning him to be careful of Leo. "He shook his finger at me," says Grace. "He said, 'You look out for this fella. He's like a snake!'"

Grace claims that he, personally, had no doubts about Leo until Sarita's final hospitalization in New York when, at the attorney Larry McKay's suggestion, the matter of succession to membership in the Kenedy Memorial Foundation was once again addressed. McKay specifically informed Leo and Grace—as he had the preceding summer—that the codicils to Sarita's will probably did not have the legal effect of conveying foundation membership at her death. A so-called corporate act, said McKay, was required to ensure that Leo, Grace, and Father Peyton inherited control of the foundation. And in light of Sarita's deteriorating condition, prudence dictated haste; McKay had the simple document ready for her signature on December 29.

Then Peter Grace received a telephone call from his lawyer.

"He said, 'You know what this guy's asking?'" Grace remembers.

"I said no."

"He wants a paper drawn up just naming him. I don't know whether or not I should draw it up."

"If he's asking," Grace recalls advising McKay, "you better draw it up."

Nearly three decades later Peter Grace and Brother Leo still disagree as to what ensued from that point. The monk insists that he took in two documents for Mrs. East's consideration—one that named him, Grace, and Peyton her successor members and another that named Leo alone. He says that Sarita chose him of her own free will and that she rejected Grace's direct entreaties to reconsider. Peter Grace alleges that Sarita was never shown the corporate act that named him with Leo and Peyton to foundation membership.

What is known for certain is that Mrs. East was too nauseated to take communion the morning of the twenty-ninth and that she moaned in her sleep that night. She was given 75 mg of Demerol "for severe pain" at 3:00 A.M. on December 30 and 32 mg of Darvon two hours later. At seven-thirty that morning she was injected with another 75 mg of Demerol "for more severe pain." She complained of constant shortness of breath and was forced to spend the entire day on an uncomfortable nasal oxygen tube to assist her breathing.

Yet Sarita's private-duty nurse, Maria Fazio, later recalled that her patient was alert and fully aware during the daylight hours of December 30. Sometime late that morning or in the afternoon, Sarita signed the second corporate act, the one naming Leo her co-member of the foundation. Mrs. East affixed her diagonal scrawl, using a Bible as her writing surface. Nurse Fazio acted as official witness and signed the corporate act, too.

"Brother Leo called me at home," says Grace. "I couldn't believe it! He didn't say, 'You're out.' He said, 'It *looks* like, technically, I have 50 percent and we divide the other 50 three ways.' "

What the monk meant was that, under his interpretation, Sarita had conveyed one full membership to him alone and that a second, via the codicil, was to be split three ways. Thus, as far as Brother Leo was concerned, he controlled one and a third votes, while Grace and Peyton had one-third of a vote apiece.

"I said, 'That's ridiculous!' " Grace exclaims. 'I never heard of such a thing! That's not what she wanted!'

"Then I got very suspicious."

On January 8, 1961, Dom Gabriel Sortais visited Mrs. East at St. Vincent's. As the Trappists' abbot general recounted in his later affidavit for the Congregation of Religious, an arm of the Roman Catholic Curia in Rome, he spoke with her, in French, for perhaps half an hour. His testimony—that Sarita told him she wanted her foundation devoted to the universal church—conflicted with Mrs. Kenedy's depiction of Sarita's distress at Cardinal Tisserant's letter. Sortais also testified that Mrs. East clearly indicated her desire that Peter Grace and Brother Leo administer the Kenedy Memorial Foundation together.

The confusion of Sarita's last weeks extended as well to her relationship with Bishop Garriga. There is little question that Garriga's tirades had alienated her; she told William Sherry at St. Vincent's that the bishop had come to see her but that she had sent him back to Corpus Christi, telling him there was nothing he could do for her.

But it was Garriga's testimony that he arrived at St. Vincent's the same day as Dom Gabriel and was at the hospital the next day, as well. He was permitted, he later said, only a few, brief moments with his parishioner, who declined, or was denied the opportunity, to elucidate her views—as she had to others—to the man she had designated her successor less than twelve months before.

Brother Leo's deathwatch at St. Vincent's continued into early February. Sarita was fitted with an orthopedic device that allowed her to sit up without shattering her ravaged spine. Until the final week of her life, she could still, for brief intervals at least and sometimes longer, summon the lucidity to recognize her callers and even share a laugh with them. Several people later remarked on her cogency until the very end.

Through these final weeks, Brother Leo wrote to the Verstraetens regularly, telling them that Sarita was experiencing wonderful, grace-filled days, that she was happier on her deathbed than he'd ever seen her, and that it was definitely wrong of Rachel Verstraeten to see Sarita's painful death from tertiary metastic cancer as cruel. "Actually," Leo wrote to her, "this is perhaps the most glorious period in dear Sarita's life."

When the end came, at about ten-thirty on the morning of February 11, 1961, Brother Leo was in the hospital cafeteria. That is what the nuns at St. Vincent's would remember, plus the monk's fury at not being called to Mrs. East's room before she expired.

In Leo's version of Sarita's death, the one he committed to paper in a letter to the Verstraetens, he was at the widow's bedside as she drew her last breath. The Verstraetens were told that her death was peace-

ful, beautiful, and gentle, with the rosary being said
"more or less continually" during her last minutes on
earth.

She was embalmed at the Abbey Funeral Home in
New York. Her remains then were flown to Texas and
arranged in a solid bronze casket within a copper vault
by the Cage-Piper Funeral Home of Kingsville. All the
night of February 13, her cowboys kept a candlelight
watch over her in the ranch chapel. The vaqueros felt
the same eerie sadness they had known on the nights
of Sarita's long-ago gun tower vigils. Several of them
later swore that sometime after midnight an old portrait of Captain Mifflin Kenedy shook loose from its
wall rivets at the San Pablo ranch house and crashed
to the floor.

Mrs. East's internment the next day in the family
cemetery should have been a solemn, tearful rite
marking the close of a life, a dynasty, and an era in
south Texas history. One hundred and thirteen years
after Mifflin Kenedy had come to the Wild Horse Desert, the last direct lineal link to the empire he founded
now was severed. The five hundred mourners included
members from every clan of the south Texas ranching
aristocracy, as well as Sarita's many cousins and in-
laws, the ranch employees, old friends, a score or more
nuns and priests, and Brother Leo Gregory, who came
down for the service from New York with Lawrence
McKay.

Bishop Garriga, however, was not in a mood for
tender valediction. He chafed at the treatment he had
received at St. Vincent's and was in an incendiary
frame of mind over the loss of his "patrimony," news
Garriga heard courtesy of Jake Floyd.

His funeral oration in La Parra's crowded chapel
was laced with purple innuendo against Sarita, a screed
verging on direct defamation of her virtue and character. "I couldn't believe what I was hearing," Major

Tom Armstrong's nephew Tobin Armstrong later told a reporter. "Obviously, he felt Sarita had turned on him."

Most of the rest of the mourners were equally stunned by Garriga's vehemence, almost every one but Brother Leo, who, by his report of the day to the Verstraetens, appears to have attended a different funeral. He wrote that the service proceeded beautifully, and added his pleased reassurances that the Kenedy Memorial Foundation was operating smoothly with no sign of legal challenges to it, or any apparent devilment from the likes of Mr. Floyd. Leo hadn't the faintest notion of the cataclysm that was about to break over him.

SEVENTEEN
✦ ✦ ✦
The Snake Strikes

Brother Leo did not plan to function as permanent master of the Kenedy Memorial Foundation. Although at Sarita's death he assumed de facto control of most of her fortune, his intent was not to spend it himself. Rather, he was determined to pass on what he had created to people he regarded as worthy custodians, such as Bishop Manuel Larrain and the others at CELAM, the Episcopal Conference of Latin-American bishops. His own destiny, he told others, was to resume his vocation as a simple monk, or perhaps as a hermit.

He disclosed the initial step in this process to Lawrence McKay in Texas at the time of Sarita's funeral. Brother Leo had spoken with one of the Kleberg family's attorneys, he told McKay, and had found that McKay was correct to suspect the invalidity of codicils as legal means of passing on foundation memberships in Texas. Consequently, Leo went on, he was going to ignore the provisions of Mrs. East's third codicil; J. Peter Grace and Father Patrick Peyton would not be accorded even their one-third vote each. The monk added that he was prepared to engage counsel to defend this position, if necessary.

"He was trying to screw Father Peyton," says Grace, who reacted to Leo's announcement by calling for an emergency meeting in Sarasota, Florida, where the industrialist was visiting a convalescent W. R. Grace executive. In Sarasota, during a long walk on the beach, Leo elaborated on his discussion with Larry McKay, telling Grace that the future perfection of the Kenedy Memorial Foundation required that the monk be given a free hand in molding its direction.

The monk told his old fund-raising mentor that he might play some adjunct role in this work but that Father Peyton had to go. Leo believed that Peter Grace admired the Holy Cross priest to a fault—was "mesmerized" by him—and explained that Sarita had had second thoughts about Peyton, too.

"In something like September or October [of 1960]," says the monk, "Sarita had a long, long discussion with Father Peyton at the Shamrock Hotel in Houston. She spoke to him about what she wanted to do and asked him if he would work with her. And Father Peyton, who is a very saintly man, he's done marvelous work with his Rosary Crusade, said that he felt she should invest this whole amount of money, virtually the whole sum, in his Family Rosary Crusade and related things.

"She and I were both profoundly impressed with his sincerity, but also by the fact that he *completely* failed to understand what she wished. The next day she said, 'This man is a holy, holy man. I would love to help him in some of his work. But he's certainly not called to be an officer of my foundation.'

"I brought that up to Peter in Sarasota. I said, 'He will never, never be [an officer] as long as I have anything to do with the direction of this foundation.' And then I said, 'Peter, if you push me into this, I sense it could destroy our relationship.' And in fact it did."

In Grace's version of their Sarasota set-to, the industrialist held his temper and even humbled himself to plead with Leo not to behave so rashly. Unlike the monk, Peter Grace anticipated trouble in south Texas and emphasized to Brother Leo the need to maintain a common front.

Then, Grace explains, he agreed to oust Peyton and to cede Leo full authority in foundation decisions—if the monk would name him his comember. "I convinced him to go fifty-fifty with me," Grace explains. "That's the best deal I could get. I knew that at fifty-fifty one guy can block everything." Ten days after Sarita's burial, Leo bestowed foundation membership on Peter Grace, thus creating the deadlock Grace desired and assuring Father Peyton, for the time being, of an advocate on the foundation.

The Kenedy Memorial Foundation board of directors was realigned, too. At the time, there were three directors: Leo and Jake Floyd and Grace, who had been added to the board in the autumn of 1960. Now the monk and Peter Grace resigned their directorships and voted the positions to two W. R. Grace & Company executives, Tom Doyle and the Grace corporate counsel Jack Meehan.

Jake Floyd remained a director as well as secretary-treasurer of the foundation, but his annoyance with having the structure of the foundation management dictated to him was profound. Father Peyton was equally irritated to learn he had been denied the membership he thought was his under the third codicil. For several weeks Peyton refused even to speak to Peter Grace, whom he accused of selling out to the monk.

Leo, true to his nature, did not pause to consider how foolish he had been to antagonize so many people, including erstwhile allies like Peter Grace. He had infuriated Sarita's bishop, affronted Elena Kenedy, and offended the ranch employees. Jake Floyd was lying in wait for him. Father Peyton was furious with him. Cardinal Spellman distrusted him. And his own abbot had tried to restrict his actions.

The monk's colossal blunder, however, came the day of Mrs. East's funeral, during a luncheon hosted by Major Tom and Henrietta Armstrong at their ranch south of La Parra. "We visited at first," recalled Bob Kleberg of his discussion with Leo that afternoon at the Armstrongs. "He was a very nice, interesting sort of fellow, and we talked about how sad it was, and things like that. And then at one point he said he wanted to talk to me privately for a few minutes. I said, 'Fine,' and, as I remember it, we just stepped in the Armstrong dining room to be away from the other people.

"He said [that Mrs. East wanted him] to come down and talk to me and talk to Tom Armstrong, first of all to get our best advice. That she wanted her ranch to continue in her father's and mother's and her family's memory, and that if there was some way that our ranch and the Armstrong Ranch would take the ranch over on some basis and operate it, that she would like to see the thing go on. We had been very close all our lives in every way. And she thought that was the best solution to it.

"At that point I said well, of course, what everybody wanted to do, as far as we could, was to carry out whatever Sarita's wishes were."

Kleberg then recounted how he and Brother Leo broached the idea to Major Armstrong. "Tom said, well, he'd be interested in taking a small area. I think he talked about thirty thousand acres, something like that."

There was a superficial logic to Leo's proposal. Mrs. East respected her two neighbors' ranching expertise, and the adjacency of their lands would allow for a smooth lease division of La Parra. But the trouble with the idea was that she had said nothing of it to either Kleberg or Armstrong at any time, including during their visits to see her at St. Vincent's. Furthermore, in her fourth codicil, executed at the same time as the third, Mrs. East had expressed her "deep respect for the ability of the present managers" of La Parra—the Turcottes. There was only the monk's word that Mrs. East had decided, as she was about to die, that her ranch should be partitioned—just the fate she had wanted to avoid when she first considered establishing a foundation. "She must be rolling over in her grave!" Elena would remember thinking when she first heard of Leo's idea.

Leo's folly, moreover, was both tactical and strategic. In the first instance he was acting in advance of his authority. The surface rights to La Parra remained at that moment in Mrs. East's estate. Although her 200,000 acres were earmarked as a foundation asset under Clause 26 of her new will, transfer of control awaited the pleasure of her executors—Louis Edgar Turcotte, Sr., Jake Floyd, and the Alice National Bank.

Strategically, the approach to Kleberg and Armstrong was foolish because it made the monk yet another enemy, Tom East, Jr., who was inflamed at the possibility that his uncle Bob Kleberg might take over La Parra. And by the same action, Leo presented Jake Floyd with a perfect rallying point around which to build a coalition.

Tom East always refused to discuss his business or his feud with Bob Kleberg with the press. But some years before his death, in 1984, the rancher did agree to a short telephone interview at his room in the Menger Hotel in San Antonio. East again declined to answer specific questions, but he did concede a fierce reaction to Brother Leo's plans for the Kenedy ranch.

"I can't say what Aunt Sarita may have wanted done with her money," East began. "But I know for a damn sure that she meant for La Parra to stay in the family. And you gotta understand Jake Floyd. He was for

Texas. Brother Leo and them raised a boil on ol' Jake's butt.''

Tom East did not have to tell his lawyer of Leo's latest gambit, not did Jake Floyd require details of East's opinion regarding the proposed lease deal. Least of all did the attorney need aid in assessing how to turn the monk's error to his, the Alice bank's, and Tom East's advantage.

Jake had not regarded his forced resignation as a member of the Kenedy foundation in June of 1960 as anything more than a temporary setback. He was content to bide his time, harrying ''the New York bunch,'' as he called Leo and Peter Grace, by shutting down the flow of new inter vivos deed transfers into the foundation coffers as he waited for his chance to strike back. It was not Jake's style to force a premature confrontation.

All the while, his local information-gathering network continued to function flawlessly. The lawyer cackled with glee whenever he retold the story of meeting the oil engineer William Sherry at Sarita's funeral and of how Sherry was dumbstruck to learn that Floyd was well aware of the oilman's supposedly ultrasecret evaluation of her mineral reserves.

But Mrs. East's sudden illness and death had reconfigured the battleground. Jake now had to contend with Brother Leo and Peter Grace as the legal comembers of the Kenedy Memorial Foundation. What is more, Jake also learned soon after Sarita's funeral that he faced a new and deadlier foe than the monk or the magnate. Floyd's doctor had found a small shallow on Jake's lung, and a biopsy confirmed that the spot was a tumor.

Jake Floyd was dying.

He was told that to prolong—perhaps save—his life he should cut out cigars, consider chemotherapy, and curtail the severer stresses of his professional affairs, which cancer therapy might anyway make too demanding for him. Floyd tried to heed the first piece of medical advice, but he would allow nothing to hinder him in his campaign to unhorse Brother Leo and J. Peter Grace and take back the Kenedy money. Jake Floyd was intent on his revenge, even if it killed him.

Yet he saw that he was going to have to proceed with great delicacy. To be successful, he needed the support of both the Kenedy family (meaning Elena) and Bishop Mariano Garriga, neither of whom figured in Jake's, Tom East's, or the Alice bank's plans for Sarita's assets. Likewise, Floyd needed to be able to count on the Turcottes and Lee Lytton, Jr. All had to play their assigned roles while Jake prepared his legal attack on Leo and Grace, a strike at the legitimacy of their memberships that would nevertheless leave the 1960 will in place and the foundation itself intact.

It was Sarita's accountant, Bill Dryden, in Corpus Christi who called Jake's attention to the more than one million dollars' worth of checks she had written to herself in the last year of her life, and to the telltale Grace Bank stamps indicating where the funds had first gone. Floyd could easily infer where the checks, none of them written on the Alice Bank, were destined. And he had a perfectly legitimate reason for asking the Grace Bank for more details. Politely, pursuant to his fiduciary responsibilities as secretary-treasurer of the foundation and as an executor of Mrs. East's estate, Floyd began to dun the Grace Bank for information.

Sarita had covered most of her heavy travel expenses (and Brother Leo's, too) with drafts on the Alice bank. A review of these canceled checks, together with the stack of hotel bills, airline statements, department-store receipts and Grace corporation travel department invoices received by W. O. Bourgeois at her office in Sarita, provided detailed documentation of where she

and the monk had been together, how often, and for
how long.

But what Jake Floyd was after was a sharper whiff
of scandal, preferably a reek, and he was willing to
manufacture the odor if the opportunity presented itself. It did, in mid-March of 1961.

One afternoon Stella Lytton went to work in Mrs.
East's bedroom on the sorrowful task of sorting
through her personal belongings in anticipation of the
Oblate fathers' moving into the Headquarters. When
Mrs. Lytton came to her late cousin's desk, she opened
a drawer to discover several neatly tied caches of let-
ters, Brother Leo's complete correspondence to Mrs.
East, plus notes from Peter Grace and Dom Edmund
Futterer.

Stella read through Leo's long, mostly typewritten
letters with growing shock and anger. Then Elena and
the rest of the family read the package of letters and
reacted just as violently. Angry as they all were at
most provisions of Sarita's new will—just entered for
probate—and predisposed to question her relationship
with Leo, her relatives read nothing benign in Leo's
repeated references to ''God's Will'' and his many re-
minders to Sarita that life on earth is a brief and chancy
travail compared with the exaltation of Christian eternity. ''Carissime'' stoked suspicions, too, as did ''your
beadsman.''

To Elena the letters' ardency was an embarrassment.
She did not think for a moment that her sister-in-law
and the handsome monk had physically consummated
their relationship, nor did anyone who knew Sarita or
Leo think so. But the letters did gush with uncommon
fervor, raising reasonable questions as to Brother Leo's
intentions. Mrs. Kenedy decided that the notes would
not be made public.

Jake Floyd and, for the time being, Mrs. East's family, agreed to respect Elena's desire to protect the dig-

nity of the Kenedy name. But the new *patrona*'s strictures did not apply to another of the documents Stella Lytton uncovered. Mrs. East apparently saved *everything* Brother Leo wrote, including his handwritten draft of the letters she copied at the Rice Hotel in June of 1960, the notes demanding their resignations. Floyd said of this evidence to an associate in his Alice law office, "I'm gonna nail their hides to the wall with it."

But Jake also had a second weapon he was about to deploy against Brother Leo and J. Peter Grace. Not long after Stella Lytton found Leo's letters, one of Louis Edgar Turcotte's five sons sat down for a long chat, in Spanish, with Sara Curiel, Sarita's maid. A report prepared from this interview was then forwarded to the diocesan offices in Corpus Christi, where it promptly disappeared.

A short while later Peter Grace heard indirectly of Sara Curiel's supposed allegations from Archbishop Egidio Vagnozzi, the papal apostolic delegate in Washington, D.C. The archbishop told Grace that he had seen evidence of wantonness in Sarita, that there were signs of a "meretricious" relationship between Leo and Mrs. East.

"What are you saying!" Grace exclaimed. "She was seventy, an old woman!"

"You," Vagnozzi replied placidly, "don't know the appetites of older women."

With his legal case against Leo coming together almost of its own accord, by mid-April of 1961 Jake Floyd was ready to act. On the fifteenth of the month, he steered his old green Ford coupe south from Alice to La Parra for a war council of the disgruntled and the disinherited in Elena Kenedy's parlor. As subsequent experience would show, the participants in the meeting were not natural allies; this was to be an ad hoc coalition of convenience, mostly Jake Floyd's.

Elena was the linchpin. Although Mrs. Kenedy forbade public disclosure of Leo's letters to Sarita, and thought all litigation unseemly, Floyd was counting on Bishop Mariano Garriga's influence over her. If the combative bishop supported a suit, Elena would follow his lead.

Johnny's widow also nurtured some old resentments. After putting up with her husband's alcoholism, then her years of subordination to Sarita, Elena Kenedy now reigned as *patrona* at La Parra. And as such, she was much more sympathetic to the aspirations, and arguments, of Tom East, Jr., then she was toward Bob Kleberg or the Armstrongs. Elena was not hostile toward her neighbors, but she had begun to call Tom East her godson, which he was not.

Stella Lytton attended the meeting but contributed little. At age sixty-eight she was assured of financial security no matter what happened to the foundation and was willing to leave possible litigation to others, even though her loss under the 1960 will of 100,000 acres, plus mineral rights beneath the land, was enormous.

Her brother Louis Edgar Turcotte, Jr., sixty-six, for many years Mrs. East's foreman, was the father of five boys and a girl and felt proportionately less satisfied with the new will, which left Turcotte to share the surface of the 70,000-acre San Pablo ranch with Stella, plus the mineral royalty interest Mrs. East assigned to her cousin during her lifetime.

Turcotte already had considered challenging the 1960 will but was dissuaded by Jake Floyd's legal argument that, as an executor, Turcotte was estopped from such action. Disconsolate, but apparently resigned to his loss, Turcotte, who was slowly failing from diabetes—the same disease that killed Sarita's parents—fell asleep during the meeting.

Tom East also had little to say. Sarita's nephew confined himself to a single moment of animation during the conversation, telling Elena, "We can't let La Parra be taken away!"

Bishop Garriga arrived with his attorney, Patrick Horkin of Corpus Christi, and wasted no time making his customary fulminations. As the members of the group discussed what they knew of Brother Leo's actions—which wasn't much—Garriga started shouting, "She was overreached! She was overreached!" and slammed a beefy fist down onto one of Elena's fragile antique tables.

Pat Horkin, large and florid faced, a onetime FBI agent, was intensely loyal to Bishop Garriga, who had seen the attorney through a long and finally successful battle with alcoholism. Horkin was as obstreperous as his client, willing to take on Brother Leo and J. Peter Grace with a lawsuit contending that Sarita's first codicil, naming Bishop Garriga as her successor member, was the single operative proof of her independent intentions. Jake Floyd, however, countered with the reasonable argument that a codicil attack held little promise for ultimate success, and persuaded Horkin to shelve such a suit for the time being in favor of Floyd's plan, which cast Lee Lytton, Jr., as the aggrieved plaintiff.

Lytton, as his friend and present lawyer, Davis Grant, explains him, held Jake Floyd in an awe bordering on reverence. Furthermore, says Grant, although Lytton was a judge, he never practiced law and actually knew very little about it, making it simpler for Jake Floyd to weave his deceits.

As a Catholic, one of Sarita's closest living relatives, and a member of her foundation until forced to resign, he was the logical choice to act as plaintiff in any action against Leo and Grace. Moreover—and here is where Judge Lytton distinguished himself from everyone else—he was neither greedy nor a liar. The day of the meeting at Elena's Lytton later explained under oath, he proposed himself as plaintiff: "I felt something should be done, and second I felt that if anything could be done about it, I was the one who had to move to do it." Lytton's lone worry was whether he, as a Catholic layman, was canonically free to sue a priest, Father Peyton, who would be cited as a nominal, alleged coconspirator with Leo and Peter Grace. Mariano Garriga quickly assured his parishioner that the diocese of Corpus Christi had no objection.

Floyd's plan was now in place. And for many months it would be nearly impossible for Brother Leo or Grace to recognize the lawyer's handiwork. Instead, the two would find Sarita's family and local bishop solidly aligned against them, all strongly supportive of a legal action filed by the bishop's attorney, Pat Horkin, on behalf of Mrs. East's nephew Lee Lytton. Tom East agreed to bankroll the suit in secret.

As Horkin, with Floyd's help, crafted the complaint, it was a small marvel of selectivity, agreeable in its wording to all the Texas principals and, at the same time, rich with unsubstantiated accusations designed to shock and panic a Catholic hierarchy that Floyd already was covertly poisoning against Brother Leo via Bishop Garriga. Archbishop Egidio Vagnozzi was not the only Catholic prelate who would be shown—or told of—the Curiel allegations as provided by the Turcotte family.

The defendants in Cause 12074, *Lytton vs. the John G. and Marie Stella Kenedy Memorial Foundation,* in the Seventy-ninth District Court of Jim Wells Country, Judge C. Woodrow ("El Burro") Laughlin presiding, were Tom Doyle and Jack Meehan (the Grace executives recently named foundation directors), J. Peter Grace, Father Patrick Peyton, and the monk, "Christopher Gregory, sometimes called Brother Leo."

Horkin characterized Brother Leo as "a man of extremely strong and persuasive personality, fully capable of influencing the judgment of Mrs. East, who was already in very bad health, in such a manner as to substitute his will for hers.'' And the essence of his case, Horkin wrote, was that ''as a result of the undue influence exercised continuously by the defendant Gregory on Mrs. East, from the time he met her until the time of her death, this defendant Gregory, in concert with the defendant Grace, with fraudulent intent, attempted to gain full control of the defendant Foundation and all of its assets.

Cause 12074 did not accuse Leo or Grace of deceits in persuading Sarita to establish her foundation in the first place, nor did it attack her new will. According to the complaint's reasoning—strictly interpreted—Leo and Peter Grace did nothing amiss until June of 1960 when the Floyd and Lytton memberships were discovered. At that point, the suit alleged, Sarita's ''letters requesting [Floyd's and Lytton's] resignations were written under undue influence exercised and exerted on her by the defendant Gregory.''

Leo's second alleged misdeed was the December 30, 1960, hospital appointment. ''It was executed,'' read the lawsuit, ''by Mrs. East on her deathbed at a time when she was in great pain because of her illness, and was under the influence of narcotics and sedatives to such an extent that she did not have the contractural [*sic*] competency necessary for her to understand the nature of the transaction.''

Cause 12074, in essence, asked the court to throw Leo, Grace, Peyton, Doyle, and Meehan out of the foundation and to restore Lytton and Floyd to their memberships. As a fillip, Horkin also asked Judge Laughlin for an immediate injunction to prevent the defendants from raiding the Kenedy Memorial Foundation ''for personal use and expenses'' and argued that "several million dollars" were at risk unless Leo and Grace and their coconspirators were stopped.

Pat Horkin produced his complaint against a deadline; on April 19 Tom Doyle and Jack Meehan were scheduled to appear at Jake Floyd's office in Alice to complete the transfer of La Parra's surface rights to the foundation in anticipation of a lease deal with Bob Kleberg and Major Armstrong. Floyd, instead, arranged for the Jim Wells County Sheriff to serve Cause 12074 on Doyle and Meehan as they walked into his office. It was another of the dramatic touches Floyd relished.

The moment Kleberg and Armstrong learned of the suit, both men dropped all interest in further La Parra lease negotiations. At the same time, El Burro Laughlin (so nicknamed for his mulish dependability) acted according to his assigned role. Judge Laughlin had been a cog in the Parr political machine but had switched his allegiance to Floyd. Laughlin granted an immediate restraining order without argument, placing a freeze on the Kenedy Memorial Foundation's assets and thus locking them under the guardianship of the foundation depository, the Alice National Bank.

EIGHTEEN

✛ ✛ ✛

The Bums in Rome

J. Peter Grace was not surprised by the lawsuit. Given the natural local antipathy to the terms of Mrs. East's new will and toward outsiders' control of the Kenedy Memorial Foundation, Peter Grace thought Brother Leo "crazy" to risk further provocation by offering La Parra to Bob Kleberg and Major Tom Armstrong. Grace also reacted with understandable concern when rumors of planned physical violence against him and the monk began circulating in Kenedy County.

In this atmosphere the industrialist wondered if Brother Leo had taken leave of his senses in late March of 1961 when the two of them were summoned by Bishop Garriga to his chancery office in Corpus Christi. Garriga castigated them both, demanded redress for the theft of his "patrimony," and warned that "some hothead" might take legal action against them if Sarita's foundation was not restored to local control. Brother Leo appalled Peter Grace with his response to Garriga's threats. If the bishop suspected chicanery, the monk told him, "get yourself a good lawyer tomorrow and start a lawsuit." Then Leo knelt and kissed the bishop's ring, asking for Garriga's blessing.

Three weeks later, when Tom Doyle telephoned Grace in New York from Alice with news of the Lytton lawsuit, the industrialist immediately called Lawrence McKay. "Aaaiii!" exclaimed the lawyer. "There's no chance down there at all!"

Grace readily concurred that to contest Cause 12074 before a south Texas jury was suicidal. In addition, he now understood that he had to worry about Sarita's Grace Bank account—details of which Jake Floyd continued to pursue—and the million dollars or so of her money that had passed through the account. Pat Horkin made it plain that he thought Sarita had been duped into spending so much on the Trappists and that he was ready to try to recover the donations in a second legal action.

"They were going to win in a south Texas court, there's no doubt about that," says Peter Grace. "Once they won, they could come after the Trappists for all that dough that was spent down there in South America. The Trappists would have gone broke. Not only were we going to lose, but they were going to put the Trappists in bankruptcy. There was *no way* any sensible person would go to court."

Grace made his appraisal of the situation known to the community at Spencer, where Dom Futterer by now was delegating many of his management responsibilities to the monastery prior, Father Joachim Viens. Grace's judgment, and Larry McKay's, carried great weight with the Trappists, who relied on the two men for advice on all their external affairs. At Grace's urging, Father Viens agreed that the only choice was to pursue an out-of-court settlement and that the only hope for securing favorable terms from the plaintiff, Lee Lytton, Jr., was to bring ecclesiastic pressure on his presumed sponsor, Bishop Garriga.

Brother Leo opposed the strategy, arguing that he and Grace should meet the lawsuit head-on in court. But under Father Viens's stern admonition the monk yielded. Brother Leo agreed to help seek a church-sponsored resolution to the Lytton lawsuit and, in the spirit of unity, suspended his insistence upon sole authority over the threatened foundation. Leo accepted Father Peyton and Peter Grace as his comembers, as per the provisions of the third codicil. A document spelling out this understanding was prepared and signed by all three.

His Holiness, Pope John XXIII
The Vatican

Most Holy Father:

We, the undersigned:Patrick J. Peyton, priest of the Congregation of the Holy Cross. Lee Gregory, brother of a Cistercian Order J. Peter Grace

request permission to accept the bequest as described in the third codicil to the last will and testament of Sarita K. East, namely all of Mrs. East's rights as a member of the John G. and Marie Stella Kenedy Memorial Foundation, a corporation organized and existing under the Texas non-profit corporation act.

Humbly kneeing at the feet of your Holiness, we beg your apostolic blessing.

With Brother Leo's ambitions for the moment contained, Father Peyton went to work cultivating his extensive contacts in the Vatican, while Peter Grace consulted with his close friends within the archdiocese of New York. Because Cardinal Spellman was then convalescing from surgery for a detached retina, Grace began with Spellman's charismatic associate, Bishop Fulton Sheen, the famous TV priest and author who was well acquainted with the labyrinthine Roman Catholic Policy-making machine.

After hearing Grace out, Bishop Sheen was foreboding. "I have only one piece of advice for you," he told the industrialist. "If this was fifty thousand dollars, it'd be easy. Fifty million? This is going to pierce the venality of all the church people in Rome, and everywhere else. This is just too much money, Peter! I want you to stay close to our Blessed Mother, because you're going to need her."

In an earlier day all that Peter Grace would have needed to do was stay close to Cardinal Spellman. Throughout most of the long reign of Pope Pius XII, Spellman had been one of the most powerful princes of the church, as well as the undisputed lord of the U.S. flock. He was known as "the American pope" and would have dictated the church's posture in the foundation case.

But by 1961 Spellman was falling into eclipse, and Grace's close identification with the cardinal was actually a liability. The decline in Spellman's power began with Pius's death, in 1958, and the succession to the papal throne of Angelo Giuseppe Cardinal Roncalli as John XXIII. Spellman was arrogantly dismissive of Roncalli—"He ought to be selling fish," the cardinal reportedly opined of the new pope—and soon found himself frozen out of the Vatican inner circle.

Spellman had also made an enemy of Archbishop Vagnozzi, the apostolic delegate in Washington. Some years earlier Archbishop Vagnozzi had headed a lobbying effort to persuade the U.S. government to name an ambassador to the Papal State, an idea Spellman used all his leverage in Rome and Washington to squelch, seeing it as a threat to his personal control of all official and unofficial business conducted between the Vatican and the United States. Now, under John XXIII's aegis, Vagnozzi was emboldened to challenge Spellman and would take keen delight in frustrating one of the cardinal's closest friends.

Grace had hoped to circumvent Vagnozzi by going directly to the Congregation of the Council at the Vatican, a body of the Curia whose authorities include the adjudication of church disputes over pious legacies. He tried to move swiftly, arriving in Rome with Brother Leo and Larry McKay before the end of April 1961, less than two weeks after Cause 12074 had been filed in front of Judge Laughlin in Alice.

But the hastily organized trip to Italy availed J. Peter Grace nothing. He and Leo and McKay were told that Archbishop Vagnozzi in Washington, D.C., was empowered to speak for the church in the Kenedy will dispute, and it was to Vagnozzi that Grace should address his arguments.

To Grace's surprise and relief the archbishop at first seemed sympathetic to his case (or at least not hostile) and indicated his readiness to resolve the matter in a more-than-acceptable way. The cardinal's proposed compromise, which he sketched on the back of a used envelope, was to expand the Kenedy Memorial Foundation board of members to five, adding Bishop Garriga and perhaps the plaintiff, Lee Lytton, Jr., but leaving Grace with Leo and Father Peyton as a voting majority.

Archbishop Vagnozzi had not yet sampled the sentiment in south Texas. Once he did, in conversations with Patrick Horkin and Bishop Garriga, the apostolic delegate rescinded his proposal and advanced a new one—a seven-member board for the Kenedy Foundation with five positions allocated to Bishop Garriga and one apiece to Peter Grace and Father Peyton. Brother Leo, on whom the Texans' fury was focused, was to be excluded from the foundation altogether under Vagnozzi's new formula for compromise.

Grace responded that the five-to-two membership split was unacceptable. However, he was more than willing for Leo to be severed from the Kenedy foundation. Under the assumption that the Trappists would be important beneficiaries of the foundation, Grace and Prior Viens thought someone from Spencer should have a seat on the board of members. In May, Peter Grace wrote Archbishop Vagnozzi that Father Thomas Keating, then abbot at St. Benedict's in Snowmass, Colorado, was a good choice to replace Brother Leo if the other sticking points could be resolved.

They couldn't.

As June arrived, Vagnozzi's attitude steadily hardened. Even the unacceptable compromise of granting Grace and Peyton minority status on the Kenedy Memorial Foundation board of members was withdrawn. Grace learned that Vagnozzi had been in touch with Rome, where the archbishop let it be known that he fully supported Bishop Garriga's claims and passed along, as Grace was informed, his opinion that the industrialist was "untrustworthy," probably primarily interested in enriching the Grace Bank. Furthermore, Vagnozzi, relying on Garriga and Horkin for his information, accused Peter Grace of attempting to bribe the Texas state attorney general Will Wilson to intercede in Cause 12074 on Grace's behalf.

On June 21, 1961, Peter Grace and the archbishop met for the last time. Their conversation quickly degenerated into a shouting match, during which the archbishop first startled Grace with his suspicion of a sexual relationship between Leo and Sarita. Vagnozzi also brushed aside as irrelevant the industrialist's strongest argument, that the Kenedy Memorial Foundation might be lost to Catholic causes altogether without an equitable, church-imposed settlement.

"Mr. Grace," the archbishop advised him, imperiously, in his slow, Italian-inflected English, "the church has existed for two thousand years without this fifty million dollars and will continue to do so quite well without it.''

When Grace continued to protest, the apostolic delegate raised the threat of excommunication.

"Fine!" Grace yelled at him. ''I'll still have the prayers of the Trappists!''

''That,'' the archbishop replied with urbane indifference, ''is all that you will have.''

Grace endeavored twice again in June to find a friendly ear at the Vatican; in all, he would travel to Rome a dozen times to plead his case that Bishop Garriga's involvement in the Lytton lawsuit was a canonical violation of abetting litigation between a Catholic layman (Lytton) and a cleric (Father Peyton) and that the Lytton lawsuit, Cause 12074, was no more than a patent power grab that invited the destruction of the foundation.

To illustrate his argument graphically, Grace personally prepared a chart, which he had translated into Spanish and Italian, for distribution throughout the Curia. The document did make Grace's case dramatically, perhaps too well. It showed unequivocally how the Lytton lawsuit was aimed not at redress of a wrong but at simple restoration of power. But the chart also vividly outlined what Grace and Brother Leo had done to bring Sarita to rewrite her will and set up her foundation; in court, it would become prime evidence of undue influence.

On the left side of his chart, Grace listed six ''Actions Taken by Mrs. Sarita K. East During Eleven Months of Her Life While Working with Father Patrick Peyton, Brother Leo and Mr. J. Peter Grace.'' They were the following.

1. Creation of the foundation
2. Execution of her new will

3. The inter vivos bequests
4. The forced resignations of Floyd and Lytton
5. The third codicil naming Grace, Leo, and Peyton Sarita's successor members
6. Leo's December 30, 1960, hospital appointment

Grace highlighted actions 1–3 in color and then connected them to a box, which read, "If Bishop Garriga's attack on actions Nos. 4, 5, and 6 is upheld by a prejudiced jury, it clearly follows that the *admitted influence* exercised on actions Nos. 1, 2, and 3 will compel, a fortiori, a decision that all six actions resulted from 'undue influence.' "

A thick arrow pointed downward from this box to one beneath it. "The Foundation and the Will," read the second enclosed text, "would thereby be destroyed, the prior Will reestablished and $50 million lost to the Church."

As Grace recalls his preparation of the chart, his object was to show that "you can't have your cake and eat it, baby. If you've got a *fair* court and a *fair* judge and you say, 'This is great, this is great, this is great, but *here was undue influence,*' and you just draw the line where *you* decide that's undue, that's dishonest. Absolutely dishonest. I thought those bums in Rome would have a conscience!"

The "bums in Rome" didn't, or at least they refused to take the definitive action that Peter Grace desired. He was positively irritated after a meeting with Domenico Cardinal Tardini, Pope John's aged secretary of state, who had served as prosecretary under Pius XII. Tardini was a gruff and wizened veteran of Vatican power politics, loyal to whichever pope he served. He listened to Grace for half an hour and then blandly refused to involve John XXIII in the dispute. Grace left his audience with the papal secretary of state perplexed and irate, muttering to Larry McKay that he thought Tardini was senile.

"They gave us the business," Grace says. "We didn't have any drag. That guy Tardini was no good at all."

It's impossible to know whether some or all of the evidence that persuaded Archbishop Vagnozzi to suspect physical improprieties between Leo and Sarita ever reached Tardini, or just who, in fact, actually glimpsed the contents of Sara Curiel's mystery testimony. The maid herself did not accuse her late mistress of carnality. According to the Turcotte brothers, Curiel did report that Sarita wanted to marry Leo, not just adopt him. If so, Mrs. East never made that wish known to anyone else. As far as charges of physical intimacy went, the Turcottes report that Curiel related how the monk sometimes went around the Headquarters in his undershorts.

Leo turns livid at any mention of such alleged indiscretions and denies them all. According to one of his many later attorneys, William Joyce of Washington, D.C., the only underwear incident at the Headquarters occurred one day when the monk came calling on Sarita. She had been washing her hair and, without thinking, answered the monk's knock at the door in her robe, or slip. Much racier behavior may have been alleged or hinted at in the Curiel dossier. But whatever the unstated charges or innuendos against Brother Leo that floated through Vatican City, nothing was proved.

In July, Archbishop Paul Philippe, secretary of the Congregation of Religious in Rome, approached Dom Gabriel Sortais. He was holding a dossier, on Leo, that the archbishop said he had received from Texas.

"Do you know this brother?" he asked Dom Gabriel.

The Trappist abbot general said that he did.

"Will you vouch for him?" Archbishop Philippe then asked.

"I will," answered Sortais.

With that, according to Father Raphael Simon, the archbishop tossed the dossier into his wastebasket.

Later in the summer, another proposed solution to the Texas Catholics vs. New York Catholics controversy, as it was thought of within the church, was raised in Rome. The new idea was to acknowledge the irreconcilability of the factions by splitting the Kenedy Memorial Foundation in two—60 percent to the New Yorkers and 40 percent to the Texans. The proposal represented a decided improvement over anything that Archbishop Vagnozzi had been willing to give the New Yorkers, but Peter Grace, Father Peyton, and Brother Leo rejected it. This set the stage for Francis Cardinal Spellman to marshal the remnants of his old power. In August, Spellman informed the Curia that an eighty-twenty split of the foundation assets was the New Yorkers' minimal acceptable decision and reinforced his position with the threat that unless Rome brought Mariano Garriga to heel and forced the Corpus Christi bishop to accept 20 percent of the Kenedy Foundation assets in return for dropping Cause 12074, Spellman would go to Texas and personally give his testimony in court.

Peter Grace was euphoric. "OVERWHELMED WITH THE NEWS," he cabled Spellman at the Grand Hotel in Rome. "WHAT YOUR EMINENCE HAS DONE IS ALMOST UNBELIEVABLE." After four months of hardball politicking within the Vatican, it appeared to Peter Grace that Bishop Garriga had been bested.

But neither Grace, nor Brother Leo, nor any of the churchly arbiters of the Kenedy Foundation fight had yet considered the possibility of that their sound and fury might signify nothing; no one had bothered to ask the prelate of Corpus Christi if he actually did control Lee Lytton, nor had the old bishop ever unequivocally stated that he did. Garriga seemed, in truth, simply to be enjoying the ruckus he was causing in church councils, and the problems he was creating for Brother Leo. In none of his remarks or actions did he betray a glimmer of knowledge that he was only another of Jake Floyd's chess pieces.

Bishop Garriga wore his innocence well, however. When, under Spellman's threat, the Vatican directed the bishop to drop all present and contemplated litigation in return for a fifth of the Kenedy fortune, he refused to obey. Garriga told the Congregation of the Council that even if he were of a mind to settle on such terms, the litigant of record, Lee Lytton, was not. Nor, said Garriga, could he force his parishioner to settle. It was the truth, but nobody in the church believed him.

NINETEEN

✛ ✛ ✛

Confrontation

Jake Floyd's war of attrition against Brother Leo and J. Peter Grace—a guerrilla campaign to distract and exhaust them until they were ready to capitulate—was telling with greater effect than the Alice lawyer could know. His most important advantage in the lengthening impasse was the strain that the passing weeks put on Peter Grace's fragile realliance with Leo and Father Patrick Peyton. The residual bitterness among the three had not dissipated, despite their outward show of unity before the pope and the various other high authorities at the Vatican. Peyton, for one, was still angry at Leo for trying to dump him from the foundation, and angry at Peter Grace for allowing the monk to do so. Grace, for his part, remained alert for signs of another attempted double cross, as he interpreted Leo's move against Peyton the preceding February. And the monk himself was growing impatient with the progress in Rome. He hadn't bolted the common front with Grace and Peyton, but he also hadn't abandoned his ultimate ambitions for management of Mrs. East's fortune, which did not include either Grace or Peyton.

Yet Leo still seemed to prize his vocation as a monk and was hesitant to imperil it. "Before Dom Edmund resigned [in the summer of 1961]," Father Raphael Simon remembers, "I had a conversation with Leo. I said, 'If, as a trustee in Mrs. East, you're put in conflict with the abbot, would you leave the community?'

"And he said, 'No, because I have discovered the value of obedience.' "

Peter Grace, however, was no longer willing to take Leo's word for anything. "You can become convinced that what *you think* is the *truth,*" Grace explains. "And he's completely that way. He could justify one thing one month, and a month later, if he changed his mind, then he'd have *that* all justified. That's his main characteristic."

Just before Father Thomas Aquinas Keating, the superior at St. Benedict's Monastery, in Colorado, was elected abbot at the mother house at Spencer, Brother Leo again tried to tinker with the membership of the Kenedy Memorial Foundation. To this point, mid-August of 1961, seven individuals (Sarita, Bishop Garriga, Floyd, Lytton, Leo, Grace, and Father Peyton) at one time or another had had some claim to, or expectation of, membership in the foundation. Likewise, eight individuals (Sarita, Louis Edgar Turcotte, Lytton, Floyd, Leo, Grace, Tom Doyle, and Jack Meehan) had been proposed, considered, appointed, or elected directors of the Kenedy foundation.

Brother Leo's idea in the summer of 1961 was to add one more of each, a director and a member, both prominent south Texans. His first selection, as a director to sit with Tom Doyle, Jack Meehan, and Jake Floyd, was the rancher Lawrence Wood of Refugio, Texas, northeast of Corpus Christi, a Catholic who, like the oil engineer William Sherry, believed that Sarita, in full possession of her senses, had entrusted her family fortune to the monk.

Also persuaded to come aboard as a third member (and thus to end the fifty-fifty voting deadlock between Leo and Grace) was Henrietta Armstrong, Major Tom's wife, Sarita's best friend, Bob Kleberg's sister, and

Tom East, Jr.'s aunt, Mrs. Armstrong, a Protestant, told Father Raphael that she thought Brother Leo had a "beautiful mind." According to a letter from Peter Grace to Cardinal Spellman, Mrs. Armstrong was invited on as a member partly as a public relations move and partly because she was a potential source of financial support should a court fight with Bishop Garriga prove unavoidable.

Peter Grace, in agreeing with Leo to vote Henrietta Armstrong onto the foundation as a member, lost his fifty-fifty checkmate veto, which hardly concerned him, since Judge Laughlin's injunction of April prevented any foundation funds from being spent on anything. Grace understood, as well, that the Texans would not idly tolerate Henrietta Armstrong's advent as a foundation member. The vote to name her and Lawrence Wood to their positions was dated August 18, 1961. Three days later Patrick Horkin, representing Bishop Garriga, went before Judge Laughlin in Alice and obtained a restraining order that enjoined Henrietta Armstrong and Lawrence Wood from taking part in any foundation decision making.

Judge Laughlin's ruling did not interfere with Brother Leo's main purpose, however. The monk had recruited a pair of prominent local partisans who trusted his intentions and would support his contentions. These included his firm opinion that Bishop Garriga was only bluffing and would cave in rather than go to trial.

Then Brother Leo shifted his position again.

In September the bishop of Corpus Christi casually let drop in a telephone conversation with Peter Grace that his animosity toward the Trappist did not extend to Grace or to Father Patrick Peyton. Grace decided to test the bishop. "Well, your Excellency," he said, "if you trust Father Peyton and me, why don't you come on the foundation with us?"

"All right," Garriga replied. "I will if you can get Leo to appoint me."

Peter Grace couldn't tell if Bishop Garriga was serious or not. Yet this apparent chance to resolve the Lytton litigation so favorably—leaving *all* the foundation money in his and Father Peyton's control—prompted a hurried call to the monk at Spencer to solicit Leo's approval.

Brother Leo's answer, conveyed in a letter of September 28, was that he thought the eighty-twenty split as endorsed by the Vatican was a superior solution, and Leo repeated his insistence that Bishop Garriga would not, if challenged, persevere in the lawsuit. But the monk also felt, at this moment, the comforting presence of a decisive new abbot at St. Joseph's. Dom Thomas Keating, he explained to Grace in his letter, "feels that for the good of my vocation, the sooner I am off the KMF, the better. While he would be willing to allow me to remain on for a bit if absolutely necessary, he would prefer me to be off. I see his point, and agree with him."

Leo left to Peter Grace the decision of whether or not to deal with Bishop Garriga. "If you would like to settle along the lines you discussed with the bishop, I will quickly step off and I'm sure that Dom Thomas would be relieved. He has great confidence in your judgment. If I step off, Henrietta will resign also. This would leave you free to appoint Father Peyton and the Bishop."

The sudden outbreak of harmony seemed too wondrous to be true. It was. On Thursday, October 5, 1961, Peter Grace had just returned to New York from a business trip in Europe when Larry McKay announced an alert from Rome. McKay informed Grace that Father Christopher O'Toole, Patrick Peyton's Holy Cross superior, was reporting that Bishop Garriga had requested an audience with Pope John XXIII to personally present allegations against Brother Leo and that the Oblates of Mary Immaculate, smarting from the loss of their oil and gas rights at La Parra, had sent a delegation to the Vatican to make their own charges against Brother Leo and Peter Grace. Even though the industrialist had touched down from Paris only hours before, by nightfall on October 5 he, together with McKay and Brother Leo, were en route by air to Rome.

Father O'Toole met them in the forenoon of Friday the sixth. By this time the Holy Cross hierarchy in Rome had decided that discussions with Grace and McKay could be conducted more fruitfully without Brother Leo present. The monk therefore did not attend Father O'Toole's briefing. He retired to pray that morning as O'Toole recounted to Grace and McKay what he knew of Garriga's expected allegations (which was very little) and of the Oblates' bill of particulars, with which O'Toole was much more familiar.

He had seen the Oblates' charges in a document shown him by Father John Walsh, assistant general of the Oblate Congregation. The Oblates, O'Toole told Grace and McKay, had started their investigation of Leo in March, and their first action had been to inquire, by mail, at Spencer whether Leo was indeed a Trappist monk at all, and not an imposter.

Their memorandum, prepared for John XXIII's attention, argued that Mrs. East could not have wished her foundation to benefit principally the church in South America as Leo claimed. The Oblates had long decades of association with the Kenedy family, and they were certain that Sarita, like her parents and grandparents, wanted her charity to stay close to home.

The Oblates also accused Grace and Leo of "kidnapping" the dying widow to New York and of trying to unload her furniture (which the Oblates had inherited with the Headquarters) even before her will was probated. They alleged further that Leo and Grace had tried to pressure Elena Kenedy to add her assets to the foundation.

When John XXIII had authorized Cardinal Spellman's proposed eighty-twenty split in August, the memo continued, His Holiness wasn't aware of all the facts. And according to the Oblates' allegations, the Vatican's impartiality in the case was severely compromised; the Holy See supposedly had a request for a contribution pending before the Kenedy Memorial Foundation membership (Brother Leo and Peter Grace) at the same time the Roman Curia was shifting away from its earlier support of the Texas Catholics to a more positive view of the New Yorkers' case.

To Brother Leo the Oblates' charges and the expectation of another salvo from Bishop Garriga were proof that the church would never successfully arbitrate the foundation dispute. If the Vatican couldn't force the bishop to concede in August, what good was it to continue bickering in October? Leo wanted to go to court. Still, he cooperated with Peter Grace during a long session in Grace's hotel room Friday night as a written rebuttal to the Oblates was prepared. The next morning the New Yorkers' defense was delivered to Father O'Toole. Then, with nothing more to be accomplished in Rome over the weekend, Grace, McKay, and Brother Leo flew to Paris, where Grace would spend Saturday and Sunday conducting corporate business.

Leo decided to fly on from Paris to Brussels, where he wanted to discuss recent events with Bishop Leo-Joseph Suenens, a close friend of Father Peyton's, whose influence within the Holy See had been responsible for most of Peter Grace's high-level access in Rome. Suenens, who had taken no part in the membership squabbles earlier in the year, told Brother Leo he had been given to understand that the monk was to be replaced on the foundation at once, an apparently minor misinterpretation of Leo's September 28 letter, in which Dom Thomas's timetable was for Leo to "remain on for a bit if absolutely necessary."

Leo himself had been the source of Suenens's information; but he chose to interpret what he heard as evidence of Peter Grace's treachery against him. According to the industrialist's retelling of the ensuing confrontation, he tried to allay Leo's anger with assurances that Leo was not being shouldered aside. But as Grace remembers it, over dinner in a Paris restaurant on Sunday, October 8, Leo accused his codefendant of bungling negotiations with Garriga and Pat Horkin and revoked his provisional acceptance of Father Peyton as a comember, as per the third codicil to Sarita's will. Only if constrained by law, said Leo, would he now allow the Holy Cross priest and rosary crusader on the foundation as a member.

Peter Grace impatiently argued back that a united defense of their memberships remained the group's only recourse. Then, when Leo disparaged the many missions to Rome as pointless, Grace defended the strategy as their single tenable option.

"He said, 'Oh no!' " Grace recalls and then adds with obvious hyperbole. " 'I'm going back to court. Fuck all these cardinals and all!'

"I said, 'You're a bunch of crap!' "

Leo answered that he believed J. Peter Grace was a megalomaniac. Grace reiterated his determination to achieve a satisfactory out-of-court settlement, with or without Leo's assistance. Once he did, Grace added, "I'm going to shove it down your throat."

TWENTY

✛ ✛ ✛

Recantation

Peter Grace labored for the next four days over a seventy-eight-page critical review of Leo's behavior. A rambling document, it touched on everything from Grace's reconstruction of his Sarasota meeting with Leo to a fretful section in which Grace detailed his many personal sacrifices over the years for the good of the Trappists. He accused Leo of reneging on his written pledge of cooperation and warned that the Cistercians of the Strict Observance stood to lose millions of dollars and might be bankrupted if the Kenedy Memorial Foundation was lost, as it undoubtedly would be unless the monk listened to reason.

But what seemed to hurt Peter Grace the most was Leo's declaration that he was "sorry" for having appointed Grace his comember in February. "Mr. Grace," read the third-person document,

feels that this is an unjust and imprudent position . . . for the following reasons:—
UNJUST 1. The Will called for Mr. Grace's appointment as a Member and Brother Leo was morally wrong in using a presumed but unproven legal technicality to frustrate the wishes of Mrs. East as contained in her last Will and Testament. In other words, Mr. Grace feels that Brother Leo merely complied with his moral obligations by ap-

pointing Mr. Grace and that he should not regret doing what he was morally bound to do.

UNJUST 2. Irrespective of moral obligations, Mr. Grace and his group of Mr. McKay, Mr. Doyle and Mr. Meehan has, since Mr. Grace's appointment, individually and/or collectively *without compensation:*

a. Had over five hours of telephonic and face to face meetings with Bishop Garriga, who will not negotiate with Brother Leo.

b. Made 12 trips to Rome, which caused great difficulties for Mr. Grace and Mr. McKay, due to their positions in their law firm and company, i/e/ their associates have been criticizing them.

c. Furnished some $30,000. of cash expenses as an advance to the cause.

d. Furnished $89,000.—cost of time devoted to this by Messrs. Grace, Doyle and Meehan.

e. Allowed $50,000./$60,000. of estimated billings of Cahill, Gordon, Reindel & Ohl to go unbilled and unpaid with nothing owed ever if the case is completely lost—an unprecedented action by this law firm—one of the outstanding law firms in the United States.

f. Taken hours of His Eminence Cardinal Spellman's time on this matter.

g. Traveled five times to Texas.

h. Spent five hours with the Apostolic Delegate in Washington on three occasions.

i. Brought family friends into the matter such as Senator Hudson in Texas.

j. Provided company airplane for travel to upper New York State.

k. Entertained twice in apartment in New York City and at home on Long Island, the Attorney General of Texas and his wife—the individual who has under his control the rulings re charitable foundations in Texas.

l. Innumerable other contributions of less magnitude.

Sarita Kenedy East
in her early twenties.
She was "strictly the
cowgirl type," says a
relative. *(Courtesy
the Missionary
Oblates)*

Mrs. East at age sixty-five, six years before her death. The fight for control of her oil fortune continues today. *(Corpus Christi Caller)*

Sarita's grandfather, Mifflin Kenedy. An authentic giant of south Texas history, the old captain helped his Rio Grande steamboat partner Richard King build the mammoth King Ranch, then founded his own 400,000-acre cattle empire, La Parra, next door. *(Corpus Christi Caller)*

Don Gregorio, Sarita's father, designed and built the monumental Headquarters house at La Parra. Its central tower housed a Gatling gun for defense against bandits. *(Corpus Christi Caller)*

Don Gregorio's formal parlor inside the Headquarters reflected the family's taste for ornate furnishings. No one ever enjoyed living in the mansion. *(Courtesy the Missionary Oblates)*

A 1947 passport photo of Brother Leo Gregory at age thirty, just before he first met Sarita on the ranch at the graveside of her brother, Johnny.

OPPOSITE: In March 1950, Brother Leo's home for twelve years, Our Lady of the Valley Monastery in Rhode Island, was gutted by fire. Suddenly, the entire community of monks was homeless. *(Courtesy St. Joseph's Abbey)*

LEFT: Abbot Edmund Futterer in 1945. He thought of the monks as his family, and "Child Leo" was one of his favorites. *(Providence Journal)* RIGHT: Francis Verstraeten, Sr., at the doorway of his Buenos Aires apartment building. He now calls his old friend Leo "a very dangerous man."

Dom Thomas Keating. Among his concerns were the several death threats made against Brother Leo in Texas.

BELOW: J. Peter Grace. The industrialist, Leo's codefendent, traveled to Rome a dozen times in the mistaken belief that the Vatican would or could force a settlement. *(AP)*

Jake Floyd. Neither lung cancer nor the hunt for his son's assassin distracted Floyd in his determination to snatch Mrs. East's millions from Brother Leo and J. Peter Grace. *(Corpus Christi Caller)*

RIGHT: Judge C. W. Laughlin, known as El Burro for the dependability of his rulings. *(Corpus Christi Caller)* LEFT: Bishop Mariano Garriga. Brother Leo found Sarita's bishop "not too smart."

John Cardinal Krol. "He was shrewd, powerful and intelligent," says Brother Leo, who repeatedly defied Krol's orders. *(UPI)*

Bishop Rene Gracida. The former monk and bomber pilot settled the fight over Sarita's money by personally seizing control of the Kenedy foundation in 1984.

Grace's statement then moved from his examination of the injustice of Leo's remark to the "poor judgment" it reflected. Grace listed four reasons for saying so.

1. Very few people would support Brother Leo if he was the only member and abandoned the Will rather than use the Will as the main point of defence.
2. Brother Leo does not have wealth or prestige whereas Mr. Grace's wealth and the prestige [sic], and the fact that he (Mr. Grace) was also accused have greatly assisted in making the charges of "fraud" look ridiculous.
3. Many of those with whom Mr. Grace, Mr. McKay and Father Peyton and others have negotiated would not negotiate with Brother Leo.
4. Many of those, including His Eminence Cardinal Spellman who have assisted Mr. Grace would not have assisted Brother Leo.

Grace's tone was hardly conciliatory, but his long dissertation had a flustered, beseeching quality to it. Upon receiving the document at Spencer, Brother Leo decided to follow the advice he had given Bishop Garriga the preceding March and hired himself a lawyer, William R. Joyce, Jr., of Washington, D.C. Together, Joyce and Leo drafted the monk's written response to Grace, an eighty-one-page text dated November 17, 1961, one year to the day since Mrs. East first had been hospitalized in Buenos Aires. Several copies of Leo's statement were reproduced and delivered to Bishop Suenens, Dom Gabriel Sortais, and other prelates in Rome and in the United States.

Brother Leo caustically rejected Peter Grace's claim of a major role in the creation of the Kenedy Memorial Foundation as "a little overdone." He reminded his

one time ally that it was he, the monk, who had discovered Sarita's wealth in 1958. "This little point,"
he wrote, "give[s] a slightly different color to the or-
igin of the Kenedy Foundation, and would indicate
that perhaps my role in the KMF was somewhat more
important that [sic] might otherwise be interpreted. It
was in 1958 that I first discussed with you the possibility of organizing a Foundation for Sarita and asked
if some of your men would like to work with me on
this work. Due to the pressure of one of the timber
deals that was going on at that time, the first actual
contact between your office and Sarita was nearly a
year later."

The monk went on to take specific exception to
Grace's assertion that the W. R. Grace corporate
transportation department had provided invaluable assistance in arranging for Sarita's various travel accommodations. To the contrary, wrote the monk, he had
been doing Grace a favor by giving the W. R. Grace
travel department lucrative commissions on Mrs. East's
heavy travel expenses.

He belittled Lawrence McKay as negligent and dil-
atory and was equally unkind to the rest of the W. R.
Grace business and legal team. "In this regard, " Leo
allowed, "I am forced to say that whereas there was
no one I would rather have worked on this than you, I
myself would not feel that the contribution given by
your men and Cahill, Gordon was essential. Actually,
had a law firm and other consultants from Texas been
chosen, for instance in Houston or Dallas, the work of
the Foundation might have been smoother."

The monk reminded Grace that expert legal opinion
in Texas held that codicils were legally ineffective for
passing on foundation memberships; then he added
that, legal issues aside, Sarita really didn't mean for
her June 1960 appointment of Grace, Leo, and Father
Peyton as a membership troika to be her last word on

the topic. "It was," he said, "done with the same sort of mentality that she had when she signed the first codicil, namely that this was an improvement over the former one, but not necessarily the way in which the matter would finally be organized."

Indeed not. Leo claimed for himself the custody of Sarita's wishes. He was to give her foundation its final direction, by assembling a management team that would dedicate the Kenedy Memorial Foundation's charity to the universal church and to the poor of Latin American.

On the equally sensitive issue of the Trappists' expectations for future foundation giving (presuming the Kenedy foundation would eventually emerge from under Judge Laughlin's injunction), Leo forgot the memos he had signed with Dom Edmund Futterer and Brother Luke Roberts at Spencer the year before, documents of agreement under which Leo was to be allowed continued, but restricted, association with Sarita explicitly because the Trappists anticipated benefiting from the foundation.

Now the monk uncorked a revisionist explanation. "At no time in 1959 or 1960," he wrote, "when I was so actively working with her in the realization of this Foundation, did I see from it any personal gain for the Trappists. I knew that Sarita in response to our generosity would more than adequately take care of our financial needs, either from the Foundation or as she actually did from her own capital. Sarita implicitly promised to help us in every possible way, and we in return assured her that we would do our utmost to help her carry out her wishes regarding the KMF."

Leo made no mention of the supposed exchange of letters between Mrs. East and Dom Futterer that presumably spelled out exactly what she wanted from the Trappists and what she was willing to pay for the service. The monk mentioned only an "implicit" understanding between Mrs. East and his former abbot, who had recently suffered a series of strokes and was not available for questioning.

The critical point, Leo went on, was that the Trappists' claims on Mrs. East's foundation somehow had expired with her death, even though in the few months during which Sarita personally authorized foundation donations as its sole member she gave $145,00 out of a total charity of $200,000 to the order's expansion program.

"My own aim," Leo elaborated, "had been to help her create as near ideal as possible a Catholic Foundation." Because of this commitment, "at no time would I be upset if I were to learn that the Foundation would not help the Trappists, although our financial problems certainly are real ones. However, I would be very disappointed were a settlement to be reached wherein the Foundation itself would not achieve the universal effectiveness that I had encouraged Sarita to plan for."

Peter Grace's reaction was immediate. He demanded to know to whom Leo's encyclical had been sent and then dispatched his executives to retrieve and destroy as many copies of it as possible. Grace also demanded a full, written retraction.

Dom Thomas Keating had in the meantime been conducting his own investigation into the affair. Tall, bearded, and soft-spoken, with a scholarly air, Abbot Keating advanced through the maze of allegations and assertions in methodical search of the truth and for an equitable end to the controversy. Keating had always admired Brother Leo and, from his vantage point as superior at St. Benedict's in Colorado, had then entertained no misgivings about the monk's mission. "I was cheering Brother Leo on," Keating remembers, "because I thought, 'This is wonderful to have developed that kind of foundation for the poor and the universal church.' ''

Keating also never doubted the character of Leo's personal relationship with Sarita; he credits the monk with enriching her spiritual life. But as time went on he came to see Leo's insistence that he alone knew Mrs. East's wishes as open to reasonable doubt. ''She kept putting Jake Floyd on and off the foundation,'' says Dom Thomas, ''and changed her new will several times by codicils. She changed the successor membership of her foundations, too. Mrs. East was at least ambivalent about Brother Leo's advice. And I don't think she knew *herself* what she wanted to do until near the very end, if then. Hence, it was a fertile field, an inevitable field for varied interpretations of her actual intents.''

The interpretations that the Texans were putting on Sarita's intents—and Brother Leo's behavior—were Dom Keating's major, but not only, concern in the autumn of 1961, and he definitely did not share Leo's enthusiasm for a courtroom showdown on these issues. ''Brother Leo,'' says Keating, ''is not one for thinking of a dark side of a situation. It is fair to say he is an invincible optimist. It never meant anything to him that there was any danger to the monastery. He thought we were just scaredy-cats, you know. He said that if we put up a bold front, the Texans would be stared down. Everyone else told us these were not the kind of people to get stared down.''

Keating also faced a severe financial crisis in late 1961. Leo's phenomenally successful days as a Trappist fund-raiser were, of course, over. As long as Judge Laughlin's injunction held, there would be no more checks from the Kenedy Memorial Foundation, no matter who controlled its membership. Patrick Horkin was threatening to charge Brother Leo with criminal fraud for the money ''washed'' through Mrs.

East's Grace Bank account and, in the alternative, was menacing the Trappists with a suit to recover the money.

On a trip to South America in the autumn of 1961, Abbot Keating found that the Trappists, altogether, were about a quarter of a million dollars in debt at Las Condes, the monastery site in Chile, and at Estancia Acosta, in Argentina, where Doña Carmen Acosta impatiently awaited completion of the abbey church so that she could retrieve Don Pablo's remains for interment in their crypt. To finish the abbey roof at Estancia Acosta, Keating says, he was forced to raid Spencer's building and maintenance fund and place the mother house in Massachusetts on an austerity budget for the next twenty years.

The dom's investigation finally led him to one of his most critical conclusions. Notwithstanding Leo's deathbed comembership appointment of December 30, 1960, Keating decided that the third codicil most clearly expressed Mrs. East's intent and that Peter Grace and Father Peyton held the same foundation membership rights as did the monk. Therefore, Keating forbade Leo any further independent action in foundation matters. When the monk ignored the order, Keating decided Dom Futterer hadn't had such a bad idea the preceding autumn when Father Edmund had thought of putting Leo back into his shoe shop—and yanking out the telephone. He also demanded that Peyton fire William Joyce.

Brother Leo's "silencing," as it was called, appeared draconian; he later decried it as an attempt to bully him into submission. But according to Dom Keating's memory, Leo evinced what the abbot took to be a sincere and sympathetic understanding of the need for Keating's action.

The two differ today on other material facts, as well. Father Keating recalls urging Leo to seek both spiritual and canonical advice in his dispute with Peter Grace. He says that he told the monk to go to the expert of his choice but that Leo said he would be content to talk with two local men—Monsignor Alfred Julien, of the Boston archdiocese, and Father Raphael Simon, at the Spencer monastery itself.

Monsignor Julien's reading of the appropriate canons was that Leo could not assert his sole control of the foundation without corroborating evidence that this was Mrs. East's wish. The monk had no such evidence. Moreover, Monsignor Julien advised, absent direct evidence that Sarita has changed her mind after naming J. Peter Grace, Father Patrick Peyton, and the monk to succeed her, it was this codicil—no matter its standing in civil law—that he was morally bound to uphold.

It was on this basis, says Father Raphael, that he and another choir priest who was close to Leo, Father John, counseled the monk. "I felt that Brother Leo was evading the obvious," says Father Raphael, "and I pressed the point strongly that Dom Thomas had supervisory jurisdiction over Leo to see that he functioned as a foundation member according to Mrs. East's wishes, which the abbot believed most solemnly reflected in her third codicil."

Some weeks later Peter Grace sent up to the Spencer monastery a draft of the retraction he demanded from Brother Leo. The monk, according to Father Raphael, once again sought him out, this time for help in recasting the document in terms Leo thought were true and appropriate. Their editing sessions, says the priest, went smoothly. "I would say to him very lovingly, 'Brother Leo, such blindness! such blindness!' and he would accept this because he saw the love and gentleness with which I said it."

Brother Leo rejects both Father Keating's and Father Raphael's versions of events. He says that he was given no choice of whom to consult and that Father Raphael tried to browbeat him.

"I swallowed that rotten junk! I swallowed almost all of it," he says. "I forced it down my gullet, 80 percent of it. I felt like I was inside an Iron Maiden! I really did. And Father Raphael really put the screws on. The poor man. I'm sure he didn't realize how much I was suffering. I'm *sure* he didn't."

Whichever version of events is accurate, Brother Leo did comment on his situation at the time in a letter to his Argentine friends, the Verstraetens. He lamented to them his self-will and pride as lifelong impediments to a closer union with God and reaffirmed his deep conviction that while a Trappist's superior may be mistaken in commanding something, "we can never be wrong in doing it, and God will always back up their orders!"

Out of this crucible emerged a new document, Brother Leo's twenty-nine-page "Recantation" of his November 17 attack on Peter Grace. It featured a twenty-two-page appendix, making Leo's apology fifty-one pages long.

He did restate his argument "that if we showed ourselves to be in earnest in defending our case, it would never go to court." But "while still appreciating the advantages of this recommended course of action, I believe now that the course of action which Mr. Grace and Mr. McKay have taken is the wiser course of action and I am in complete accord with them and wish to retract my previous opposition."

"The second issue," Leo continued, "was the question of scandal. We disagreed on the extent and seriousness of this danger. However, in view of the opinions of American observers, I now am in accord with Mr. Grace and Mr. McKay in their estimate of the extent of damage that could be done by scandal."

The recantation next turned to the matter of foundation membership, and Leo retreated—again—on this issue. "Let me say," he wrote, "that I now fully acknowledge that the co-Membership of December 1960 [his deathbed appointment by Sarita] did not in any way change the obligation of appointing Father Peyton and Mr. Grace as co-Members with me as designated in the Last Will of Mrs. East and specifically in the Third Codicil of that Will, which she never revoked or altered. Therefore, we are now in complete accord."

TWENTY-ONE

✝ ✝ ✝

An Apostolic Visitation

His recantation brought Brother Leo back into the fold just in time for his first testimony in Cause 12074, Lee Lytton's suit alleging undue influence—three days of questioning in mid-February 1962 by Patrick Horkin at the W. R. Grace & Company boardroom in New York. When Horkin's grilling was over, Peter Grace was pleased to inform the nervous community at St. Joseph's Abbey in Spencer that Brother Leo had been more than equal to Horkin's toughest questions, even though it was news to Grace and everyone else when Leo explained to Horkin that Abbot Futterer had assigned him to help Sarita set up her foundation in answer to her direct request for the monk's assistance. Mrs. East's "implicit" promise "to help us in every way possible" as the monk had described it in his November 17 statement had become, under oath the following February, an explicit deal in which her donations through her Grace Bank account were her quid pro quo for Brother Leo's aid and attentions.

The monk's expressed contrition for his written attack on Peter Grace, and then his poised performance under Horkin's examination, were the only bright spots in an otherwise grim early 1962 for J. Peter Grace. On January 8 there came word from Texas that Kenneth Oden, acting on behalf of his senior law partner, Jake

Floyd, had filed a so-called "intervention" in Cause 12074, entering Floyd's name as a coplaintiff and appropriating Lee Lytton's charges as his own. According to Ken Oden, the decision for Jake Floyd to step out of his anonymous role was made at Pat Horkin's request; the attorney for Lee Lytton wanted a non-Catholic plaintiff as insurance should more pressure be brought by the church for Lee Lytton to desist in the suit.

But Jake Floyd's direct entry as a litigant raised the pressure on the New Yorkers to settle in another, more immediate way. Ever since Lee Lytton filed his original suit, in April 1961, it had been a shared assumption on both sides of the case that the allegations in 12074 might invite a separate civil action aimed at undoing the 1960 will, or parts of it. The reasoning was, first of all, that Sarita had plenty of relatives who were now angry at what had happened to their inheritances and, second, that the selective way undue influence was alleged to have been applied in 12074—only in connection with the third codicil, the Lytton and Floyd resignations, and Brother Leo's deathbed appointment as Mrs. East's comember—was patently self-serving. Peter Grace had pointed this out in detail in his chart for the Roman Curia.

Some smart lawyer, somewhere, was going to see how the residual clause (26) in Sarita's will, for instance, might also be vulnerable to legal attack as a product of undue influence, and that to have it thrown out might benefit certain heirs or ex-heirs. When, after just a few months, no fewer than forty south Texas lawyers wrote Judge Laughlin's clerk in Jim Wells County for a copy of Cause 12074, as well as the Kennedy County clerk, Faye Chandler, for a copy of the 1960 will, the question no longer was whether a challenge of some sort was going to be made but when.

Here was the possibility that Peter Grace feared

most, a successful suit to dismantle the 1960 will and the foundation, which would deprive the church of the millions Grace had been at great pains to secure for it. Not only did Jake Floyd's intervention in 12074 as a coplaintiff with Lytton lend important weight to Lytton's charges (Floyd was an executor of Sarita's estate), but under Texas law the action further estopped Jake Floyd from aiding in the defense of the will and foundation should a legal challenge come. Jake Floyd and Pat Horkin, in effect, were daring Peter Grace to a game of chicken: capitulate, or risk losing everything.

The next setback for the New Yorkers came in February, thanks to Pope John XXIII. Four months earlier (and just after the name-calling episode with Leo in Paris), Grace had received from the Reverend Edward L. Heston, the Holy Cross procurator general in Rome, a copy of Heston's notes of a meeting with the new Vatican secretary of state, Amleto Giovanni Cardinal Cicognani. Cardinal Tardini had died the preceding summer, not long after his meeting with Peter Grace and Larry McKay.

"Having occasion to call on His Eminence for other business," Heston's memo began,

Father Heston brought up the question of the controversy between the Bishop of Corpus Christi and Mr. Peter Grace and companions in the Kenedy Foundation. Cardinal Cicognani had just come from his regular daily audience with the Holy Father, and in the course of this audience had briefed His Holiness on the background of the points at issue, since Bishop Garriga was to be received in audience that very morning. The Holy Father concurred most energetically in the necessity of taking steps to stop the lawsuit before it involves the Church in a vast-scale scandal. Mentioning that the Congregation of the Council had proposed during the summer a settlement on the basis of 80/20, Cardinal Cicognani expressed the opinion that this might be broadened to a 75/25 settlement, but not any more.

When His Holiness suggested that the settlement might be 70/30, Cardinal Cicognani objected that this was too much, but was over-ruled when the Holy Father replied that the Pope could afford to be liberal!

Heston went on to report on his later discussion with Father Walsh of the Oblate Congregation, also in Rome to complain of Leo and Peter Grace. Walsh had heard directly from Bishop Garriga on the outcome of his audience with John XXIII. "From the account of the Bishop," wrote Heston of what Father Walsh told him, "His Holiness began to see the question in another light." The pope told Bishop Garriga that he would be willing to hear more about the Texans' side of the case. "Undoubtedly," Father Heston closed, "there will be further developments."

There were, the following February, when Pope John XXIII at last lost patience with all the unseemly wrangling. The pope named Archbishop John Krol of Philadelphia as his apostolic visitator, a sort of papal special agent. Krol was invested, as Archbishop Vagnozzi in Washington explained in a letter to Dom Thomas Keating at St. Joseph's Abbey in Spencer, with "plenary power to take such measures, including canonical penalties, as he deems to be necessary to remedy the regrettable situation that has developed in the matter of the 'Kenedy Foundation.'"

In other words, Archbishop Krol had full authority to review the case and then impose whatever solution he saw fit on the squabbling Catholics. No Roman Catholic in the affair could chance opposing the archbishop's decisions without also hazarding the direct church sanctions.

John Krol had his detractors within the church. "He's primitive," says William Joyce, Brother Leo's Washington attorney, who would be among the first individuals threatened with excommunication by Archbishop Krol in the unfolding controversy. "Krol's straight out of the coal mines. Guys like him don't even know how to use forks."

Krol, a burly six feet one inch tall and fifty-one years old at the time of his appointment as visitator, had a sharp face, a sharper mind, and a reputation for rigid absolutism in doctrinal and hierarchical matters. He was also a dedicated opponent of nuclear armaments, which he considered immoral.

The fourth of eight children in the Polish immigrant family of John and Anne Pietruska Krol, he was born and raised in Cleveland, where, after high school, he worked as a butcher and as a Kroger Stores supermarket manager. He discovered his vocation for the priesthood in his early twenties and studied at St. Mary's Seminary in Cleveland, where he supported himself, in part, by selling cigars to his fellow seminarians.

After his ordination at the comparatively advanced age of twenty-seven, Krol rose steadily in the Cleveland diocese. By 1961 he was prominent enough to be called to Rome to serve on a bishops' commission charged by John XXIII with laying the groundwork for the epochal Vatican II Council, scheduled to begin in 1963. While working in the Holy City that January, Krol learned that he was soon to be named archbishop of Philadelphia. A month later, on February 11, 1961, the day Sarita died at St. Vincent's Hospital, John Krol was installed as head of the United States's sixth-largest archdiocese.

A year later the new archbishop wasted no time familiarizing himself with the Kenedy foundation dispute. Krol considered the Texans' and the New Yorkers' contentions and conducted personal interviews with Bishop Garriga and with Brother Leo.

Soon Peter Grace discovered that the papal appointee was even less congenial toward his point of view than Cardinal Vagnozzi had been. The industrialist importuned the archbishop with long letters—which Krol for many weeks refused to acknowledge—impatiently asking how His Excellency intended to handle the matter. The longer Krol persisted in ignoring him, the more irate Grace became. "I hated the sonuvabitch at the time," he recalls. "Krol treated us as absolute dirt. I thought that was terrible, and I told him so."

It wasn't until some years later, Grace now claims, that then Cardinal John Krol at last explained his hostile indifference to him. "It's very simple," Grace remembers the cardinal telling him at a dinner. "When I first met Brother Leo, I decided he was a crook. And I don't deal with crooks. I decided he was dishonest, and that's the end of it. You were in bed with a dishonest man."

The apostolic visitator's opinion of the monk may have been formed even before they met. Leo reported at the time to Peter Grace that Krol had alluded to, but would not disclose, a five-inch stack of affidavits that allegedly attested to Leo's wrongdoing. These reports were supplied to the archbishop by Mariano Garriga and presumably included Sara Curiel's testimony.

With his last hope of a favorable church-sponsored settlement now gone, Peter Grace reconciled himself to salvaging what he could of the Kenedy Memorial Foundation. From the 80 percent share of the foundation he had hoped to retain in the summer of 1961, Grace was forced to keep retreating through the spring of 1962 until May, when both the Trappists and Cardinal Spellman advised him to take Patrick Horkin's nonnegotiable last offer. Under it, the New Yorkers, along with Mrs. Armstrong and Lawrence Wood, would concede the Kenedy Memorial Foundation in its entirety (to Bishop Garriga, they assumed) in return for oil revenues up to a total of $14.4 million, exactly half the artificially low assessed value of Sarita's estate that Jake Floyd had negotiated for tax purposes with the Internal Revenue Service. This money would flow into Grace's Serra Fund, to be renamed the Sarita K. East Foundation.

The tentative settlement left Leo no voice whatsoever in either the old or the new foundation, and no amount of pressure could bring him to accept it positively. Instead, the silenced monk made a gesture of protest by signing a May 30, 1962, resignation, intending it as a signal to Henrietta Armstrong of his passive resistance.

Peter Grace's acceptance also was conditional. He wanted letters from Lee Lytton and Jake Floyd exonerating him from any alleged wrongdoing, and he balked at Archbishop Krol's insistence that the Holy See approve all disbursals from the new Sarita Kenedy Foundation, a demand that the apostolic visitor also put to Bishop Garriga, who accepted it.

Pending a solution to Grace's objections, Krol journeyed to Alice in July of 1962 on what he believed to be a pro forma visit to the south Texans. The archbishop assumed that whatever was agreeable to Bishop Garriga would satisfy the supposedly nominal plaintiff, Lytton and Floyd, and assumed further that Elena Kenedy was interested solely in restoring the Kenedy foundation to local Catholic church control. With Peter Grace nearly ready to accept Pat Horkin's offer and Brother Leo's resignation in his pocket, Krol anticipated no further obstacles to a satisfactory settlement.

His first surprise came from Jake Floyd. Sitting at his office desk and scratching his ear with a paper clip,

Floyd nodded toward Lytton, Tom East, and Mrs. Kenedy and casually explained to Krol that the group had decided to form its own Kenedy Memorial Foundation membership board. Bishop Garriga was to be allowed a single vote as the fifth member of the foundation.

Two days later at a second, tempestuous gathering with Garriga at his Corpus Christi chancery, Floyd's bloc held firm. The visitator warned the Catholics present that their souls were imperiled. Garriga, his fragile pride again wounded, sputtered for an explanation from Elena, who sat in silent discomfort. Tom East, who rarely spoke at all, only shrugged at Krol and reminded the archbishop that he was a Protestant and therefore couldn't be excommunicated.

By the end of the meeting, Garriga and Krol were reduced to asking—not demanding—that the foundation board be expanded to seven members with the addition of the diocesan vicar general and a designee from the Holy See, still a voting minority of three with the bishop. Jake Floyd said he would consider the proposal.

Back in Philadelphia, Krol pondered this unhappy reversal for the church and decided to probe Jake Floyd's coalition at what he guessed to be its weakest point, Mrs. Kenedy. "Dear Mrs. Kenedy," he wrote Elena on July 25, "It was very kind of you to see me so graciously and to give me the opportunity of representing the interests of the Church.

"Everyone agrees that the Church is the principal beneficiary of the Kenedy Memorial Foundation. Everyone also agrees that in life Mrs. East time and again sought advice and counsel from bishops and priests about her charitable donations. It is only reasonable that the pattern which she followed in life should be followed after her death."

Elena's reply, typed on Jake Floyd's office typewriter, was curt. ''I cannot help but believe that you have been misinformed,'' the letter read. ''During her life, Mrs. East and I discussed and considered such matters together, and usually gave half and half. When we decided to make a charitable donation, the checks would be written by our office manager and the checks would go out from the office. Neither Mrs. East nor I ever consulted Bishop Garriga or his predecessor or any priest about such matters.''

Mrs. Kenedy could not have been altogether pleased with the tone of the typewritten note, for she appended a personal message in her own hand. ''All through this case,'' she wrote to Krol, ''we have tried to protect the bishop as we do not want him hurt in any way. You know also we have no personal interest in the Foundation assets, we have had only work and heartaches. It is most regrettable that this matter has caused hurt feelings amongst old and trusted friends.''

It pained Elena Kenedy to side against her bishop, and the memory of the difficult moment in his chancery was fresh many years later when she agreed to speak of the events of July 1962. ''You'll understand,'' she said in a halting voice, ''Sarita founded the *Kenedy* Foundation, not the Archbishop Krol Foundation. Bishop Garriga was a good man, and I wanted him to understand that nothing would change. It would be as it was.''

Actually, there was one critical change on July 25, the day the visitator wrote Elena from Philadelphia. That afternoon the attorney William Wright of Laredo, Texas, down on the Rio Grande, filed an action on behalf of members of the Rodriguez family, direct descendants of María Concepción Vidal de Rodríguez, Sarita's grandmother Petra Vela de Vidal's third child by her first marriage.

Wright's suit, Cause 348 in the Kenedy County probate court (Judge Lee Lytton, Jr., presiding), charged that the undue influence allegedly exerted on Mrs. East by Peter Grace and Brother Leo extended to the creation of the 1960 will. But Wright, knowing his clients would fare poorly if the entire 1960 will was thrown out and replaced by its predecessor document—Sarita's 1948 will—argued that only the residual clause of the 1960 will was a product of undue influence. He wanted all the assets included under it to be split by Mrs. East's relatives on a pro rata basis, according to the nearness of their blood kinship.

The sums to be divided would exclude income from the inter vivos transfers of mineral rights to the foundation—about a quarter of the total Kenedy fortune—because these were outside the probate court's jurisdiction. But there was no doubt that if Wright was successful in attacking the residual clause, a second action alleging undue influence in obtaining the inter vivos transfers would follow.

On the same day, Wright attempted to intervene directly in the original suit. Judge Laughlin in Alice denied the lawyer standing in the case. Nevertheless, the long-expected will contest had now begun. Unless it could be defeated, or unless Wright would accept a settlement, everything was lost.

TWENTY-TWO

✠ ✠ ✠

Shifting Allegiances

Until the showdown in Bishop Garriga's office, and then William Wright's will-contest suit, Cause 348, the contenders for control of the Kenedy fortune more or less sorted themselves into two opposing camps—the Texans and the New Yorkers. Suddenly, however, all the existing alliances dissolved as individual interests and allegiances shifted. At the time, Jake Floyd and his junior partner, Kenneth Oden, were probably the only two people in Texas or New York who could keep all of the players straight.

In the summer of 1962 Lee Lytton fired Patrick Horkin—who had thought Archbishop Krol's terms acceptable—and immediately hired Ken Oden to take over as lead plaintiff counsel in Cause 12074. Ken Oden, a native of Yoakum, Texas, served as a bomber pilot in World War II. He joined Floyd's Alice firm in 1950 at age twenty-six and spent the next decade learning the practice of law from the masterful Mr. Floyd, whom Oden remembers as "a moral and a juridical giant."

Pat Horkin, whose first loyalty always had been to Bishop Garriga, then filed his own intervention on Garriga's behalf in 12074, a petition that argued that Sarita's first codicil, naming the bishop her successor,

was not only legal but also the clearest indication anywhere of her unimpaired judgment.

Jake Floyd, his cancer so far in abeyance, meanwhile approached Bill Wright to see what it might cost
him to make the Laredo attorney—and his forty-three
Rodriguez family plaintiffs in Cause 348—go away.
Wright wouldn't say, except to indicate it was a lot
more than Jake was prepared to pay him. "Maybe I'd
give 'em a hundred thousand," Floyd remarked in an
off-the-record conversation with James Rowe, an editor at the *Corpus Christi Caller.* "But they want a lot
more. We gotta fight 'em." According to John Fitzgibbon of Laredo, one of Wright's associate attorneys
in the case, Floyd was immovable. "We were never
offered anything by Jake," says Fitzgibbon. "He told
Bill Wright that he would live to regret the suit. And
sometimes we almost did."

Floyd's first move was to amend the allegations in
Cause 12074 so that they were no longer sworn; in this
way, he deprived Wright of sworn testimony and therefore forced the Laredo lawyers to try to build their
case for undue influence from scratch. Next, Jake as-
sessed the recent adversity for any opportunities it
might afford him.

His potential problems included Peter Grace and
Brother Leo, who suddenly had gained some apparent
leverage with the filing of the will contest. Their sworn
testimony could prove vital to the defense of the will
and the foundation, key evidence for which Grace
might demand a better deal than the $14.4 million he
tentatively had agreed to take. Second, Archbishop
Krol was holding Brother Leo's May 30 resignation
and had indicated his unwillingness to release it unless
the settlement offered improved terms to the Vatican.
Finally, Bill Wright and his clients, the "Mexican
heirs," were not going to back down in their demands
unless Floyd could scare them into it.

What Floyd required was a handy, all-purpose weapon, and he found it in Tom East, Jr. On November 15, 1962, Tom East, represented by the attorney Walter Groce of Corpus Christi, filed his own intervention in 348, the will contest. This pleading contended, as did Wright's, that Leo and Grace had applied undue influence on Mrs. East from the very start. But instead of arguing that only the residuary clause was invalid, East asked that the entire 1960 will be dismissed and replaced by the 1948 document, under which he, together with his brother, Robert, and their sister, Alice Hattie, were given Mrs. East's San Pablo ranch and all the oil beneath it.

Jake, through Ken Oden, told Peter Grace and Archbishop Krol that East had bolted the coalition and was now a renegade faction unto himself. The rancher was rich, Oden explained, and determined to get a lot richer unless he could be prevailed upon to drop the will-contest intervention. If the settlement could be resurrected, Oden went on, Grace would be obliged, as the industrialist recalls, to "play ball."

East's specific terms for withdrawing his intervention were that Peter Grace take $5 million, not $14.4 million, and that Grace negotiate and settle with Bill Wright. To Wright, Fitzgibbon, and their associates, the message of the East intervention was also a threat. "Jake and his bunch used Tom East as an ogre, a bogeyman," says Frank Nesbit, who in 1963 would become a central figure in Cause 348, the will contest, representing members of the Turcotte family. "East had no intention of goin' through with it. But he wanted to show all the Mexicans, 'Forget it. If you set aside this will I'm right behind ya to probate the '48 will, and you know that you get part of nuthin'.' It was nothing but a legal maneuver."

There was substance, however, to still another developing rift. Following Wright's initiation of the will

contest, the ailing Louis Edgar Turcotte's family notified Patrick Horkin that they wanted the as-yet-
undisclosed letters from Brother Leo to Sarita returned
to family custody, *their* custody. If the will itself was
now to be disputed, the Turcottes wanted control of
what certainly would be critical evidence. When Horkin temporized, the family went to Bishop Garriga
with their request, only to be rebuffed again. Disappointed as he was with the meeting in July, the bishop
would not violate Elena Kenedy's sternly expressed
desire that the offending letters remain secret.

As this dispute festered, new trouble broke out
among the easterners. Brother Leo's May 30 resignation from the Kenedy Memorial Foundation had been
written as a form of protest, not a surrender. Nor did
he fire the attorney William Joyce as Dom Thomas
Keating had directed.

That spring Leo acquired a new ally, Father Dominic Hughes, a moral theologian who had been teaching
at Spencer. Hughes was a portly priest with a full head
of curly black hair, a fine elfin wit, and a reputation
for brilliance and fractiousness. He was a maverick
Catholic intellectual who, according to Bill Joyce,
never once showed any interest in the foundation fight
but was outraged at what he regarded as Dom Thomas's dictatorial abuse of Leo's basic human rights,
especially his freedom of conscience. Hughes also
concurred in Bill Joyce's low opinion of Archbishop
Krol and of Peter Grace.

He became a conduit between the silenced monk
and his attorney, shuttling messages and information
between them and advising Leo on spiritual and canonical issues. When fragmentary reports of Archbishop Krol's failed mission to Texas reached Leo at
Spencer, it was Father Hughes who relayed to Bill
Joyce the monk's desire that a letter be sent to the
visitor.

Krol, who already had decided that Leo was a crook and who had emphasized to Dom Thomas his approval of Leo's silencing, assumed that the troublesome lay brother had been removed from the picture altogether. Krol did carry, after all, Leo's resignation from the foundation.

The archbishop was thus astounded in July to receive from Bill Joyce a letter on Leo's behalf informing the visitator that there was "a solution to this impasse." "From my own experience as counsel for Brother Leo," Joyce wrote, "and from conversations with the Armstrongs (They together would control the Board of Members of the Foundation as it exists today) I am certain they both would be willing to accept the solution Your Excellency has devised."

Krol could scarcely believe what he read. Nor could he fathom how the monk, commanded to silence, had somehow remained sufficiently informed to hatch this gambit, or was possessed of the effrontery to hazard it.

"Can you offer any information or explanation about this gentleman and the statements he makes?" Krol queried Leo in an August 27, 1962, letter on his official archdiocesan stationery. "Would you know how he learned of my position in the controversy, and offer [*sic*] to share his views with me? I shall appreciate any information or explanation you may be able to supply, and I would appreciate having it in writing." After an equally frosty telephone call from Krol, Leo withdrew his suggestion to the archbishop that management of the Kenedy foundation be returned to his control.

The action then shifted back to Texas, where the Turcotte family, locked in its feud with Bishop Garriga over access to Leo's letters, surveyed the rapidly balkanizing battle for Aunt Sarita's estate and decided to join it. In November of 1962 Louis Edgar, still believing himself estopped from suing as one of Sarita's executors, offered his late brother Andrew's son, Andy, Jr. (the Kingsville mortician), up to $100,000 in legal fees if Andy wanted to file an intervention. Four months later Louis Edgar Turcotte died from a diabetes-related heart attack (Bishop Garriga was excluded by the family from the funeral), and within two weeks of his death Andrew Turcotte, Jr., represented by the local lawyer Burch Downman, became the first of fourteen Turcottes to file separate pleadings in Bill Wright's will case. Andrew's uncle Louis Edgar had expected, according to his son Patrick, that the family would seek to have the 1948 will probated. But since Andrew and the rest stood to inherit more under a pro rata division of the estate according to blood ties, they all appropriated the Laredo attorneys' argument that only the residual clause was invalid because of undue influence from Brother Leo and Peter Grace.

Then came the deluge. Over the next several months the number of separate contestants in Cause 348 swelled to 181 with the entry of the rest of Petra Vela de Vidal's numerous descendants, plus a clutch of surprise litigants. These included the verifiable descendants of Mifflin Kenedy's younger brother Elisha, who also had been a Rio Grande steamboater, as well as a group claiming descent from Mifflin's alleged brother Charles, whose existence in fact they could never prove.

Kenedys, Kennedys, Kendys, and Kennys from all over the United States mailed inquiries to the Kenedy County courthouse, some complete with family genealogies. "We are not the type of people that wish publicity and to become involved in a bitter court battle," wrote a man from Warren, Ohio. "The bitterness, acrimony and accusations are for those who put money ahead of love and respect for our beloved blood relative."

"My great-great grandmother," wrote a woman in

Pennsylvania, "was the aunt of Captain Milford Kenedy. Our families were separated and never had the opportunity to meet often."

This correspondent claimed to recall the old captain himself. "I heard him speak often of the falling water level. He dreamed of the day when boats again could sail up the Rio Grande throughout the whole year. If there is a spot where a dam could be built . . . then use one third of our inheritance to build this dam."

Still another letter writer was upset about the church's involvement in the case. In his eighteen-page submission he wrote, "No one has the right to allow Capt. Kenedy's fortune to be seized by the Catholic Church. The U.S.A. would be destroyed by such inconsiderate and ungrateful persons."

But the most interesting new contender was a resident of Texas City, near Galveston, who called herself Sarita Kenedy and who based her and her brother's rights to inheritance on her assertion of direct descent from Sarita's uncle Tom, the one murdered by Deputy Sheriff José Esparsa in Brownsville. As was revealed in court, on the night of Tom's 1887 marriage to Irene Yznaga at the Immaculate Conception Cathedral in Brownsville, the Kenedy family maid, Ramona Gonzales, appeared at the cathedral as well. She was carrying an infant she called Roberto, who, according to what Ramona told the priest, was Tom's son. She wanted the boy baptized as Roberto Kenedy.

The priest refused the maid's request, but Ramona gave Roberto the Kenedy surname anyway and later revealed his father's identity to him. Roberto's daughter, the litigant Sarita Kenedy, and her brother also grew up certain of their lineage, which ultimately was accepted in court. However, under Texas's complex rules for assigning heirship, Tom Kenedy's grandchildren were both the strongest and the weakest claimants to the estate of his niece. They were Mrs. East's closest blood relatives among the Kenedys. Yet because of their father's illegitimacy, they were debarred from standing in the will contest and could not inherit no matter how the case was decided. Save for the illegitimacy of Sarita Kenedy's father, a major portion of Sarita Kenedy East's estate would have gone to her.

Pat Horkin intervened Bishop Garriga—that is, entered him as a litigant—in Cause 348, the will contest, just as he had in the suit he originally filed for Lee Lytton, Cause 12074, pleading that codicil one, naming the bishop Sarita's successor, should be probated, and challenging codicil three as a product of undue influence. While this action caused no more than a ripple in the dispute, Horkin's second move, his attempt to serve Leo, Peter Grace, and Father Peyton with summonses, created a brief panic. Alerted by Ken Oden that process servers in Albany, New York, headquarters for Peyton's Rosary Crusade, in Spencer, and in New York City were about to be dispatched, Peyton and Grace both arranged to be out of town that day. Brother Leo boarded a jet for Chile; a trip he made willingly. As the monk explained in a letter to his mother, Lotus, he hoped the rustication would open a new and glorious phase in his vocation. His single disappointment, he wrote, was that Abbot Keating had refused his request to be known henceforth as Brother Joseph.

As Edwards ——

TWENTY-THREE

✠ ✠ ✠

A Plea to the Pope

The summer of 1963 was a relatively quiet period. The prime defendant, Brother Leo, was once again lost in contemplation in the Chilean monastery Sarita had bought for the Trappists in 1960 and the arch manipulator Jake Floyd was now rapidly losing ground to his cancer. With Jake and Leo absent, the blitz of litigation that their warfare touched off ceased briefly.

Lee Lytton recused himself as presiding judge in the will contest and was replaced, under gubernatorial appointment, by a special probate judge, William R. Edwards, thirty-one years old and just five years out of the University of Virginia Law School. Muscular and athletic, a native of New Jersey, Edwards had moved to Corpus Christi to set up a civil practice. The fact that he had most recently practiced law as an associate at Baker, Botts in Houston, Peter Grace's Texas counsel, led some in the courthouse crowd to assume the appointment was an arrangement. If so, no one thought to tell Bill Edwards how he was supposed to behave. "I was here in town," he says in his Corpus Christi office, "and I was the only one around, as I understand it, that didn't have any interest in the case, the one that everybody in the lawsuit would accept either because they didn't have any objection or they didn't know me. I hadn't made anybody mad at that time.''

As Edwards began to grapple with the welter of claims and counterclaims, motions, and hearings, another player, Archbishop Krol, slowly worked to revive some version of the settlement he thought had been negotiated to everyone's satisfaction a year before. The one legal impediment to closing the deal had been removed; Bill Wright's attempted intervention in 12074 had been rejected by the higher courts, meaning that Lee Lytton's original suit could be dissolved if everyone was amenable.

Of course, everyone would also then have to join together to face the 181 will contestants. And until their claims were disposed of, no allocation of the Kenedy foundation's resources would be possible. Years later some lawyers would speculate that Jake Floyd, in fact, had invited Bill Wright to file his suit, knowing that as long as it was pending the Kenedy estate and Kenedy foundation assets would remain in the Alice National Bank's custody. Such was Jake's reputation for deviousness that the accusation seemed plausible.

The negotiated peace that aligned Lee Lytton, Tom East, the Alice bank, Elena Kenedy, and the bishop with Grace, Father Peyton, and Leo (all the original disputants) against Bill Wright and the Mexican heirs was a tribute to Archbishop Krol's patience and diplomacy. Realizing that he could not dictate terms, the visitator wisely settled for a series of compromises that would prevent, he thought, an embarrassing spectacle of Catholic suing Catholic for a Catholic fortune.

The bishop of Corpus Christi, for example, was to receive guaranteed membership on the Kenedy Memorial Foundation, but the Corpus Christi diocese would not control the charity. Tom East would continue his intervention in 348—his suit was useful for keeping pressure on the Mexican heirs—but the rancher did give up his demand that Peter Grace settle the will contest himself, and East agreed that Grace could receive the negotiated $14.4 million for his Sarita K. East Foundation. East, in return, would manage all 400,000 acres of La Parra under a Kenedy foundation contract. J. Peter Grace did not get his letters of full exoneration from the Texans, but he got his $14.4 million and an agreement from Krol not to quibble over the makeup of the new Sarita K. East Foundation board. For the time being, Grace would run it along with Father Peyton, Cardinal Spellman, and a representative from the Trappists, possibly Leo.

Under a formula stipulated by the new Texas attorney general, John Ben Sheppard, the original John G. and Marie Stella Kenedy Memorial Foundation would have five members, at least three to be Catholics and at least one a non-Catholic. Elena would serve, as would Lee Lytton and Bishop Garriga. The board of members would also include Ken Oden and Bruno Goldapp, a vice-president of the Alice bank. Ten percent or more of the foundation's annual charity was to be set aside for non-Catholic causes. And all the money had to be spent in Texas.

Everyone, in short, got what he or she wanted, or reasonably hoped to get, under Krol's new deal.

Except for Brother Leo.

The monk, who turned forty-six that summer, had spent a placid several months in Chile writing to the Verstraetens across the Andes in Buenos Aires and to his mother, who had moved back to southern California and was living with Leo's older brother, Jackson, Jr., and his family. Leo favored them all with a stream of spiritual advice, rarely mentioning the foundation fight in his correspondence. The subject of money surfaced only twice in his many notes. In the first instance, he told Lotus that the Graces' aged cook Anna, whom she knew well, was sending him $100 a month out of her salary. So that Peter might not discover this, he asked if perhaps Anna could address her envelopes to Lotus for forwarding to Chile. The second mention of money was Leo's suggestion to Lotus Gregory that she consider donating a $1,200 royalty check she expected from Dodd, Mead, one of her late husband's publishers, to a water-well-drilling project for the monastery.

Brother Leo's serenity was abruptly shattered on September 10, 1963, with the arrival in Santiago of Father Vincent Dwyer on the noon Panagra flight from New York. Father Dwyer, a Spencer monk, was carrying letters for Leo from Archbishop Krol and Abbot Keating, plus a copy of the settlement for Leo to sign.

"After long and arduous effort," wrote the visitator, "we have succeeded in promoting some co-operation among the various parties." Krol informed the monk that "my superiors"—meaning the new pope, Paul VI, elected by the College of Cardinals the preceding June after the death from stomach cancer of John XXIII—understood the settlement and shared the archbishop's "anxiety to conclude this phase of the controversy as quickly as possible." "Your signature to the agreement is requested," Krol went on, "and I wish to assure you that you may in good conscience co-operate in the request."

Dom Thomas's message also urged compliance and included his personal wish that neither Leo nor any member of the Spencer community take an active part in Peter Grace's new foundation. "Would you also write me a note suggesting whom you would like to succeed you?" the abbot asked. "Peter will want some representative of the Order to be on the Foundation for at least six months, but I am hoping we can persuade him to accept someone else. If you can think of anyone who would be pleasing to you and acceptable to him, it would be a great help to me, both in satisfying you and in reconciling Peter to the Trappists dropping out.

"May the good Lord and St. Joseph bless you and give you the grace to bear whatever disappointment is involved in this situation for their honor and glory. With much love and prayers, and looking forward to seeing you soon, Father Thomas."

Father Dwyer was under orders to secure Leo's signature and then to pouch the signed settlement on Panagra's return flight at 3:00 P.M. to Lawrence McKay in New York. But once Leo read the terms of the agreement, which cut him out of the picture entirely, he stalled his fellow monk with the excuse that he needed time to consult his conscience and to consider his civil responsibilities in the matter. Dwyer protested but could do nothing to force Leo to sign.

Then Leo set to work. He immediately contacted William Joyce in Washington, who cabled Jake Floyd in Alice: "HAVE BEEN REQUESTED TO ADVISE YOU THAT BROTHER LEO HAS EXECUTED REVOCATION OF RESIGNATION AS MEMBER OF KENEDY MEMORIAL FOUNDATION AND AM FORWARDING SAME TO YOU UNDER SEPARATE COVER."

Next the monk visited Father José Aldunate Lyons, the Jesuit superior in Chile, who was sympathetic to Leo's situation, according to what Aldunate knew of the matter from Leo himself. Once the monk laid out his dilemma to Father Aldunate—how to foil the settlement without risking loss of his vocation—the Jesuit suggested a clever stratagem.

The idea was for Leo to sign the settlement papers as ordered, but instead of returning them to McKay he would send the settlement directly to Paul VI with an accompanying letter. This note would explain that despite what His Holiness might have been led to believe, the settlement contradicted Mrs. East's plans for her foundation, as she had confided them to Leo. The monk declared that in conscience he could not agree to the settlement unless Paul VI publicly invoked his canonical power to reverse Mrs. East's true last wishes. Certain that Pope Paul would never directly embroil himself in such a way, Leo enclosed his letter with the signed settlement and entrusted the papers to a priest for delivery in Rome, where Bishop Manuel Larrain of the Episcopal Conference of Latin-American Bishops (CELAM), already in the Holy City for the autumn's opening sessions of the Vatican II Council, had promised that the envelope containing the signed settlement and Leo's letter would be hand-delivered to Paul VI.

When Father Dwyer came home empty-handed, Archbishop Krol began firing increasingly irate tele-grams to Leo in Chile from Rome (where he also was attending the Vatican II meetings) demanding to know why the settlement had not been returned. At first, Leo allowed only that he'd sent the settlement "else-where." "I DIRECT YOU," Krol cabled late in Sep-tember, "TO IDENTIFY PERSON OR OFFICE TO WHOM AGREEMENTS WERE SENT AND HOW SENT."

Waiting until he could be sure the packet had reached Bishop Larrain in Rome, Leo finally wired back: "YOUR CABLE JUST REACHED ME. DOC-UMENTS DIRECTED TO HIS HOLINESS. TAKEN BY HAND."

Krol deduced that Larrain was holding the papers. As both he and the Chilean bishop later told the story, he accosted Larrain at a council session and demanded to know if he had the documents. Manuel Larrain, in truth, did not know that they had been delivered to his hotel and so denied that he had the papers. However, on returning to his room that day, the bishop discovered them on his desk and telephoned Archbishop Krol at once.

Together, the two then visited the papal secretary of state, Cardinal Cicognani. The cardinal read Leo's covering letter to the pope and then handed the settlement agreement with Leo's signature on it to Archbishop Krol, saying that the monk's condition as contained in his letter to Paul VI was fulfilled.

Leo's ploy failed, as Peter Grace later pointed out to him, because he hadn't attached his condition to his signature on the settlement paper. If he had, Archbishop Krol would have retrieved a useless, altered document.

The archbishop, who had not yet heard of Bill Joyce's cable to Jake Floyd informing the attorney that Leo was revoking his 1962 resignation, stayed on in Rome for the autumn's Vatican II sessions, expecting the settlement to be a fact by year's end. There still seemed to be a chance for the affair to be closed without serious damage done to the church.

This hope evaporated in late November when Brother Leo's photograph and a story headlined "A Will & Two Ways" appeared in the religion section of *Time* magazine. *Time* told its readers of an intrachurch power struggle, "a bitter battle of words and wits that echoes all the way to the Vatican," over what the magazine's research indicated were potential oil revenues "which may be worth as much as $300 million." Sarita was described as "an aloof and eccentric widow who liked her whiskey" and Brother Leo as a "personable monk" who, in *Time*'s paraphrase of the allegations, had "exercised a Svengali-like influence over a sick old woman of unsound mind."

Brother Leo, in a letter to his mother, tried to minimize the story's negative impact, calling it a "good little humiliation for me" and assuring Lotus that he was grateful for "this affliction," which he read as a sign of God's kindness toward him, a heaven-sent experience in character building.

Archbishop Krol also read the *Time* article as a humiliation, but not a welcome one. When apprised by Bishop Garriga of Bill Joyce's revocation telegram sent to Texas the preceding September, the vexed prelate wired Brother Leo in Chile, ordering the monk to meet with him in Palm Beach right after the New Year's holiday.

Leo, braced for trouble, arrived in Florida on the first Friday of 1964 and met the visitator that afternoon. He found Krol reserved and quite civil at first. On Saturday morning, however, Krol directed Leo to write out a new resignation from the foundation and to sign, as well, a power of attorney giving a lawyer of Krol's choice authority to act in Leo's stead.

"I," Leo later testified, "respectfully as I could, pointed out to him that in conscience I didn't feel that I could do so. He became quite indignant, and I remember he turned on his heel and went over to the door and shut the door. Then he came back and assumed all the authority that he is capable of assuming—he is a fairly impressive man, a large man—and ordered me with all the powers that the Holy See can convey to an apostolic visitator to sign the two documents."

As Leo tells the story, Krol spent an hour or more trying to cow him into surrender. Then, when Krol stalked out of the room to take a telephone call, the monk raced to a second phone, where he dialed Father Luke Anderson, the prior at Spencer, asking Father Luke to find Father Dominic Hughes and to fly down together to his rescue that night.

They did, and spent the next several days in Florida, according to Anderson, declaring to Krol that a monk had the right to refuse a command if it violated his conscience. In the end neither side would concede. "It got terribly repetitious," says Father Anderson. "Father Hughes, who was a very well educated man, kept saying simply, 'I think that Leo has a valid point.' And then the archbishop's answer to that was, 'Yes, but a good religious will yield to obedience.' And that's pretty much where it stayed."

Krol also arranged for Ken Oden and Robert Jewett from the Baker, Botts office in Houston to meet with Leo in Florida; both attorneys would be involved in the preparation for the will-contest trial before Judge Bill Edwards, and Brother Leo was a key prospective witness. "We were met at the airport in Miami by Krol and Leo," Jewett recalls. "The archbishop was driving a big Cadillac rent car, and Leo tried to direct him on how to get to our hotel. All the way, Krol would just sort of brush him off. But we *did* interview Brother Leo.

"We were just trying to develop facts, just trying to nail down facts. I did say to Leo, because I thought it might be helpful if we ever found it necessary, 'Tell us of any circumstances you can recall where you requested that Mrs. East take an action and where she said, "No, I don't want to do that." '

"And Leo became incensed! My question was an affront to him. I remember very distinctly that he became very highly incensed that I would even suggest he might ask her to do something and she would not do it."

TWENTY-FOUR

✛ ✛ ✛

Dom Thomas Acts

Ken Oden's report of the truculent monk's behavior in Miami was the last word Jake Floyd would hear of his nemesis. On February 26, 1964, three years and fifteen days after Sarita's death, the Dry Snake, aged sixty-nine, expired at the Methodist Hospital in Houston. Floyd's single greatest regret, he told a visitor, was that he wouldn't live to enjoy his complete revenge on Leo and Peter Grace. But he did hang on long enough to see all the necessary settlement documents executed and placed in an escrow account at the Corpus Christi State National Bank.

Brother Leo, back in Chile, was aware that Archbishop Krol had intercepted his signed copy of the papers, but he assumed, mistakenly, that since he had revoked his foundation resignation of May 1962, no final settlement was possible for the present. The promised confirmation of Bill Joyce's telegram had not arrived in Alice.

Further emboldened by his canonical standoff in Miami, he proceeded to bury Joyce and Father Hughes under an avalanche of memos and notes outlining strategy after strategy to recapture control of Sarita's fortune. Just trying to keep Leo's many plots straight, Joyce remembers, "was like chasing a drop of mercury across a tabletop."

One of the monk's notions was for Joyce to file an undue-influence suit on Leo's behalf against Peter Grace's Sarita K. East Foundation, alleging some sort of corporate culpability in coercing the monk's signature on the settlement. Another idea was to approach Ken Oden with a plan to set up a *third* foundation, one controlled by Leo and Henrietta Armstrong. In return for the monk's cooperation in defeating Bill Wright's will contest (a given, Leo reasoned, if Bishop Garriga testified on the monk's behalf), Leo and Henrietta would take the $14.4 million Grace was supposed to receive, together with a sum equal to the amount Oden figured it would otherwise cost to settle with Wright. This plan was predicated on Leo's claim of exclusive foundation membership conferred on him by Sarita on her deathbed. If Grace wanted to advance his claim, Leo pointed out, he would have to do so in an unfriendly Texas venue.

A grander strategy sprang from Leo's belief that the Mexican heirs' will challenge, Cause 348, would be heard before the escrowed settlement to 12074 could be filed in Judge Laughlin's court in Alice. In this scenario Garriga and the rest of the Texans would testify to Leo's rectitude, thus destroying their case against him in Cause 12074, the original Lytton complaint. Once Wright was defeated, Leo then wanted Joyce to file a revocation of the settlement document Archbishop Krol had taken from Bishop Larrain in Rome. To neutralize the visitator's authority, Leo suggested a means for persuading the Curia in Rome to assert itself.

He asked Joyce and Hughes to recast his November 17, 1961, statement castigating Peter Grace as a memo to be proffered, in Latin translation, to the Congregation of the Religious. As part of his strategy, Leo wanted to get the Latin-American bishops involved, enlisting their self-interested support for the reestablishment of a foundation devoted to their causes. The Jesuit Father Aldunate in Chile, the monk suggested, might be given copies of the memo for circulation among CELAM members and other prelates in Latin America who should know that "$200,000,000, or more destined by Mrs. East for Latin America is being hijacked by Corpus Christi and the Visitator."

Leo, acting on erroneous information from south Texas that Judge Edwards would call Cause 348 to trial in mid-June of 1964, flew from Chile to Washington in late May to help Bill Joyce and Father Hughes assemble the many requisite papers. When he learned that the trial date had been postponed some days before, he flew back to Chile via Argentina, where he had other business he wished to attend to.

Los Laureles, the property Mrs. East had purchased northwest of Buenos Aires at Entre Ríos, had become another focus of contention. It was controlled by Sarita's Argentine foundation, originally styled the Asociación Auxiliar de la Obra Cisterciense, but renamed by Leo the Fundación Sarita Kenedy de East.

Peter Grace, a member of the Argentine foundation board, concluded in 1963 that with the Lytton lawsuit and Dom Keating's suspension of the Trappists' Latin-American expansion program for want of funds, the most prudent course of action would be to liquidate the partially completed foundation at Entre Ríos. In the face of Argentina's currently ruinous inflation rate and the unavailability of money to complete any sort of permanent installation there, Grace argued that it was best for the Trappists to take what they could for the property.

Brother Leo disagreed and countered Grace's proposal with the assertion that the Trappists no longer enjoyed any claim on the land. Sarita, he said, meant for Los Laureles to *someday* become a monastery if possible, but since Dom Keating had decided not to build one there, the property reverted to its original purpose, a model breeding cabana for Santa Gertrudis cattle. Leo's abbot thought he had settled this difference of opinion when he ordered Leo to resign from the Argentine foundation, but he discovered otherwise in June of 1964 when the monk, working through his loyal friend Francis Verstraeten, Sr., another board member, engineered Peter Grace's ouster along with that of his allies on the board.

In all, Brother Leo was back and forth between Chile and Argentina four times in 1964, a series of trips that prompted a severe reaction at Spencer. "It was with deep sorrow that I recently learned of Brother Leo's four trips to Argentina," Dom Thomas wrote Verstraeten in early July of 1964,

> all made without the permission of his superiors. This constitutes, as you will realize, a very grave violation of his obligations as a religious, no matter how good his intentions were.
>
> In accordance with his own desires and mine, I located Brother Leo in Chile with the view of affording him the opportunity to return to his monastic vocation. It was for the good of his soul that I, as his abbot, directed him to resign from the [Argentine] Foundation a year and a half ago. This resignation was accepted by the meeting of the members of the Association on October 28, 1963. In persuading you and other members of the Foundation to neutralize . . . Peter Grace . . . he is obviously trying to gain effective control for himself.
>
> Saint Joseph's Abbey is ultimately responsible for the substantial funds given to the Foundation which passed through the abbey account in the Grace National Bank, the legitimacy of which gift has been questioned in the pending litigations.
>
> I am convinced that Brother Leo's vocation as a

monk is being seriously endangered by his renewed activity in this affair in direct opposition to his abbot.

I trust you will understand, therefore, why I am convinced I had no alternative but to recall Brother Leo permanently from South America and to refuse him all communications with persons in South America.

Keating's letter to Francis Verstraeten did not do justice to the abbot's extreme displeasure with Leo or to the severity of the monk's punishment. He was summoned to Boston's Logan Airport on Thursday, July 2, 1964, and there issued a canonical warning, called a precept, to obey his superior or suffer the possibility of dismissal from the Trappists. Leo was then sent into exile at Notre Dame du Calvaire, a forlorn French-speaking Trappist foundation near the little town of North Rogersville, in New Brunswick, Canada. "Father Hughes," wrote Bill Joyce to one of Leo's Argentine friends, "told me that for the first time Brother Leo had been thoroughly shaken by this turn of events and seemed to be frantic."

Within a week of his arrival at Calvaire, Brother Leo sat down with Father Hughes to produce a memo for Dom Keating. Noting in his first sentence that the memo "may be at any time used by the person to whom it is addressed in any manner that he in conscience sees fit," Leo went on to explain he was "convinced more by interior assurance than external argument" that he should capitulate in order to preserve his vocation as a monk.

"Since I have signed [the settlement]," he wrote further on,

and since the only alternative to me is a suit of intervention to set aside the "settlement," since moreover, in the present situation such a suit would mean the loss of my status as a religious, I acquiesce to the unfortunate state of things. In the present situation I accept the decision of events in light of the above, without condition and thus I shall initiate no further action whatsoever concerning the Kenedy Memorial Foundation. The word "initiate" does not preclude my cooperating in such actions as my superiors may judge to be necessary for the finalizing of the settlement already agreed upon.

Lest there be room for doubt that he was giving in, Leo and Hughes included two more sentences of surrender toward the bottom of the memo.

I cannot expect to do more than I have done to see to it that the true and complete wishes of Mrs. East, known only to myself, should be fulfilled. I accept the fact that my obligations to her have ceased, and I commit to the conscience of others the administration of her wishes.

TWENTY-FIVE

✚ ✚ ✚

The Good Thief

Brother Leo later repudiated his July 1964 letter to Dom Thomas, claiming that the memo had been Father Dominic Hughes's work, that he had hardly read it, and that his spiritual adviser had talked him into signing it for some unspecified reason of his own. "I thought that memo was awful," says Leo. "I promise you that to me it was revolting. I shouldn't have signed it."

Father Thomas Keating, on the other hand, was delighted with Leo's letter, as well as with the several other notes the monk wrote, and sent, to his abbot from Canada that summer. All contained assurances of Leo's obedience and words of gratitude for Abbot Keating's strong action to restore Leo to his vocation. Dom Thomas, on the advice of Monsignor Julien, considered that Leo's memo authorized him to act in the monk's name; that is, Leo had ceded decision-making responsibility to his abbot. Accordingly, on the afternoon of August 31, 1964, Father Keating telegrammed the attorney Robert Jewett at Baker, Botts in Houston:

I THE UNDERSIGNED AS THE SUPERIOR OF CHRISTOPHER GREGORY (BROTHER LEO) IN VIRTUE OF AN UNDERSTANDING WHICH I HAVE WITH HIM HEREBY AUTHORIZE YOU TO

TAKE THE STEPS NECESSARY TO EFFECTUATE
THE SETTLEMENT WHICH THE SAID CHRIS-
TOPHER GREGORY HAS HERETOFORE SIGNED
IN THE CAUSE PENDING IN THE DISTRICT
COURT OF JIM WELLS COUNTY STATE OF
TEXAS 79TH JUDICIAL DISTRICT NUMBER
12074. THOMAS KEATING ABBOT OF ST. JO-
SEPHS ABBEY SPENCER MASS.

The next day, the settlement papers were released
from escrow in Corpus Christi and presented to Judge
C. Woodrow Laughlin in Alice along with Keating's
telegram. Unusual as it was for a district judge to accept a religious superior's bona fides on behalf of a
monk, Laughlin did so, and entered the settlement as
an interlocutory decree, meaning that it was entered
contingent upon the resolution of the will contest,
Cause 348, to be heard by Judge Bill Edwards at the
courthouse in Sarita. When Cause 348 was settled, the
agreement in Cause 12074 would become final.

Leo himself did not learn of Dom Keating's action
until several weeks later. Ever since then Leo has argued that the filing was illegal. He claims to have earlier informed Bob Jewett at Baker, Botts in Houston
that Jewett did not have the power to represent Leo in
court or in any legal proceeding. Jewett denies ever
having been told this by Leo, or by Leo's lawyer Bill
Joyce, prior to the filing of the settlement. The monk
further argues that Dom Thomas overstepped his authority in speaking for him in the telegram to Jewett,
that Dom Keating knew Leo opposed the settlement
and would not have agreed to it. Father Thomas re-
sponds that Leo's memo of July 1984 explicitly
empowered him to act as he saw fit, that he double-
checked his actions with Monsignor Julien, Larry Mc-
Kay, and the apostolic visitor, and that he had heard
nothing from Leo to contradict the memo between the

time he received it and the day the settlement was entered in Judge Laughlin's court.

Leo did not at first believe that the settlement had been, or could be, filed. Because of the restrictions on his correspondence, and the remoteness of the Calvaire monastery, it wasn't easy for him to gain reliable intelligence on the events in Texas. Apart from letters to Lotus, the only outside correspondence he was allowed was with Father Hughes, and this dialogue, by Dom Keating's order, was supposedly restricted to moral topics and questions of conscience. It wasn't, of course. By labeling each of his letters to Hughes "Conscience Matter" (so that the abbey censors were forbidden to inspect them), Leo was able openly to discuss the foundation with the priest and to query Father Hughes for information. To be doubly safe, he instructed Hughes, "Destroy This," at the bottom of the notes. And when the priest wrote back, he was instructed to use a code.

If the settlement had truly been entered, Leo instructed in an early letter, Hughes was to reply, "My poor auntie is dead." If Bill Wright in Laredo was aware of the conflict between Leo and his superiors, Hughes was to use one postage stamp; if not, two. If the priest, who once again was acting as Leo's go-between with Bill Joyce in Washington, advised the monk to refuse to sign any further papers, he should place the stamp upside down. The monk directed that if Hughes and Joyce believed that the appeal to the Curia they had prepared from Leo's November 1961 statement should now be sent on to Rome, they should send him a postcard bearing a water scene.

He entertained high hopes for the appeal, originally part of his plan to upset the settlement once the will contest had been won. "Liberalization" had become the catchword for the ongoing Vatican II reforms, and the role of conscience in religious life was being sympathetically reviewed in Rome. An appeal to the Curia that the settlement violated Leo's conscience seemed likely to benefit from this new mood within the hierarchy. Moreover, a mandatory retirement age of seventy for bishops was being discussed. Leo sensed a shift in church attitudes against "old bishops," such as Mariano Garriga, now nearly eighty and failing fast from a variety of chronic ailments.

The monk was cautious in his letters to Dom Keating that autumn, never complaining of his situation and often thanking the abbot for taking from him the burden of worry over Sarita's foundation. But to Hughes he pressed for action on all fronts, vowing at one point to risk excommunication if that might help redirect Sarita's money to Latin America. "How can I relinquish this whole bag to anyone?" he asked in another note.

On November 5, 1964, Hughes warned Bill Joyce, "Leo is beginning to gather steam again. Everybody had better be careful." A few weeks later, the monk seized the occasion of a short stay in the local hospital (his ulcer was acting up) to telephone Harry Gibbons and Pierre Jacomet, two friends he had known from Latin America. He persuaded them to act as his "delegates" to assess the situation in Texas and, if possible, to hire him an attorney. Instead, Gibbons and Jacomet visited Ken Oden and came back to Canada firmly convinced that Leo was misguided to oppose the settlement. According to the monk, he treated his two friends to a tirade for what they had done counter to his wishes, and was sternly rebuked in return.

"To be *condemned* by the world is a most precious grace," Leo wrote to Lotus in a letter in which he compared himself to the "good thief" who hung next to Jesus on Calvary. In this spirit, he authorized Bill Joyce to write Ken Oden, and to send copies to Larry McKay and Denman Moody, chief trial lawyer at

Baker, Botts, that he had not freely agreed to the settlement and had not been represented by his counsel of choice at the time of its filing. Enclosed with Joyce's letter were copies of a letter written, but never mailed, from Leo to Robert Jewett, informing the attorney that he did not represent the monk, as well as the revocation of Leo's May 1962 foundation resignation. In the autumn of 1963 Joyce had telegrammed news of the revocation to Texas. But the promised confirmation apparently was never sent.

The letters, and Leo's abortive attempt to make Pierre Jacomet and Harry Gibbons his agents in Texas, provoked Abbot Keating to issue another precept. He commanded Leo, again, to fire Bill Joyce and canceled the monk's correspondence privileges with Father Hughes. Leo also was told to desist from contact with Jacomet and Gibbons, who had refused him any further assistance anyway.

The "condemnations" continued, as well. Peter and Margie Grace, Leo reported to his mumsy, visited him at Calvaire in the early winter of 1965, and both, in his term, warned him that he was headed for the "gutter." Father Aldunate in Chile wrote, "I think that before the crib of Our Lord you must forget all the complications and problems that you are mixed up in." And Bishop Manuel Larrain of Talca, for whose ministry to the Latin-American poor Leo was flirting with expulsion from the Trappists, informed him by letter that the bishop wished he would stop mentioning CELAM in connection with the foundation fight.

One quiet voice within the Trappists was raised in Leo's defense. Abbot Futterer, who himself had originally been sent to Calvaire, now was staying at the monastery in Snowmass, his physical health partially restored. Futterer had chosen to forget, or could not recall, his own battles with Leo or the financial and legal woes the monk had caused Futterer's successor,

Dom Keating. "Leo," the old abbot wrote to Francis and Rachel Verstraeten in Buenos Aires,

> would seem to be taking his reverses in a very realistic and wonderful way. He who could speak so convincingly about the cross and one's need of carrying that cross in union with Our Lord, is now living that basic principle to the hilt in his own daily life. While I personally look upon Brother Leo as a great soul, even heroic, I am well aware that this heroism of his strikes its roots deep in a spirit of faith that realizes "one can do all things in Jesus" Who alone constituted a Christian's greatness and strength. Brother lives his faith. His life of seclusion, hard work, habitual prayers, submission to God in the person of a man—never to a man as such—all this is Leo's theory put into practice by himself. He derives peace and the courage to go on from looking at the Crucifix.

It was another ally, Father Dominic Hughes, who extricated Brother Leo from Calvaire. From the moment the monk was shut away in Canada in early July, his friend the priest had tried to spring "our boy," as he often referred to Leo in his letters to Bill Joyce, hoping to gain Leo's transfer to a less remote foundation in a more hospitable climate. Leo naturally concurred and told Father Hughes his first choice for relocation (since he had no chance of being returned to South America) was Spencer's daughter house near Lafayette, Oregon, Our Lady of Guadalupe, where his old novice master, Columban Hawkins, had been abbot since 1955.

The Australian-born Hawkins, sixty-two, was receptive to the idea but took a jaundiced view of the monk's conscience problems. "You are aware," he wrote Hughes in September of 1964,

that Brother eagerly desires to come to our monastery
and that I am very willing to receive him. However, I
have made it clear to Brother that it is my firm belief
that he should have done with this KMF and all such
business if he is to settle here and to be directed by
me.

Hawkins added that he had had reservations about
the expansion program from the start and that Leo's
conscience would never have become a problem if he
had "refused to go out of the monastery on this
treasure-hunting business. From his own confidences
I can affirm this."

Father Hughes's reply was eloquent. "You may regret," he wrote a week later,

establishing any prior conditions to taking Brother. He
is as he is and no statement about the changing situation around him can have much validity. I cannot
clear him of responsibility that is not my doing in the
first place. Not even Dom Edmund could clear him of
the responsibility he once imposed on him. At least
Brother has the dignity now of not having sold himself
for a mess of porridge—of having sought some temporary advantage for himself at the cost of denying a
truth. In the last three years he has shown a strength
that is astonishing. Those opposed to him will resent
it, but they are impressed. This is the man Mrs. East
did and could trust. He is not always right—or even
honest perhaps—but he is a man and worthy to be
treated as such.

Dom Hawkins was so moved by Father Hughes's
pleas and the subsequent letters he received from Leo
that he suspended his misgivings about the monk and
asked Dom Keating to set up a meeting for all the
contentions and concerns over Leo's behavior to be

aired. Four months later, in February of 1965, the conference was called for New York City. In all, Hawkins would remember under questioning, there were at least three rounds of discussion involving himself, Keating, Leo, Father Hughes, Peter Grace, Larry McKay, Jack Meehan of the Grace corporation, and even Margie Grace.

Hawkins and Hughes were outnumbered but not outargued. The days of talks ended much to Leo's advantage, with Father Hawkins agreeing to assume responsibility for the monk at Our Lady of Guadalupe under his pledge to continue restricting Leo's outside contacts. Dom Keating was dubious that Hawkins could deliver on this promise; he shared Archbishop Krol's belief that the only way to keep Brother Leo off a telephone was to rip the device out. But Keating reluctantly went along. In return, Peter Grace was to keep Leo, and Dom Hawkins, informed of any developments in Texas, where the will contest still loomed. It was not decided then whether Leo would be asked to testify or be prevented from doing so. But the monk was obliged to promise that he would do nothing on his own without first notifying everyone else of his intentions.

Dom Hawkins returned to Our Lady of Guadalupe with his ward in mid-February, a few days before Bishop Mariano Garriga died at age eighty in Corpus Christi and was replaced by Bishop Thomas Drury of San Angelo, Texas. Garriga's demise changed nothing as far as the litigation was concerned. Patrick Horkin simply inserted Drury's name for Garriga's on motions and pleadings as he filed them before Judge Edwards in the will contest. Under the terms of the settlement, Drury also assumed his predecessor's seat on the Kenedy Memorial Foundation. Now, just four years after Sarita's death, her foundation carried but a single member, Lee Lytton, Jr., appointed, however fleetingly, by its founder.

Leo was assigned to work in the carpentry shop at Our Lady of Guadalupe. The Oregon monastery supported itself, in part, by manufacturing church furniture. He made his usual, positive impression on the Oregon community. "I think he's a wonderful person," says Father Paschal Phillips, then the prior at Our Lady of Guadalupe. "He always kept faith with his ideals and continued to be a better monk than most of us."

But assembling pews and sanding altar tables did not consume Leo's energies for long. Slowly, he brought Dom Hawkins closer and closer to his point of view—that Dom Keating had abused his abbatial authority and violated Leo's right to his conscience when Keating empowered Robert Jewett to act in the monk's name and conclude the settlement.

By late spring 1965 Dom Hawkins had relaxed many of the restrictions on Leo, allowing him (with Abbot Keating's permission) to take up his correspondence with the Verstraetens again and abetting his penchant for intrigues (without Keating's knowledge) by permitting him telephone and postal contact with other friends, particularly Major Tom and Henrietta Armstrong, in south Texas. By the summer Dom Hawkins's own letters mimicked Leo's in their disparaging references to the "pseudo-settlement" of the foundation dispute and to the Oregon abbot's wishes for a "providential" reversal of the injustice, as Hawkins now saw it.

True to the ad hoc nature of his thinking, Brother Leo's game plan came together willy-nilly. In August he flew together with Dom Columban to Texas to meet with the Armstrongs. Both the major and Henrietta still believed in Leo, and their strong support for him impressed Abbot Hawkins. The major also offered his opinion that if the settlement had been fraudulently entered, as Leo said it had been, the monk had a duty in conscience to inform the court in Alice, Judge Laughlin.

This observation served to justify seeking a legal opinion on the matter. Within weeks the need for an attorney had evolved into the idea, which Leo shared with Bill Joyce and Father Hughes, that he might engage Melvin Belli, the San Francisco-based criminal lawyer then famous for his 1964 defense of Lee Harvey Oswald's slayer, Jack Ruby, in Dallas.

Father Hughes dissuaded Leo from hiring Belli, while Dom Hawkins, on his own, conferred with one of Leo's staunchest admirers, Judge James Dougherty's son and Beeville, Texas, rancher, Dudley Dougherty, a major contributor to the Trappist expansion program. Dougherty, in turn, put Hawkins in touch with his cousin Frances ("Sissy") Farenthold of Corpus Christi, a lawyer, well-known feminist, future candidate for governor in Texas, and keynote speaker at the 1972 Democratic National Convention, who agreed to represent Brother Leo in association with her colleague the attorney Marshall Boykin, also of Corpus Christi.

"I must say I was critical of Brother Leo at the time," Farenthold recalls. "I read the newspapers regularly, and he certainly was pictured in an unholy light. My cousin was always trying to get it through my hard head that there was something there and so forth, but my feelings were that this monk was some kind of scoundrel."

Then Sissy Farenthold began discussing the case with Leo by telephone, calls the monk often placed from the monastery in Oregon at the start of his day, about five or six in the morning, Texas time. Gradually, like Dom Hawkins, Sissy came to see her new client as a victim instead of a scamp. "He has very close and personal relationships with people," she explains. "Brother Leo contributes far more to people than he ever receives. If anything he's childlike, to the point of being aggravating, if you know what I mean."

At about the same time, and again through Dom Hawkins, Leo also acquired a new canonical adviser, Father Thomas Brockhaus of Mt. Angel Abbey, in Mt. Angel, Oregon. Father Brockhaus, Leo informed Dom Keating, believed there was room within canon law for a legal challenge to the settlement, inasmuch as the Kenedy Memorial Foundation was not, strictly speaking, a "pious Foundation."

Dom Keating had seen it all coming; a month or two earlier the Spencer abbot began considering moving Leo again before it was too late. But if nothing the monk might try any longer surprised Father Thomas, his willingness to abide Leo's intrigues had come to an end.

On November 19, 1965, Keating wrote Brother Leo from Spencer, expressing his pleasure that the monk had availed himself of canonical advice but adding that he, as Leo's superior, had never based his claims of authority on the "pious Foundation" argument. Contrary to Father Brockhaus's interpretation, the abbot wrote, this was a "pious cause," a fight to preserve Sarita's foundation, or most of it, for the church. Portentously, Keating continued, "there are a number of factors involving morals in this case."

First of all, I have an obligation to see that Mrs. East's wishes are carried out, at least insofar as this is reasonably possible. The present settlement at least assures that the bulk of Mrs. East's estate will go to the Catholic Church, which was certainly her primary intention. The action which you contemplate to set aside the settlement is likely to jeopardize the defense of the 1960 will to such an extent that the whole of this donation may be lost to the Church. I don't see how in conscience I can permit you to do this and fulfill my role of supervisory power in a pious cause.

Secondly, the Abbey is presently responsible for a million and a quarter dollars which you placed in an account which you opened in the Abbey's name at the Grace Bank without the knowledge of our corporation and in an illegal manner. Over four hundred thousand dollars of these funds you transferred to a non-profit foundation in Argentina. In a memorandum to me in 1961, you stated that the property was eventually to become a Cistercian monastery and that the income from the cattle operation to be developed there was to go to the expansion of the Trappist Order in South America. You have since denied that the Abbey has any rights to this foundation. You effectively removed from the board of directors through certain friends of yours those who could represent the interests of the Abbey, making at least two trips to Argentina without permission in order to arrange this underhanded maneuver. This was a scandal to the devoted benefactors of the Abbey who had worked very hard to set up the foundation for you, yet whom you did not hesitate to subject to this humiliation. Thus the Abbey is held responsible, in case the Will contestants win this suit, to return to the estate of Mrs. East at least four hundred thousand dollars, which it has no way of recovering. This is a serious injustice to your community.

Abbot Keating's third and fourth complaints covered Leo's secret contacts with Bill Joyce, as well as certain of the tales the monk had told Archbishop Krol. One was that Peter Grace had his own interests, not the church's, in mind when he opposed Leo's usurpation of foundation control in 1961. "When you visited the Apostolic Visitator," charged Keating, "you allowed this false and calumnious impression to remain and indeed you strengthened it.'' The dom was also personally upset that Leo had led Krol to understand that Abbot Keating's father, a well-known New York admiralty lawyer whose firm had done work in the past for the Grace corporation, was personally in Peter Grace's pay. "It is evident from all of the above," Keating wrote, "that your continued activities in this case are causing you to place acts which are immoral and unjust. Your spiritual welfare, as well as the safeguarding of innocent third parties, demands that you desist from all further action in the case unless explicitly authorized by me in writing if you wish to remain a member of the community and of the Order."

Fifthly, your attempt to set aside the settlement is going to increase the scandal which has already taken place because of the imprudent way in which you functioned in relation to Mrs. East, including the extraordinary manner in which you made use of your power of attorney from her. Since your name is inseparably linked with that of the Abbey, the public can only think that if you place an act to set aside the present settlement that the Abbey is seeking to obtain a larger share of the settlement and to gain control of the Foundation. The name of the Abbey has already suffered a great deal in the eyes of the hierarchy because of its involvement—or more precisely your involvement—in litigation. If you now question the settlement you have signed, the hierarchy can only conclude that this is being done with my permission, since it would not be believed that a religious would act in such an important matter without the approval and permission of his religious superior.

. . . The faithful are embarrassed to see religious, especially contemplatives, disputing over large amounts of money. The case is far too complicated for people to unravel all the intricacies of rights in conscience which make you feel that you can act independently. It will be assumed that whatever you do is being done in the name of Saint Joseph's Abbey, and nothing you say or I say can change that impression unless you do this precisely as a private citizen, that is, as one who has been dismissed from his Order.

TWENTY-SIX

✛ ✛ ✛

Gone to Texas

Brother Leo's looming confrontation with Abbot Keating was momentarily delayed on the morning of December 3, 1965, when two carloads of sheriff's deputies pulled up at the Lafayette monastery in search of the monk. The uniformed posse had a subpoena for Leo, commanding his testimony in the will contest—Cause 348—plus photographs of the monk supplied by the attorney Frank Nesbitt, who at that moment was contentedly enjoying a cup of coffee and a menthol cigarette in the sheriff's office. After two years of tracking Leo from monastery to monastery, Nesbitt had his quarry, he thought.

Nesbitt, of slight frame, wiry and baldish, was a civil lawyer in Corpus Christi, but not a specialist in estate work. He was respected for possessing one of the keener legal minds in the community and for his pugnacious approach to litigation. "Frank was and is a very good attorney," says Marshall Boykin. "He's like a bulldog."

His clients were the late Louis Edgar Turcotte's sons—Bobby, Edgar, Jr., Jack, Joe, and Pat, each burly like their father. One of them was responsible for threats of violence against Peter Grace. "I won't tell you which one it was," Jack Turcotte says of his brothers. "But he was just trying to make Grace nervous, make him look over his shoulder once in a while.''

"My clients," observes Nesbitt, "were somewhat strange people. They didn't get along with anybody that didn't agree with 'em. I guess Bobby was the most violent one. He was very vitriolic about Leo and what would happen to him."

"Bobby," Jack Turcotte agrees, "was irrational at that time. He became mentally obsessed about that damn lawsuit."

Apart from his clients' combativeness, Frank Nesbitt's intervention in December of 1963—two years before he finally caught up with Brother Leo—alarmed and angered most everyone else for what it alleged. His pleading exactly paralleled Tom East's, filed the year before by East's attorney, Walter Groce, as part of Jake Floyd's strategy to scare both William Wright and Peter Grace. But whereas Tom East was bluffing in his suit, which asked that Sarita's 1948 will be probated, Frank Nesbitt and the Turcotte boys were in deadly earnest. If successful, the brothers would come into the share of La Parra, including mineral rights, that their late father would have inherited under the 1948 will, half of Sarita's half of the ranch, or about 100,000 acres, and untold millions in oil income.

Nesbitt's suit imperiled the plans of just about everyone—the "Mexican heirs," the other Turcottes, the Alice National Bank, Peter Grace, and Brother Leo and Tom East. By contrast, if Nesbitt succeeded, the Oblate fathers would prosper with the restoration of all oil rights beneath the congregation's 10,000 acres surrounding the Headquarters. Lee Lytton would inherit his mother's share of La Parra, a portion equal to the 100,000 acres the Turcotte brothers would receive. And the Catholic church would do all right, as well. Though the church would lose whatever it ultimately might have gained out of the 1964 settlement, a reversion to the 1948 will would restore to the Corpus Christi diocese the 13,000 acres of La Parra (with mineral rights) that Sarita had originally earmarked for her local bishop.

Mindful of what their respective clients, the Alice bank and Peter Grace, might have to forfeit, Ken Oden, together with Denman Moody of Baker, Botts, opened settlement negotiations to kill Nesbitt's challenge. Pat Turcotte, a petroleum engineer, and his brother Bobby (who was thinking of writing a book about Leo and Sarita, entitled *The Rape of an Empire*), told their lawyer that they would handle the discussion. "You couldn't ask for a worse bunch to be together at one time to talk settlement," says Nesbitt.

Pat Turcotte told Oden and Moody what the brothers wanted. "Well, Pat!" Moody replied. "You want more than what you'd come out with if you won this case!"

"Sure!" Turcotte replied. "So do *you*. If we win this case, you get nothing. This way, we leave you with *something*."

Angriest of all with Nesbitt's rambunctious clients was Elena Kenedy. When Nesbitt filed his intervention in December of 1963, Mrs. Kenedy knew that Archbishop Krol had secured Brother Leo's signature on the settlement papers and that her "godson," Tom East, was due to take over La Parra's cattle management. Bishop Garriga, then still alive, had been pacified with a seat on the foundation. And it appeared as if Leo's letters to Sarita and the embarrassing insinuations being aired in the newspapers could be suppressed if Bill Wright and the rest of the will contestants were brought to terms.

But the Turcottes were intent on exposing everything to upset the 1960 will and foundation, including the letters. According to several sources, they even contemplated raising as an allegation the old rumor that their father, Louis Edgar, wasn't really Sarita's cousin but her half brother, the product of an extra-marital liaison between Don Gregorio Kenedy and Louis Edgar's mother (Sarita's aunt), Amilie Turcotte.

Frank Nesbitt came to accept unexpected drama as part of doing business on behalf of the five Turcotte brothers. His focus from the outset was on controlling the outcome of Cause 348. "He was without a doubt the best lawyer in the case," says Joe Day of Fort Worth, who represented three of Petra Vela's grand-daughters. "Frank was the best operator in the court-room, and he was the best prepared."

Joe Day's major role in the case was to research each plaintiff's background in search of those who alleged descent from Petra Vela but could not prove it. In the course of this work, he uncovered the truth about Sar-ita's uncle Tom Kenedy's illegitimate son, Roberto, in-formation that prevented Roberto Kenedy's daughter Sarita Kenedy from inheriting a major portion of Mrs. East's fortune. As a matter of purely historical inter-est, Day also discovered that Mifflin Kenedy fudged the date of his marriage to Petra Vela. All the extant accounts Joe Day could find fixed the day as April 16, 1852. Yet Mifflin's marriage certificate, still on file in the Brownsville city hall, clearly marks the date of the Catholic ceremony as May 10, 1854, more than two years later, and a year after the birth of Thomas, his first child by the Mexican widow.

Frank Nesbitt did most of the rest of the work, con-centrating on building the case against Leo, something Bill Wright and the other attorneys had so far ne-glected to do. He subpoenaed hotel, telephone, and bank records, interviewed clerks and accountants, and pressed Pat Horkin, in a lawsuit, to yield the letters and other material kept secret since 1961. He went after Peter Grace's files, where he found a trove of the industrialist's correspondence, including what would prove to be one of his key pieces of evidence, Grace's undue-influence chart prepared for the Catholic hierarchy in 1961. Nesbitt also submitted written interrogatories to Archbishop Krol and Cardinal Spellman.

But his main concern in two years of steady work was to locate the monk. Legally, Nesbitt could not force anyone to disclose Leo's location. Nor would it have done him any good to know that Leo was in Chile or Canada, since there was no way to compel the monk's testimony in a civil matter if he was out of the country.

Nesbitt assumed that Leo's superiors, with Ken Oden's and Peter Grace's encouragement, were deliberately keeping Leo hidden. This was why the attorney was startled, gleefully so, in November of 1965 when Sissy Farenthold, as he remembers, let slip Dom Columban Hawkins's name as the abbot who had taken over Leo's control. Nesbitt went to the library and consulted the *Catholic Directory* for Columban Hawkins's address and then considered how he might corner Leo at the Oregon monastery before the monk was moved again.

The necessary papers would have to be filed at the Kenedy County courthouse in Sarita, where Nesbitt feared that the county clerk, Faye Chandler, would alert Ken Oden and thus Leo's superiors to his subpoena. So the attorney prepared the documents, gave them to Bobby Turcotte, and then flew to Oregon. Turcotte was to file the notice of intent to take Leo's deposition and then immediately telephone Nesbitt at the Yamhill County sheriff's office, where a hundred-dollar donation had made the sheriff agreeable to serving the subpoena at Nesbitt's signal.

On the appointed day, December 3, 1965, Bobby Turcotte filed the notice as agreed and then added a touch of his own. Still concerned that Mrs. Chandler might alert Ken Oden before the subpoena could be served, Turcotte surreptitiously rewired the courthouse switchboard. After he called Nesbitt and the posse was dispatched, Bobby flipped a switch and scrambled all telephone communications out of the Kenedy County courthouse for two hours.

Up in Oregon, Brother Leo was on garbage detail that morning, assigned to drive a truck full of wood scraps and sawdust to the monastery dump. Ordinarily, he would have taken his load directly across the Trappist property to their dump, but it had rained the night before and most of the back trails were too muddy. Therefore, Leo took the long way around, heading out the monastery's main gate and then south to reach the dump via paved highway. He had traveled about a quarter mile when the monk saw the armed deputies in their cruisers coming the other way. Innocent of their mission, Leo gave the lawmen a friendly wave and continued on.

At the dump, a quaggy natural depression, Leo managed to get his truck stuck in the mire. He decided to leave the vehicle and head back on foot. In the meanwhile, Frank Nesbitt's posse had arrived at the monastery porter's lodge, brandishing a subpoena and threatening to search the cloister if Father Paschal Phillips, the monastery prior and that day's acting superior, didn't produce Christopher Gregory, a.k.a. Brother Leo, for service of his summons.

Father Paschal, a former attorney, recalls being informed by Dom Columban that Leo was staying at Our Lady of Guadalupe "under wraps," and being "told to say that he wasn't around." This is what the priest told the sheriff's men.

"So pretty quick they got in their car, breathing threats, and left," Father Paschal continues. "Well, in about three quarters of an hour I'm called back to the porter's lodge again, and here are the same gentlemen, this time looking very stern. They were quoting

Supreme Court law cases about people who spend the rest of their lives in jail. And then suddenly one said, 'Look under that big oak tree over there. What do you see?' And I looked, and to my amazement there stood a sheriff's deputy in full uniform with a shotgun!

"He then says, 'Now look over there, under that other tree.' And there was another sheriff's deputy with a shotgun. And then they took me out on the road and showed me their roadblock. Everyone going in and out of the monastery was being stopped and interrogated. It was kinda wild. I couldn't believe it."

Father Paschal left the porter's lodge again, still unwilling to admit to Leo's presence at the monastery, and returned to his office to consider the situation. "I was sitting there thinking, 'What the hell do I do now?' " the father recalls. "Is this constitutional? Can they do this?' and who walks into my office, quite shook up, but Brother Leo.

"I said, 'It's only a civil subpoena. You might as well take it if they're gonna get this excited.' "

But Leo would have nothing to do with the sheriff's men. "Oh, no, no!" Father Paschal remembers the monk pleading. "I don't want to get the civil subpeona. It'd be awful and terrible.'

"I couldn't see why. I thought he was a little nutty. But that was all right. I had orders to go along with the nuttiness and not ask questions. So I went along."

The prior developed a plan for Leo to take off, on foot, across the three-mile-wide monastery property—literally, over the hill—and to wait for one of the monks to drive out the front gate and around to fetch him to the Portland airport. Meanwhile, says Father Paschal, the sheriff put a tap on the monastery telephone and began demanding to see Abbot Hawkins, who was on a trip to Canada. Quite by coincidence, a French-speaking Trappist abbot from Canada arrived at Our Lady of Guadalupe at just that moment and was grabbed by the deputies. "They jerked him out of his car and said, 'We've got the abbot! Oh boy! And he's trying to answer us in French!' "

Once this case of mistaken identify was rectified, Father Paschal put a young monk, Brother Raymond, in a truck and sent him through the roadblock to pick up Leo. Together they drove to the airport, where, in another complete coincidence, they met Abbot Hawkins returning from his trip. Leo explained to Hawkins what he knew and why he was standing in the airport with a travel bag. By now it was midafternoon, and if the abbot and the monk had remained at the Portland airport much longer, they would have encountered an irate Frank Nesbitt on his way home to Texas. They decided that Leo should at least get out of the state to avoid the subpoena while he and Hawkins considered their next move. Thus the monk and abbot rented a car and drove over the Columbia River into Washington State and the river town of Longview, where they took rooms for the night.

Meanwhile, back at the monastery, the Yamhill sheriff, Bud Mekkers, had reinforced his posse with several deputized citizens. Gazing out at the crowd from his office, Father Paschal recognized members of the party, including the monastery's dentist, who looked sheepish carrying around his large rifle.

"By now the monks were singing vespers," says Father Paschal, "and what followed should only occur in a grade C movie. Rain was falling, and I'm out there saying, 'You shall not pass,' to the sheriff and his armed troops. The monks are going *'Dominus, domino-mayo do-do-do-do'* and all of them curious as hell. I mean they could hardly sing! They were all trying to see what was going on.

"So finally I got Mekkers, and I said, 'Let's make a deal. I will get you four monks and you pick two cops for each monk and I'll let them search the place. Then, if they don't find anything, you'll all go away?'

"He agreed. So I go into the choir, and I grab four monks and say, 'Take 'em anywhere they want. Don't ask questions. Just do it.' So off they go, each pair of policemen with a picture of Brother Leo. And I think the funniest part was Brother Girard downstairs on the toilet. All of a sudden there's Bang! Bang! Bang! on the door of the toilet stall. So he pulls up his pants and opens the door, and here's two big policemen. They hold up their picture next to Brother Girard and say, 'Nope, that's not him. Thank you, sir. We're very sorry.' And they close the door. They went all through the place and, of course, they found no Brother Leo. Finally, the troops dispersed, though I must say they left the guys out under the trees with the shotguns all night long. Idiots! So, that was the end of it.''

Almost. Later that evening the switchboard at Our Lady of Guadalupe took a call from a reporter. The "reporter" was Frank Nesbitt.

"I was so irritated and disappointed when I found I'd missed him that I called the abbey," Nesbitt recollects. "They answered the phone out there, and I said, 'Can I talk to Brother Leo?'

" 'Oh no! We don't have a Brother Leo here!'

" 'Who's in charge out there?' I said. 'This is a newspaper reporter, and I want to get a little information. We hear there's an awful ruckus goin' on out there.'

"Oh, you should have heard them! 'Oh no! No! No! No! Nothing is happening here!'

"It tickled me to hear 'em frettin'. I just wanted to get a little fun out of the damn thing after all the trouble I'd gone to.''

The next morning, December 4, Dom Hawkins and Brother Leo telephoned the monastery from Washington State and then called Dom Keating at Spencer with their news that the monk was now a fugitive. Since

Leo had already evaded the subpoena, Dom Keating agreed with their plan that Leo continue on north into Canada for the next several days. The monk would first stay in Vancouver at a Benedictine monastery and then move out to the town of Courtenay, on Vancouver Island, and an eremitical colony, the Hermits of St. John the Baptist, overseen by a Father Jacques Winandy. Once his proper course of action was agreed to, Leo would return to Our Lady of Guadalupe.

Brother Leo made his visit to Dom Winandy and the hermits of Vancouver Island serve more than one purpose. No matter what the outcome of the subpoena, he was irreconcilably set upon going to Texas and filing suit to upset the settlement. Since Dom Keating's letter of November 19 had been unambiguous as to the consequences of filing, Leo took the opportunity of his days with Winandy to discuss the eremitical life, an option for the future he had been thinking about anyway. When the monk's expected dismissal came, he would turn to Winandy for help and guidance.

After consulting with Peter Grace, Dom Keating decided that Leo should accept a new subpoena but ordered him to be prepared to answer written questions in Oregon, not to present himself to Nesbitt in Texas. In a letter written January 6, 1966, just as he was leaving for a short trip to Argentina, Father Thomas spelled out his reasoning. ''I am concerned about your physical welfare,'' his letter said.

> Serious threats continue to be made, which may be carried out if you go to Texas. These threats are not being made with the object of keeping you out of Texas, nor have they been passed on to me with that objective. I think you probably have the family in mind from which these threats principally emanate.
>
> These same persons are most active in the Will contest. It seems certain that they will try to bring crim-

inal charges against you—probably charges involving federal offense.

Your religious vocation is not likely to prevent these charges, since, as you have yourself indicated in your last letter, these people are out to embarrass the Church, at whose hands they imagine they have suffered during this case. This gives me additional concern for your welfare. We wish to stand by you at this time with every help and assistance we can muster.

Dom Thomas reiterated his patient appreciation for Leo's efforts to assist the poor and his shared belief that prayers alone were not enough to ensure the salvation of the world's destitute. But he added that the monk's plans to upset the settlement would in all likelihood destroy the only available instruments to aid the downtrodden—the foundations. "I must," he wrote,

take all measures that are within my power to prevent [these] disasters . . . from taking place, including also the grave detriment to the community, Order and Church which would befall.

Your going to Texas is so charged with serious danger, that to prevent it, I am hereby giving you a precept in virtue of your vow of obedience not to leave the Abbey of Our Lady of Guadalupe without my explicit permission. . . . In my absence from the country, Father Owen, Prior of Spencer, alone can grant permission for you to leave the monastery.

Violation of this precept will render you subject to immediate dismissal from the Order in accordance with Canon 668.

Believe me when I repeat that it grieves me very much to be compelled to take this position, and it would grieve me much more should I be compelled to take such action.

Leo left Our Lady of Guadalupe on the afternoon of January 7, 1966, ahead of Dom Thomas's precept and therefore, technically, not in violation of it. To protect Dom Columban, who would have been obliged to try to prevent the monk's departure, Leo said nothing of his plans to go. When the abbot walked into his office that evening, he found a sealed envelope from Leo on his desk. Inside was a penciled note informing Hawkins, "I have gone to Texas to see my attorneys."

TWENTY-SEVEN

✦ ✦ ✦

"Monk Gets Boot"

Brother Leo's decision to go to Texas to testify was predicated, in part, on two mistaken beliefs. One was that he could undo the 1964 settlement when Ken Oden held his 1962 resignation from the Kenedy Memorial Foundation, his 1963 signature on the settlement papers, and his letters from Calvaire to Father Keating in 1964. "I had all kinds of written statements from Brother Leo furnished to me by the New York group," says Oden. "They all showed his *consent* to the settlement agreement. To attack the agreement put him in a duplicitous position, to say the very least. A hypocrite. A Texas jury wouldn't stand still for that."

The monk's second clouded notion was his firm conviction that the charges against him of undue influence could be defeated. All that his trip to Texas was going to accomplish was to create acute embarrassment for the church and for his order. It would also cost him his monk's habit.

Marshall Boykin and Sissy Farenthold were Leo's attorneys of record and would appear as such during the deposition. But with Lawrence McKay and Peter Grace's approval, it was decided to bring in Denman Moody from Baker, Botts in Houston, a very experienced trial lawyer, to coach Leo through his testimony to Frank Nesbitt and also, when it came time for

Moody to question the monk directly, to put as much favorable evidence as possible on the deposition transcript. Brother Leo accepted Moody's help without demurral. He had it in his mind to use Moody to assist him in defending his behavior with Sarita (a goal they shared), while at the same time using his testimony to Nesbitt to taint the settlement. But for his ill-informed grasp of the situation, Leo might have seen that both strategies were going to backfire.

Yet Leo gave a bravura performance. His interrogation began at 9:30 A.M. on January 17, 1966, in office space rented for the occasion at the old Driscoll Hotel in Corpus Christi. At least a dozen attorneys plus a court reporter were crowded into the room, and all at first were edgy about the presence of Bobby Turcotte. Some, including Joe Day, worried that Bobby might be carrying a gun. But no one in the room, with the exception of Pat Horkin, who had conducted Leo's first deposition, in New York in 1962, had yet felt the full weight of the monk's extraordinary presence, and not even Bobby Turcotte was immune to his charm.

"First day, Bobby sat there lookin' mean, you know," says Day. "Bu after about two hours we had our first coffee break, and there was ol' Bobby right up there with Brother Leo, just *jabberin'* with him. Leo just about mesmerized Bobby. I swear Leo had the qualifications of being the best con man goin'. Believe me, you had to be pretty well trained not to be convinced by what he said. That's the truth!''

Frank Nesbitt knew he had his hands full, too. "I remember,'' he says, "one day when I kept pushing Leo about something. Kept pinning him down, trying to get an answer. And he always had some way of getting around it. And during recess he said—he and I got along all right, we weren't enemies—he said, 'Frank, when I want to tell you something, I'll tell you. And when I don't want to tell you something, you're not going to hear it.' And it was true. He was sharp enough to keep putting me off and putting me off and not give me an answer. Or else half an answer.''

The complexity of Nesbitt's questioning, and Leo's prolix responses, resulted in a marathon deposition that would stretch into two months. Its twenty-six-volume transcript ran to more than five thousand pages and a million words. The attorney's direct examination of the monk lasted for twenty-four days, during which time he gave Leo all the latitude he desired to attack his treatment by Dom Keating and Archbishop Krol and to denounce the settlement as unjust. Leo's accusations that his superiors had tried to muzzle him— and tinker with the truth—couldn't hurt Nesbitt's case.

Nor did an exchange between Nesbitt and the monk on the murky ethical doctrine of ''mental reservation,'' the willful withholding or distortion of a truth, even under oath, to protect a higher truth. Nesbitt read a detailed description of the doctrine from a text written by a Jesuit scholar, and then asked Leo if he ever used mental reservations. The monk allowed that he did, although he was unfamiliar with the specific term. He added, ''I can conceive of no fact that the courts of Texas have a right to know, which is related to this particular case, that I would have a right to conceal or distort in any way.''

Nesbitt jumped on the answer. ''Do you set yourself up in any sense as a judge of what people have a right to know in this case or not?''

Leo emphatically said that he did not and rephrased his answer to say that he thought it would be ''wrong, morally wrong,'' to lie. But the damage to his credibility as a witness had been done.

The monk also got himself into trouble under Nesbitt's close inquiry into his relationship with Sarita, the pivotal issue in all the litigation. He asserted, as always, Sarita's concern for the poor of Latin America. Nesbitt asked if she had indicated how much of her money should go to this cause, and Leo could not say that she had. The attorney then asked if this charity was supposed to begin at her death, and Leo answered no, Sarita wanted to help the poor in her lifetime, unfortunately cut short by her cancer. Did Leo have any specific examples of this? Nesbitt asked. What percentage of the more than a million dollars she did spend in Latin America before her death went to projects for the poor? Leo couldn't answer.

He did assert—as he had in his November 1961 statement—that none of the Kenedy Memorial Foundation money, unlike Sarita's direct philanthropy, was to go to the Trappists and that Dom Edmund Futterer knew this. Then Leo testified to the existence of the supposed letters between Mrs. East and Dom Futterer, written in late 1959 or early 1960, which spelled out the deal. He claimed to have seen the one Sarita wrote to Futterer and to have heard, from Mrs. East, a description of the abbot's reply. Because of this exchange, Leo now said, he was acting under his vow of obedience to Dom Edmund. He was duty-bound to see that Sarita's foundation was set up as she wished, even though his new abbot, Dom Keating, was bullying him to break this sacred vow by invoking a contrary demand.

The problem with this line of reasoning remained its lack of corroboration. Leo couldn't produce the letters, and there was no one else who could vouch for their existence, a situation not unlike that created by his assertion that he alone knew Mrs. East's true wishes.

Nesbitt had already elicited from Leo strong, righteous denials that he had in any way cozened the widow, and the monk's testimony that she was a practical, levelheaded woman who certainly knew her own mind. The attorney therefore couldn't resist exploring Sarita's decision to seek Leo's help in setting up her foundation.

"Now you mentioned," he asked about three weeks into his direct examination, "that from sometime late in 1959 up until the time she died that you had the permission of your abbot to be with Mrs. East at any time she desired, to aid and assist her with reference to her work with the foundation. During all this period of time and up until the time she died, what services did you render to her in connection with the foundation?"

"Whatever services she asked me to render," Leo replied.

"What services did she ask you to render? Of what nature? Were they legal?"

"No, I am not a lawyer."

"Were they medical?"

"No."

"Was it an advisory capacity with regard to her ranching problems?"

"No."

"Was it an advisory capacity with regard to her oil property?"

"No."

"Well," Nesbitt queried politely, "what was it that she wanted?"

"To help her in any way that I could," Leo answered a little unsteadily. "To actually do the work that she had wanted to do for a long time and which she actually did, to a fairly large degree, succeed in doing by the time she died in February '61. I introduced her to as competent a Catholic businessman as I know—namely, Mr. Grace—and through him she was introduced to the Cahill, Gordon law firm, which is one of the most reputable law firms in the country, as well as their associates in Houston. And I discussed whatever matters connected with the foundation she wished to discuss with me.''

''Well,'' Nesbitt went on, giving Leo a thoughtful, curious glance, ''what kind of advice did she look to you for in your discussions of the foundation matters?''

''Well, just whatever came to her mind on a day-to-day basis,'' said the monk. ''As I say, it was actually during that period that she had her lawyers draw up her new will, and set up the foundation, make the original appointments of the directors.''

''That's what her lawyers did. What did you do?'' For once, Nesbitt had Leo cornered.

''Well, I really didn't do very much, Frank. I mean, when you, when it boils right down to it, I didn't actually do—I didn't do very much.''

The attorney asked if Leo had seen a recent *Corpus Christi Times* article that described him as Sarita's ''companion and spiritual advisor.'' Leo had, and he disapproved of the description.

''I don't feel that I was her companion,'' he said, ''as much as a lot of other people were during the last years of her life. And I certainly was not her spiritual director . . .''

''Well then, let's go back to what you did do,'' Nesbitt said. ''Will you tell us what it is that she wanted you to do over all this period of time, that you did do for her?''

''Well, she wanted to meet Mr. Grace, and I arranged for that.''

''All right. That took just one meeting for that, didn't it?''

''Right.''

''But of course you were with her an awful lot of times when Mr. Grace wasn't there, weren't you?

''Would you repeat the question?''

"You were with her on quite a number of occasions after you had introduced her to Mr. Grace?"

"Yes I was, Frank," Leo answered and then mentioned another of the tasks he fulfilled for Mrs. East, helping to send a small load of Santa Gertrudis cattle down from Texas to Los Laureles in the summer of 1960.

"All right," said Nesbitt. "From 1959 until the time she died, you introduced her to Peter Grace, got her connected with the Cahill law firm, and you got a shipment of cattle off. Now, what else did you do, in all the time you spent with her, and all the moneys that she was supposed to finance your South American expansion program for?"

"Well, I guess that—gee, I can't think of anything else right now, Frank. There were little things. For example, I recall making certain travel arrangements for her."

Finally, Nesbitt asked, "Can you recount for us any services you rendered to her during the entire period of time from 1959 and 1960 until she died that, in your opinion, would warrant her paying a million dollars or more for your assistance?"

"No," Leo had to admit. "I can't, if you put it that way."

Nesbitt was never made aware by his clients of Sara Curiel's supposed accusations against Leo. He believed that the strongest evidence against Leo was in the monk's own hand, the letters that Sarita had saved and that Pat Horkin finally had been forced to divulge. "That's your proof," he says. "That's your evidence. Not each individual letter. Bu if you take the whole series, they paint a broad picture. You can read what Leo was telling her against what she did, like heading for South America, setting up the foundation, or writing checks for him."

The attorney turned to the correspondence early and

often in his questioning, seeking to establish for the record the links between what Leo urged on Sarita and her subsequent actions. He could show how a note predated a donation, or how "God's Plan" seemed to crop up in the letters whenever Sarita was making key decisions about her foundation. But Nesbitt got nowhere with Leo himself. Holding the monk's handwritten letter to Sarita of April 7, 1959—sent as she was first deciding whether to visit his prospective monastery sites in Argentina and Chile—Nesbitt asked, "Now, there is at the top of the letter a sign of a little cross, with the letter *M*. Would you explain what that means?"

"Surely," Leo answered. "The cross, of course, is the symbol of our redemption and salvation effected by Christ, and the *M* stands for the mother of Christ, who in a very real way assisted her Son in the work of our salvation."

"I presume that you anticipated Mrs. East would know what that meant?"

"Yes."

"Had you been around her enough and talked to her enough on religious matters to feel that she would understand that without explanation?"

"Mrs. East was considerably older than I, and had been trained as a child as a Catholic, and I knew that she knew what that meant before I was born."

Nesbitt then quoted a line to Leo. " 'You are kept very deep in our thoughts and prayers, that God may pour out upon you an abundance of His best gifts.' Was there some reason for having her in your prayers and thoughts at that time?"

"There certainly was."

"What was the reason?"

"Her very great generosity to our order over the past almost ten years. When a benefactor makes gifts of a very substantial nature it certainly places a very heavy obligation upon us to show our gratitude. The benefactors of the Trappist order have a very special place in the daily lives of our monks.

"Perhaps one of the special attractions that the average benefactor would have in assisting a Trappist monastery is the security of knowing that their intentions would be remembered in a very special way in the thoughts of the members of all the communities that they have helped to establish. That is why, for example, that 'our' actually refers not only to my own community at Spencer but to all those other communities that Mrs. East and her sister-in-law had helped to establish."

"Now, did you know Mrs. East well enough to believe that she was of such a religious nature herself that she would understand and appreciate the thoughts and prayers?"

"I would even go so far as to say that if it wasn't for the thoughts and the prayers that I don't think that she and her sister-in-law would have ever made us any of the contributions that they so generously made. In other words, I think it was uppermost in her mind."

Leo calmly characterized his letters to Sarita, at length, as innocuous collections of religious verities. "I would say this, Frank. On the one hand, obviously, this hasty note wasn't written for the broad coverage that it has received, but that those truths [in it] are very basic ones to Christianity and they could be expressed to anyone, any Christian who had reached the midpoint of life. They are nothing else but the truths, for example, that you find in the gospels and the epistles of St. Paul reiterated over and over. 'Of ourselves, we can do nothing, our Lord has said,' [and] 'With My help, you can do all things.' I am sure I have said those same things to quite a few people. And they would be as applicable, I am sure, to perhaps yourself as they would be to anyone else that I have ever met."

Denman Moody, the trial expert from Baker, Botts took over Leo's questioning on February 12. Moody skillfully framed his examination to emphasize Peter Grace's and Father Peyton's spiritual qualities, as well as Leo's testimony to Sarita's care for the poor. He also placed in evidence hundreds of snapshots and color slides, most taken by Sarita, of her several trips to Latin America, some showing slum scenes, but the great majority depicting scenery. There were several shots of Mrs. East enjoying herself in the company of grinning monks.

Moody had noted Leo's polished defense of his letters under hostile questioning and decided the monk would do even better if led by a friendly hand. He took Leo back to the April 1959, handwritten note and asked what Leo had meant by "an *act* of sincere Trust." Nesbitt had endeavored to characterize the phrase as Leo's direct attempt to wheedle money from Sarita.

"The few simple thoughts in this note," Leo replied, "paraphrase thoughts of our Lord as expressed in the Bible, and in particular the thoughts of the author of the little book *Confidence in God,* which has been introduced into the record, where he speaks of confidence in God's mercy as being the key to that mercy, which allows God to pour that mercy into our hearts.

"For example, the author says in speaking of the soul's trial when brought face to face with its own limitations and shortcomings, 'To bear with one's self is an act of great virtue.' And I would say that when I used the word 'act' in this particular letter, I was referring to those internal acts of faith and love, and especially trust in God's mercy, whereby a soul acknowledges it is totally dependent upon God for all the good that it has and for all the good that it needs. And that act of accepting our limitations [and confiding] our needs to God's love and mercy is an act of supreme importance and supreme effectiveness.''

"When you used the word 'act,' '' Moody then asked, ''were you there asking Mrs. Sarita East to make a donation, was that the intent of your expression?''

"No, obviously not," said Leo. "I say, 'Make an act of sincere trust in His love for us and in His desire to help us and to have mercy on us.' In other words, the whole strength of that act that I am describing in this letter is the same as the acts of confidence that the author of the little booklet *Confidence in God,* is speaking of. It is an act of our soul, directed exclusively toward God as, indeed, I make clear in that very sentence, 'Then He'—and He of course refers to God— 'Then He wants us to turn away from ourself, toward Him, and make an act of sincere trust in His love for us.' In other words, that act is the act of confidence, which is a wholly interior act, directed by the soul toward God in an especial way toward God's love and mercy for us.''

"Now, Brother Leo," Moody continued in a fatherly voice, "in the event that someone should point out that language and the word 'act' and claim that that means that you're asking Mrs. Sarita East for some type of donation, would that just simply be a mistake?''

"Yes," Leo answered. "I would distinguish between an act of confidence in God, which is referred to in this exhibit, and an act of generosity toward one's neighbor, which seems to be what you are referring to.''

The monk's effortless disquisitions provoked snickers among the other lawyers, who nonetheless marveled at Leo's command of nuance. "Leo didn't fool us," says Joe Day, "although I appreciated his logic and, sometimes, just the beauty of the finesse of his approach to things. I mean, he could make things sound so logical." Engrossed as he, too, was by Leo, Frank Nesbitt was not going to let the monk turn the witness chair into a pulpit without some salty rebuttal.

"The mere fact," he asked on redirect examination, "that any religious sits and writes and spouts forth biblical teachings of Christ does not necessarily mean that he is a sincere man of Christ, does it?"

"No," the monk answered.

"His motives and what he has done by way of fact must be investigated to determine his sincerity, do they not?"

"Yes."

"Brother Leo," Nesbitt went on, "would it be fair to say that any religious who would prostitute the scriptures of the Holy Bible, or the religious truths of Christianity, to take advantage of a sincere, faithful, trusting believer for the purpose of acquiring money and only that, that such a religious that would do anything like that should be subjected to scorn as a charlatan?"

"Yes, it certainly would."

"Yes, sir. And as we have just gone over, Christ teaches us that there will be such people, isn't that true?"

"Yes."

Nesbitt did fine with Leo until he returned to the letters themselves. Holding the monk's note to Sarita of January 19, 1960, written as she was about to establish her foundation, he quoted: "Christ told us that loving God means to do His will. 'If you love Me, you will do My Will, even as I love my Father and always seek to do those things that give him pleasure.' Loving God means to try all day long, and in all that we do, to please Him, by doing the duties of our state in life for His sake, and by accepting all that His will sends into our daily lives with trust and love."

The attorney paused and then addressed the monk. "Are you telling her," Nesbitt asked, "or do you have reference in any way that if she wants to do God's will she must carry out this plan of hers that you said she had already formulated, to create this foundation for the benefit of the impoverished areas of the world, with special emphasis to Latin America?"

Leo reread the passage aloud and then fixed Nesbitt with a calm gaze. "Nowhere do I refer to the Kenedy Memorial Foundation," he said. "Nowhere in there do I refer to anything, as far as what she should do, except whatever are the duties of her state of life, which her own conscience was the one to judge what they were. The thoughts in this paragraph could be said to anyone and certainly have no reference, for example, to the Kenedy Memorial Foundation, except insofar as she might have felt that God wished her to set up such a foundation."

Of all the attorneys, Pat Horkin (representing the diocese of Corpus Christi) questioned Leo most closely on his financial dealings. Two Grace Bank accounts that particularly interested Horkin were the Spencer "Incorporated" and the Spencer "Inc." accounts Leo opened in September of 1959, just before Sarita left on her first trip to South America. Horkin, whom Archbishop Krol had taken into his confidence, may have been told that the "Incorporated" account was Leo's secret money channel. If so, it seems likely that Horkin pressed the issue for the hell of it, just to see how Leo would explain his financial innovations. Horkin's first question was why two accounts were necessary.

Leo began by answering that the abbey maintained as many as five or six accounts in several banks, each established for a specific purpose. Then he ignored Horkin's specific question. "This particular account," he said, referring to them both, "as nearly as I can recall now was an account that my abbot asked me to open in the Grace Bank in connection with the South American expansion, where contributions that were given for the specific purpose of our expansion work in South America could be received by the account of St. Joseph's Abbey within the United States so as to afford the donors of those contributions adequate proof for any tax deductions that they wished to obtain.''

"Brother Leo," Horkin then asked, "which of these accounts did you use to transfer funds from Mrs. East's account into the Cistercian abbey account?"

"I really don't recall now, Pat," the monk answered. "I might have used either." The purpose in either case, he said, was "to give evidence to Mrs. East's bookkeeper that those gifts that she was making were exempt from any federal or state gift tax."

Horkin went on to ask if he understood Leo correctly on another point. Had it been at Sarita's instruction that Thomas Doyle of the Grace Bank received all her canceled checks and statements on *her* Grace account?

Leo replied that that was right.

"Do you know what her reason was for treating this one bank account differently from numerous other checking accounts that she had?" Sarita's object, of course, was to hide her donations from Jake Floyd and her relatives.

"Well," said Leo, "as far as I can tell, this account was a very special account, unlike any other account that she ever had. No funds were ever transferred by her into this account until she had already decided that those funds, in that amount, were to be used in some phase of the expansion work in Latin America. I would say it was a very special account, totally different in nature from all her other accounts."

But Horkin wanted to know why Sarita didn't just transfer the money directly into the Spencer account, which the monk had testified was established to provide her a tax record.

"I am not a tax attorney," Leo answered. "I would say that perhaps she could have done it, had her bookkeeper been willing to support those transfers with all the necessary information that the U.S. government probably would have required to have shown the reality of the various nonprofit corporations in Latin America which were being established at that time, that the money was going to."

Horkin took a moment to digest this answer.

"Brother Leo," he asked after the pause, "you had not only the power to draw checks on Mrs. East's account, but you also had the power to draw checks on the Spencer corporation's account in the Grace National Bank, did you not?"

"That is correct."

"So, as far as the transfer of these funds to South America was concerned, there would have been no reason why the checks could not have been deposited directly into the Cistercian Corporation account, and you could then have checked them out, could you not?"

"That would be true, yes. It could have been done that way."

"Do you know of any reason why Mrs. East's accountant would have raised objections, during 1960, if he had known about these transactions in these large amounts of money?"

Leo said that Sarita told him her accountant, whom he never met, feared the tax-exempt status of the Latin-American foundations, then newly formed.

"I understand that, Brother Leo," Horkin replied. "But I also understand that most of the funds from Mrs. East's account were transferred by you, under your power of attorney, from her account to the Cistercian Corporation account in the same bank. That's true, is it not?''

True enough, Leo answered, and the reason for it was the need for Sarita to establish that a bona fide U.S. charity, the Trappists, was receiving her donations.

Horkin rejoined that checks made out directly from her to the Trappists would have sufficed to meet most legal requirement.

"That is true," Leo agreed. "That is absolutely true."

"So there is no real explanation of why this very special account was set up, then?"

"Yes," Leo answered brightly, "I think there is a very obvious explanation. Number one, Mrs. Sarita East wanted it that way. And number two, I think I can guess at least one reason, and it was simply that the money could be more securely controlled by herself. In other words, had she deposited, say, a large amount of money in the Trappist general account, it would have required, perhaps, a corporate action on our part to have accepted it. And she might have felt that, since she left those funds in some instances for a month or longer in the New York City account, that some way or another they might have been diverted to another use. At least I presumed that she felt that she had better control of those moneys by handling it in the way that she did.''

Leo was apparently implying that Abbot Futterer or Brother Blaise might be tempted to misspend Sarita's money if it were made too readily available to them. And Sarita appears to have concurred in this assessment, at least as far as the monk's explanation goes.

"By better control," Horkin asked, "would you explain what you mean? Isn't it true that she didn't write a single check on that account during its entire life, in the year 1960?''

"She instructed that those moneys be withdrawn and, as I recall, at least certainly in general, as soon as they were withdrawn from her account and transferred through the Cistercian Corporation's account they were immediately cabled to whatever purpose in Latin America that she wanted those funds to go to."

"But you were the one who handled those funds."

"I handled them as her agent, as a result of the power of attorney that she gave me. As I said before, she never placed anything in that account until she had decided that it was to be transferred to one of the various works that she was interested in in Latin America [the two monasteries and Los Laureles]."

Horkin also established that Sarita wasn't in New York when her account was first opened, on January 13, 1960. Leo called the action "just another example, corroborated by all of these exhibits that you have introduced, of the favors that were afforded to her by that Grace Bank." Nowhere in his testimony did Leo concede the slightest impropriety in the way Mrs. East's money was handled.

Then there was the question of Leo's "washing" operations, as he innocently referred to them in his letters to the Grace Bank. Horkin entered some of these into the record. "Now, Brother Leo," he asked. "Will you explain to us what the term 'wash' means?"

"Yes," said the monk. "An object which is washed is passed through a process without being substantially altered, and that, exactly, is what Mrs. East wanted done with these deposits which she made in her own account in New York City, before those moneys were sent down pursuant to her instructions to South America. In other words, they were passed through a recognized U.S. nonprofit corporation so that that corporation became responsible, in the eyes of the Federal Bureau of Internal Revenue, for whatever happens to those moneys afterward."

"Now, Brother Leo," Horkin said, "do you know or not whether this term 'wash' is frequently used to describe the process whereby funds are transferred through multiple bank accounts for the purpose of concealment in tax fraud cases?"

"No," Leo answered. "I don't know about that. The most common use, of course, of that term has to do with washing your hands. As I say, an object can be looked upon as being washed, as I have said before, if it passes through a process without being substantially altered, and that is exactly what happened with the checks."

Preposterous as the monk's questioners found the content of his testimony, Leo delivered it in confident tones of unwavering conviction. The only time he lost his poise was in private, on Sunday, February 27, when Sissy Farenthold told him that Dom Thomas had acted. "A priest handed me the signed dismissal at the cathedral in Corpus Christi that Friday," she recalls. She read the document, dated January 12, noting that it was worn looking, as if it had been handled by several people.

Dear Brother Leo,

I deeply regret that you have persisted in your decision to disregard the precept I gave you under threat of dismissal by continuing to place or to allow Mr. Joyce to place actions designed to set aside the settlement agreement in the KMF. As I repeatedly told you, this action would leave me no choice in trying to protect the common good of our community but to dissociate you and the actions over which I have no control from the Abbey.

With great sorrow I hereby inform you that you have been dismissed from the Order according to Canon 668.

You, of course, have the right of appeal. Your vows

remain intact and you have the obligation to return to the Order as soon as the cause for this dismissal is removed.

The precepts which I have heretofore given you also remain intact, except the one which I recently sent to Oregon but which must have arrived after your departure. . . .

You are further obliged to put off the religious habit and to live in the world, and you must continue to live in the world until you can prove that you have actually removed the cause of this dismissal for a reasonable length of time.

With my prayers and sincere affection in Christ,

Thomas Keating, Abbot

That weekend Farenthold and the monk were to fly to Nashville to visit Lady Florence East, a prospective witness on Leo's behalf. "I didn't see any point in giving him that letter until we made the trip," says Farenthold. "And so it was Sunday when I finally gave it to him. And it was like giving a person a death message. He was just distressed about it. Deeply. Deeply."

"Monk Gets Boot for Estate Work" reported the *Fort Worth Star-Telegram* a week later when Leo was formally notified of his dismissal, on the last day of Denman Moody's questioning. The nearly two-month delay from the date of the dismissal's execution to its official delivery, Leo speculated, could be explained by Archbishop Krol's or Peter Grace's desire that Moody put all his positive evidence on the record before the monk learned his fate.

The next day, March 8, 1966, Leo authorized Marshall Boykin to file his legal challenge to the 1964 settlement of the Lytton lawsuit. This petition, formally known as a bill of review, named the Kenedy Memorial Foundation, the Alice National Bank, and thirteen individuals as defendants or parties to Leo's action, including the new bishop of Corpus Christi, Thomas Drury, and Jake Floyd's widow, Edie, executrix of her husband's estate.

The twenty-four-page petition complained at length about Dom Thomas Keating's and Archbishop Krol's behavior toward Leo. "From November 1961," it read,

> petitioner was not informed of any of the negotiations for settlement or progress of the case except insofar as same may have been reflected by the instrument submitted to him for his execution; was never furnished copies of pleadings in said cause; was not fully informed as to the terms of such settlement; was refused free communications with regard to such suits; was required to remain silent with regard thereto; was refused permission to seek his own advisers; was refused permission to seek advice or assistance of lawyers of his own choosing, and particularly, lawyers licensed to practice in the courts of Texas; was refused permission to go to Texas and, in fact, was directed not to go to Texas. . . . During all of this period of time petitioner has been subject to constant threat of dismissal and other censures unless he complied with the orders of and submitted his will to the direction of his superiors.

"Wherefore," the bill of review asked, "that upon trial hereof that judgment entered in Cause 12074 . . . be set aside and held for naught; that the issues made by the parties' pleadings . . . be tried, and that petitioner have judgment naming petitioner a member and director of The John G. and Marie Stella Kenedy Memorial Foundation." Leo also pleaded for court costs, expenses, attorneys' fees, "and such other and further relief to which he may be entitled either at law or in equity.''

"Leo Risks Career for Vast Fortune" the *Houston Chronicle* announced in a series by the reporter Tom Mulvany, who scored a news beat by getting Archbishop Krol to agree to an interview. "I am not familiar with all the allegations that Brother Leo has made in Corpus Christi," said the archbishop. "It is a bit unfortunate that he has apparently lost his sense of religion. These are matters wholly incompatible with religious life, and he has violated his instructions in a whole series of incidents."

At Spencer, Leo's dismissal and lawsuit brought down a crush of press inquiries, forcing Dom Thomas to issue a statement. "By his course of action," it read, "Christopher Gregory effectively withdrew himself from his religious life in our Order. And since his course of action was seriously harmful to the common good, there was no choice left but to dissociate him from the Order."

On March 15, four days before the deposition at last was over, the Congregation of Religious in Rome issued a rescript, or edict, confirming Brother Leo's dismissal from the Trappists and freeing the monk from his vows. Leo refused to accept the dispensation from obedience, poverty, chastity, and the rest, although it took effect nonetheless. But he did take advantage of the chance to become known as Brother Joseph, which Dom Keating had denied him permission to do four years before. On his new passport, issued April 1, 1966, he listed his full name as Roderick Christopher Gregory, a.k.a. Brother Leo Joseph, and signed it Joseph Gregory.

He had hoped to find shelter as a hermit in Dom Winandy's Vancouver Island conclave, but the stir the monk had created in Texas had frightened Winandy's bishop. "He heard me very attentively," Winandy wrote to Dom Hawkins in Oregon; "then he said to me that without judging the Brother himself he thought I cannot receive him into the colony. 'If the newspapers should talk again about the Texas affair,' he said, 'that may do the colony heavy harm.' " Winandy suggested that Hawkins erect a hermitage for Leo near Our Lady of Guadalupe.

Six weeks later Winandy came up with another idea. He indicated that Leo, or Joseph, could occupy a mean hovel Winandy himself had used as a hermit's cell on the Caribbean island of Martinique. Living conditions at the site, known locally as Fond Canot, or "bottom of the canoe," because it rested in a swampy, trough-like depression on a mountainside about a thousand feet above sea level, were primitive. It was infested with mosquitoes and spiders. There was no plumbing of any sort—potable water was to be had from a nearby river or the cell's rain barrel—and the weather on that side of the island alternated between scorching sun and drenching downpours.

When Leo arrived on Martinique, in early July, he discovered that the cell itself was a stone-and-concrete, tin-roofed rectangle about ten feet by fifteen feet, furnished with a cot, a chair, and an altar. On its small porch he installed a portable kerosene stove to prepare his meals, mostly lentils and carrots and breadfruit, which he found edible if well boiled.

For clothing, he would wear sandals and Dom Winandy's old hermit's habit, a gray flour sack with holes cut in it for head and arms. It was a forty-five-minute walk to 7:00 A.M. mass in the village of Morne-Vert. In all, as he wrote Lotus Gregory, he was ready to settle into a life of secluded prayer and reading, done for now with the tumult of the foundation fight and eager to take up his new hermit's vocation.

✛ ✛ ✛

TWENTY-EIGHT

Undue Influence

Back in Texas, Marshall Boykin understood that with Ken Oden pulling the strings in C. W. Laughlin's Alice courtroom, anything was possible. "Ken Oden," he says, "was a smart, shrewd lawyer. He had a sort of sixth sense of knowing what was the tactically expedient thing to do."

A case in point was the 1964 settlement that Boykin wished to attack for Brother Leo. "I went over to Alice and the courthouse and went through the files," Boykin says. "I never saw so many things filed in a case! Everybody was filing something every other day. Then when I read the settlement agreement, it clearly looked to me that all the issues had been disposed of, although it had language that said this agreement was interlocutory [that is, temporary]. It was, I think, a clever little job of trying to be *either* final or interlocutory, depending on what Mr. Oden wanted it to be."

Boykin explains that he had to be careful; if he attacked the settlement with a petition assuming it was interlocutory, Judge Laughlin might gavel it down as final. If that had happened, says Boykin, "I would have been out, just purely out."

Therefore he crafted a bill of review (which can be filed only if a judgment is final, or appealable) that forced Ken Oden to respond, one way or the other.

The Alice lawyer chose to argue that the judgment was still interlocutory. Judge Laughlin held for Oden, as did the appeals courts. "And that was fine with me," says Boykin, who felt he had case law that would allow him to demand a trial on Leo's allegations. "It established that there wasn't a final judgment, and since there wasn't a final judgment I was entitled to a complete trial of the facts, even though my client was alleged to have signed a settlement agreement."

Marshall Boykin's bill of review was, however, a backburner item to Ken Oden. It was the other case, the will contest, Cause 348 to be heard by Judge Bill Edwards in Kenedy County, that made Oden nervous. Under the 1964 settlement, Oden was a member of the Kenedy Memorial Foundation (along with Lee Lytton, Bishop Drury, Elena Kenedy, and Bruno Goldapp) as well as the foundation's lawyer and chief counsel for the Alice National Bank, depository for all Kenedy foundation assets (still under injunction). The bank, in turn, had contracted with Tom East for East to operate La Parra.

All of these arrangements were contingent upon maintenance of the 1960 will, the foundation, and the 1964 settlement against the concerted attacks from William Wright on behalf of his "Mexican heirs," Frank Nesbitt for the Turcotte brothers, plus Joe Day from Fort Worth, and all the rest of the lawyers representing 181 claimants in Cause 348. Each approached the suit a little differently, but all basically were arguing the very allegations that Oden's client, Lee Lytton, and his law partner, Jake Floyd, had made against Leo in the first place.

"It was sort of a paradox I was in," Oden laughs. "In the original suit I was tryin' to get deadwood on Leo, to show fraud and undue influence practiced on Mrs. East. In the will contest I was trying to show that fraud and undue influence was *limited* to two codicils to the will relating to membership in the foundation *only*. Well, that's walkin' the chalk line.''

During the lengthy pretrial process of motions, depositions, petitions, and hearings, Frank Nesbitt emerged as the major legal competition for Oden. Judge Edwards seemed willing to give Frank Nesbitt every opportunity to pursue his case and, in the process, to shed unwelcome light on the Alice National Bank's financial dealings as depositor for Kenedy Memorial Foundation funds. With Jake Floyd and Louis Edgar Turcotte now dead, the bank was also the sole remaining executor of Sarita's estate.

Because of Edwards's rulings, Nesbitt was able to force disclosure that the foundation's assets had swelled to about $14 million in cash and bonds, and that total was increasing by more than $100,000 a month from mineral royalty payments. Perkins & Floyd, Oden's law firm, had collected $200,000 out of estate funds to probate Sarita's will, and had billed the bank another $29,000 for its lawsuit work. Thirteen thousand dollars had gone to Denman Moody's firm, Baker, Botts, also in connection with the defense of the will and foundation.

''They [Ken Oden and his allies] didn't much like me,'' recalls Edwards. ''I later suggested that the Alice bank wasn't performing very well as executor, and I even entered an order removing them and appointing another bank as executor. That got appealed and overturned. They also filed a lawsuit against me, saying I was not qualified to be the probate judge, because I didn't live in Kenedy County. They were just trying to get rid of me. So I hired a lawyer and beat it.''

Judge Edwards, who was being paid $16.65 a day—1/365 of a county judge's annual salary—fought his dismissal on principle. ''That maneuver just irritated me,'' he says. In the end, all that it accomplished was to delay the beginning of Cause 348's public trial until June of 1967.

Due to a peculiarity of Texas law (which would be changed as a result of Cause 348), the proceedings in the Sarita courthouse were essentially a dress rehearsal; no matter how Edwards ruled, the case automatically would be tried again, before a jury, in Corpus Christi district court.

This was a serious obstacle to the plaintiffs' attorneys who were working for out-of-pocket expenses and contingency fees—a percentage of whatever award they might ultimately win for their clients. Two trials meant twice the time and effort expended for the same potential fee, with the prospect of further retrials and appeals stretching the case well into the 1970s.

For Frank Nesbitt, who with Joe Day had developed almost all the evidence in the case, Cause 348 was an even greater personal burden, because it consumed him to the detriment of the rest of his practice. "Nesbitt was almost insanely dedicated to his clients," says Day. "He'd go days without sleeping if necessary. He left no stone unturned anywhere."

Nesbitt had another problem, too. Ordinarily, once a legatee such as the deceased Louis Edgar Turcotte accepts an inheritance from a will, he and his descendants are legally estopped from attacking the will under the legal theory that a person cannot enjoy the fruit of a tree and then say the tree should be cut down. Nesbitt got around this issue by arguing that his clients' father had been ignorant of the undue influence practiced on Sarita; he didn't know that the tree *should* have been cut down, and therefore his sons were within their rights to try to do it themselves.

To bolster this claim, Pat Turcotte went in search of an heir or beneficiary under Sarita's 1948 will who did not inherit under the 1960 document. According to law Turcotte could buy a portion of this person's 1948 inheritance rights and thereby purchase legal standing to sue to have the 1948 will reinstated. In Brownsville, Turcotte found Robert Putegnat and his sister, Marie Walker, who stood to inherit about $1,000 each if the 1960 will was overturned. They agreed to sell the Turcottes a 10 percent interest in each of their inheritances, for a total of $4,400. This was more than twice the amount that Putegnat and his sister would realize if the Turcottes were ever successful in reinstating the 1948 will, but the amount would also be a bargain for the Turcottes if it ensured their standing to sue and led to a victory, which would be worth millions of dollars to them.

Judge Edwards accepted Nesbitt's clients as litigants, but their right to sue would be contested again in district court and for as long as the case wound through its inevitable appeals, until finally adjudicated in the Texas Supreme Court, putting their attorney in jeopardy of winning every battle but the last and thereby losing the war.

Ken Oden, by contrast, could win while losing, as long as the key issue of the Turcottes' legal standing ultimately was decided in his favor. The inter vivos gifts to the foundation, for now, were not at issue. They had been made during Sarita's lifetime and could not be attacked in probate court. Oden had no worries about compensation for his time and efforts, either. He was not a contingency lawyer working for a percentage of what he might win. His fees for defending the will were covered by the Alice National Bank, which in turn simply billed Sarita's estate for legal expenses. Also, the two-trial format offered Oden a tactical edge.

He knew that Frank Nesbitt was critical for making the case for undue influence; Nesbitt had developed the evidence against Leo and had the required courtroom skill to present it. Yet Oden also knew that a time of crisis lay ahead for the plaintiffs in Cause 348.

At some point Oden could count on Wright and Johnny Fitzgibbon to recognize that although they shared Nesbitt's aim of proving undue influence, they were sunk if the Turcottes' attorney went on to persuade the courts to reinstate Sarita's 1948 will, so favorable to his clients. Wright and the rest hung their hopes on the more tenuous argument that Leo and Peter Grace's undue influence over Sarita was confined to the residual clause of her 1960 will, and nothing more. It was the income from this major portion of the estate that the attorneys were eyeing for themselves and their clients.

"You see, I was their common enemy," says Oden. "But they also had differences. At first, I guess for their own convenience, Wright and his group let Nesbitt take the lead. But he was cuttin' their throats for 'em, and they didn't know it! It wasn't too smart. I guess they had a lot of faith somewhere in Nesbitt. But anyone with one eye and half sense could see it comin.' "

Judge Edwards convened his court on Monday, June 19, 1967, in the cramped second-floor courtroom of the Kenedy County courthouse, in Sarita. Earlier in the spring the boxy, three-story white brick edifice rose up from a pretty garden of wildflowers that Sarita herself had sown years before. But by the middle of June the flowers had long since wilted in the dust, and the courthouse shimmered alone in the south Texas heat. There were no businesses in Sarita, except for the La Parra ranch office, and no other multistory edifices save for the tall town water tower, visible from several miles away. Besides the Our Lady of Guadalupe Church, built for the ranch employees, there were only a few low houses and then nothing but Route 77, the railroad tracks, and beyond them boundless miles of sun-blasted rangeland.

Above the judge's high bench, framed by the state

of Texas and the United States flags, Elena Kenedy had hung a glowering oil portrait of Captain Kenedy, the same one that by the testimony of Sarita's vaqueros had crashed from its moorings the night before her funeral. To the immediate rear of the bench were the open barred doors of the small county jail. Empty of prisoners at the time, one of the two cells housed someone's dog, as Edwards recalls. The jailer's wife used the other cell to hang her laundry.

The courtroom, which most days would be filled with up to twenty attorneys and eighty or ninety spectators (including the press seated in the vacant jury box) was not air-conditioned. The south Texas summer by early afternoon turned the room into a sauna, obliging Judge Edwards to curtail court hours to from 9:00 A.M. until 2:00 P.M., with three twenty-minute breaks, the third for lunch.

When Edwards announced this decision, Major Tom Armstrong, a Kenedy County commissioner, approached the judge with a question. "He asked me if I could ride a horse," Edwards remembers. "I asked why. He said, 'Well, the way I understand it, you come down here and work half a day and get a full day's pay. I was thinkin' maybe that you could check fences or something in the afternoon.'"

Since there was no time to drive anywhere to eat, Judge Edwards and most of the will contestants bought cold venison sandwiches from one of the courthouse employees; they were available with or without onions. Those who were defending the will, led by Ken Oden, usually enjoyed a quick hot lunch provided to them in the ranch office, which was air-conditioned.

Neither Brother Leo nor Peter Grace appeared as witnesses to defend their actions. Although Judge Edwards remembers seeing the monk from time to time during the course of the trial, all that Leo had to say for the record was contained in his million-word deposition, which the judge read at night at home, rather than aloud in court, to speed the case along. Indeed, very little direct oral testimony was offered at all. Most of each day's proceedings was taken up with the entering of exhibits, such as Leo's letters to Sarita and Peter Grace's undue-influence chart (a total of 1,886 exhibits were offered into evidence) and transcripts of the various depositions.*

The exhibits and transcripts revealed, in their totality, not just the germane evidence from which Edwards would decide the issue of undue influence. The massive documentation also traced the fluid history of the litigation in which allies and enemies continually adjusted their allegiances as expedience and self-interest dictated.

The single exception to this pattern was Judge Lee Lytton, Jr. What set Lytton apart was that even though he had taken, over time, a number of contradictory positions in the controversy, he had consistently supported a single objective, the preservation of his aunt Sarita's foundation for the primary benefit of the Corpus Christi diocese. Tough as Frank Nesbitt felt constrained to be in exposing Lytton's shifts from one legal argument to another, he came to respect Sarita's nephew for not giving in to personal greed.

"Lee was put on the spot," say Nesbitt. "I can't blame him for doing what he did, and, not only that, I am convinced that Lee was a strong believer in what he was doing, that it was honest and right. He could have joined us very easily, because after all his mother

---

*Courts usually will not accept sworn depositions in lieu of personal testimony if a witness is physically capable of testifying in person. However, under Texas law at the time Judge Edwards was not required to impose that condition. Also, since the case was certain to be heard de novo in district court, Edwards saw no reason to require witnesses like Leo to repeat their hundreds of hours of prior testimony in probate court.

was my clients' aunt and Lee had exactly the same claims that we had. But he didn't. He didn't seek anything that I know of, individually. He was actually for the church.'' Some years later Ken Oden would learn how uncompromising his client, Lee Lytton, was in this commitment.

One of the few witnesses whose testimony was taken in court was Elena Kenedy. She provided some uncomfortable moments for Ken Oden. During the time before 1964 when it appeared that Lee Lytton's original suit, Cause 12074, might go to trial, Elena was interviewed and coached as to the content of her possible testimony against Brother Leo and J. Peter Grace. But now that Ken Oden had to defend their conduct, at least in part, someone neglected to deprogram Elena Kenedy's evidence.

In the courtroom, under Frank Nesbitt's questioning, Mrs. Kenedy told the story of how Sarita, on her deathbed at St. Vincent's, had been so distressed by Cardinal Tisserant's letter. Mrs. Kenedy quoted her dying sister-in-law as saying, ''Elena, that is a mistake and should be corrected. You know I would not treat Texas like that.''

The Turcottes' lawyer was amazed. ''She just came out with it, and I almost fell over,'' he recalls. ''I couldn't believe it! They had her all primed and cocked, but I guess they forgot she was still ready to go off.''

The Turcotte brothers did not get along with Elena Kenedy, and they never had. During her testimony that summer, she suggested that Sarita held their father, Louis Edgar Turcotte, Sr., in low esteem. The Turcottes resented what they took to be Elena's demeaning reference to their father and retaliated by telling Nesbitt to ask her what Sarita thought about Arthur East, her husband, whom she put on the ranch payroll—a question certain to irritate Mrs. Kenedy, who was always hypersensitive to any blot on the family name, no matter how minor or how remote in time. "So he asked her if Arthur was more or less a hired hand," Jack Turcotte recalls. "And Mrs. Kenedy turned white! I was then keeping some of my cattle on her land. The next day her local lawyer told me to get them out of her pastures and to get my own tail out of there, too."

The most entertaining of the few witnesses to testify personally was Tom East, who took the stand in late July, toward the end of the trial. East came to court straight from the range in full cowboy regalia, including boots and a bright red bandana. "Someone from the *National Observer,* I think, wanted to take a couple photographs of him," remembers Judge Edwards. "He pointed his camera at East, who just stopped and said, 'What are you pointin' at me?'

"I told him, 'It's just a camera, don't worry about it.'

"And he said, 'You know, Judge, in this part of the country if someone points something at you, you gotta worry.' "

Frank Nesbitt, for one, believes that East's rusticity was mostly an act. "When Tom got on the witness stand," says Nesbitt, "he looked down at the court reporter and said, 'What's that there fella doin' down yonder?': country-like, you know, this dumb country attitude. And he was *anything* but dumb. He and Jake were three-fourths of the brains behind the whole thing, and East was also the money and the strength."

The rancher admitted on the stand that he had financed the Lytton suit after hearing that Brother Leo was negotiating with his uncle Bob Kleberg and Tom Armstrong to take over La Parra. "I didn't like that," he said. But East denied that he and his uncle had been at war with each other. "I don't think we've ever been unfriendly,'' he testified. ''We've had differences of opinion like everyone else.''

Nor did Tom East give Frank Nesbitt any opening to explore the rancher's cozy relationship with the Alice bank, of which he had been a director until shortly before the bank, acting for the foundation, hired him to manage La Parra. He acknowledged that other bank employees had been fired when they challenged the will. But his case was different, he explained to Nesbitt, because East's intervention in 348 predated his employ. ''They hired me,'' he said. ''The others were already hired when they fired 'em.''

East appeared as the opening witness in Ken Oden's brief, two-day defense of the will, a counterattack consisting in the main of depositions in support of Leo's conduct and Sarita's mental competency. This sworn and transcribed testimony included that of the oil engineer William Sherry, then sixty-seven, who was unhesitant in his admiration for the monk, part of whose legal costs he was paying. Sherry sometimes referred to Leo as ''the boy.''

Testifying in his Tulsa office before Denman Moody, Pat Horkin, and Frank Nesbitt, Sherry recollected that he saw Mrs. East three times in the final months of her life: once, in September of 1960, when she asked him in Houston to conduct the secret evaluation of her mineral holdings; once, in October in New York, where Sherry delivered his findings; and the last time, at St. Vincent's Hospital, just days before her death.

On the basis of these meetings (about three hours of conversation in all), Sherry claimed to know Mrs. East's mind very well and was certain of her intention that the bulk of her estate go to the poor of Latin America. ''She felt strongly about this,'' he swore, ''and I did, too.'' She had complained to him, the engineer said, that her family and bishop didn't understand that the word ''Catholic'' means universal.

She also indicated to him that she felt she had done quite enough for her family and local church. Sherry added that he had "smoldered" at Leo's later treatment, believing the monk "the victim of some cruel decisions."

Major Tom and Henrietta Armstrong—she was a nominal defendant in, or a party to, all three lawsuits, 12074, 348 and the bill of review—agreed with Sherry's point of view. Their strongest feelings were contained in a letter to the Vatican composed and hand-delivered to Rome by the major himself in May of 1966, just after Leo's dismissal.

"The Sarita Kenedy East we knew was a devoted daughter of her church," it read.

That she had a strong loyalty and love for her church is shown in the many gifts that she made. In her last years she became also more concerned with the universal church as distinguished from the more parochial church. I think that before her death Mrs. East realized that she was the stewardess of her possessions for a larger and more universal cause than she had theretofore realized. This was certainly clear in the establishment of her Foundation which she wanted to be unlimited in its possibilities.

There is no doubt in my and Mrs. Armstrong's minds that Mrs. East was her own boss, that she made her own decisions, and that she knew her own will at all times prior to and after she executed her last Will and created her Foundation, and before she died she exhibited the clarity of mind and purpose of a woman who knew very well what she wanted to do. There is no doubt that she let others help her and be her instruments in effecting her Will; however, it would be an insult to Mrs. East and her memory to say that she was unduly influenced by any person. Mrs. East's works were her own creation of which she was justly proud.

There is also no doubt in the mind of Mrs. Armstrong and myself that Brother Leo was God-sent to help Mrs. East in the performance of some of the greatest actions she ever took in her life. I think the relationship of Mrs. East and Brother Leo could be talked about in terms of the providence of God. Certainly Mrs. Armstrong and I feel that Brother Leo brought Mrs. East immeasurable peace and happiness during the last years of her life.

The last of the depositions for Judge Edwards to read was that of Bob Kleberg, aged seventy, the lord of the King Ranch, who gave his testimony in early 1967 at the Baker, Botts offices in Houston. Beginning with a happy recollection of getting drunk on champagne at Sarita's 1910 wedding to Arthur East—"An old priest there led me up to it," said Kleberg. "He had on long underwear. He passed the champagne around and I got a glass of it. I thought it was damned good."—the rancher described a lifelong friendship with Mrs. East. "She and her brother, Johnny, were about the closest friends we had," Kleberg testified. "I would say she was a very, very wonderful woman in every way. I would hate to put a limit on it. I don't know where to stop. She was a very fine woman, a very strong person, a very clear thinker, and I would say with a head full of common sense."

Kleberg described Brother Leo as "a very nice, interesting sort of fellow," whom he hardly knew. "There were all kinds of religious people back and forth around that ranch all the time," he said. "I can't remember who they all were, but they were comin' and goin' all the time. There wasn't anything new [about Leo's visits] that I knew anything about."

"Did Mrs. East ever explain to you the nature of

the relationship that existed between her and Brother Leo?'' Frank Nesbitt asked.

"No,'' the rancher replied. "I don't know why she would.''

What about the several stories of Sarita's drinking problem?

"I would say no, positively.''

"Have you ever heard of it?''

"No.''

"So if it existed—''

"That does not mean that we wouldn't take a drink,'' Kleberg interrupted. "Or that she couldn't go to a party and have quite a lot of fun, just as any of us would. But I would say no problem.''

"So if one did exist, you weren't aware of it and hadn't heard about it?''

"I think I would have known it, and I didn't know it. Now, her brother did have. He drank a lot. But he had just as much sense when he was drunk as most people have when they are sober, but he liked it. I used to love to drink with him.''

Final oral arguments were waived in Cause 348, with a deadline of January 15, 1968, given for the various attorneys to submit their written arguments. In the meantime Judge Edwards began to sift through the huge mass of evidence presented.

"I was worried,'' he says. "I wondered how I could ever decide this. There was so much evidence, so many people. But by the time it came down to making a decision, I had no problem at all. I mean, it just jumped out and hit you in the teeth!''

As Edwards remembers his deliberations, among the more persuasive facts were these:

1. The hundreds of color slides, most snapped by Sarita on her tours of Latin America, that Denman Moody entered into evidence during Leo's depo-

sition and then screened, for hours, in Edwards's courtroom.

"It was a travelogue," says Edwards, "and they just insisted that I look at it. After a while it felt as though they wanted to put the same hit on me that they'd put on her. All this tranquil scenery and the poor people of Latin America. I'm sitting there thinking, 'C'mon guys, we've got enough poor people around here. You don't have to traipse off to Argentina to help.' We could have found all the needy beneficiaries she could want within fifty miles of her ranch."

2. The missing cowboys' surnames from letters H to S in the will's list of "Accounts Receivable" to be forgiven. The judge concluded that a page of the will had been lost in the rush to get it rewritten and signed. He did not believe that Sarita had somehow decided to disinherit people with surnames beginning with H through S. "Putting down all those little people was the act of a thoughtful person," says Edwards. "But to arbitrarily eliminate a page was contrary to my image of a woman with all her faculties. To me, that was telling. It was like she was told, 'This is good for you. Go ahead and sign it.' "

3. Leo's decision to take the dying widow to New York. "At that time," the judge points out, "M. D. Anderson in Houston was one of the world's foremost cancer centers. And they take her to New York! That disturbed me. It just wasn't right. You don't take a person who's spent her entire life in south Texas to New York City to die. You just don't do it! Somebody was doin' things they shouldn't have been doin.' "

4. The monk's testimony as to the pressures put on him by Peter Grace, his superiors, and attorneys to do as he was told. "They apparently tried to give him an attitude change, that kind of business. This

'We're gonna talk to you, boy, and get you to testify right' stuff didn't sit very well with me. I said, 'Well, son of a gun, I'm going to have to look hard at what these people have done and said, because I know they want to change things around.''

5. Leo's equivocation on the doctrine of mental reservation. ''That meant I couldn't accept anything he was saying. Not that he wasn't telling the truth, but I was only hearing from him what he believed I needed to hear.''

6. Peter Grace's undue-influence chart with all its boxes and arrows, which concluded that the *''admitted influence''* practiced by him and Brother Leo on Mrs. East, taken together with the allegations in 12074, ''will compel, a fortiori, a decision that all six actions resulted from 'undue influence.' '' Says Judge Edwards, ''That chart was as telling a piece of evidence as there was. Ol' Peter Grace outlined the fraud, and, by gosh, he was right! You'll never convince me that that old lady wasn't overreached. And it was just a shame.''

On Friday, February 23, 1968, the judge announced his decision. ''The court finds,'' he wrote, ''that undue influence flows to the execution of the entire 1960 will and its codicils. All must fall.''

TWENTY-NINE

✦ ✦ ✦

Peter Grace Speaks

Judge Edwards's decision was a bitter surprise to Brother Leo. In a letter written to Father Dominic Hughes after the verdict was handed down, the monk ascribed it to Edwards's politics, calling the judge a "bagman" for south Texas liberals whose agenda, Leo explained, was shaped by narrow Texas chauvinism. Among these liberals, one of the most dedicated was Leo's attorney Sissy Farenthold.

His new life as Brother Joseph, the hermit of Martinique, seems also to have fallen short of his expectations. Whether because of the harsh conditions on the island, his fondness for travel, or his pressing business concerns away from his tin-roofed cell—including the liquidation of the Argentine proto-monastery and breeding station, Los Laureles, for something less than $50,000—Brother Leo found frequent cause to absent himself from Fond Canot.

According to his passport, he flew to New Orleans in August of 1966, about six weeks after putting on his flour sack habit. In November he visited Argentina, reentering the United States on the twenty-second of the month. In March of 1967, and again in August and September, he returned to Argentina (with a side trip to attend part of the trial in Sarita, as Judge Edwards recalls; then he came back to the United States in November, as he had the year before.

December 1967 and early January 1968 he spent in Chile and Argentina. On June 11, 1968, he flew to New York. His next stop was Argentina; then it was back to the United States and again to Argentina. He wound up 1968 in Miami, waiting for a plane back to Martinique. All told, from July 1966 until December 1968, Brother Leo spent at least a third of his time anywhere else but at his swampy hermitage. "He's peripatetic, that's what I'd call him," says Peter Grace.

Leo's attention began to stray, too. As a lay brother at Our Lady of the Valley, in Rhode Island, and through his years of travel on behalf of his order, the monk's reading diet had been more or less restricted to Scripture and spiritual books, including biographies of saints. While he kept up with his devotional reading, in his new life as a dissociated Trappist, Leo also began to digest novels like Pasternak's *Dr. Zhivago,* which Leo admired, and psychological literature; he read and recommended to his friends Erich Fromm's *The Art of Loving.*

Psychology in general interested him, as did Far Eastern philosophy and religions (notably Buddhism) and the disputed practice of graphoanalysis, the study of handwriting for clues to personality. Leo had had his own handwriting analyzed by a "Zytron" computer at the 1964 world's fair in New York. The punch card he retained for several years listed 150 possible "characteristics revealed by your signature." Leo fit 25 of them, from "frank" to "energetic," "shrewd," "proud," and "purposeful." The machine did not find him "patient," "tolerant," "practical," or "lazy." It did suggest he had "executive ability."

Brother Leo's special fascination, however, one that he discussed in detail in letters to Rachel Verstraeten and her sisters in Buenos Aires, was with Jungian depth psychology and its concepts of the collective unconscious, individuation, and the anima—the feminine side of man's nature that, according to Carl Jung, is a projected image of womanness that a boy first encounters incarnate in his mother. Leo explained in his letters that he began consciously to comprehend his anima while in Oregon at Our Lady of Guadalupe. He called her Helen. By 1971 the monk's immersion in Jung's ideas would draw him away from Martinique again to study the psychologist's thoughts at an institute in Switzerland.

The cost of the trip would be underwritten by Margie Grace, who, unlike her husband, felt no alienation from Brother Leo. Kenneth Oden remembers interviewing Margie Grace as a potential witness in the will contest. ''She told me,'' he recalls, ''something like, *'Well!* We just *love* Brother Leo.'* That attitude was not going to be useful in a case where the monk is accused of exercising Svengali-like influence on an older woman. I sure couldn't use her as a witness. I saw that right off. That sort of thing was just what I was trying to play down. I'm not surprised to hear that she kept donating to him.''

Grace, who was not told that his wife paid for Leo's trip to Switzerland, was himself still under siege in the will controversy that he blamed Leo for causing. Peter Grace's most faithful friend and confidant in the hierarchy, Cardinal Spellman, had died in 1967, and his nemesis, Archbishop Krol, had been elevated to the rank of cardinal in Philadelphia the same year. Grace's worst fears from the outset, a public trial, were realized, too. As he predicted in his chart, Judge Edwards decided that Peter Grace, the much-decorated, image-conscious lay champion of the Catholic church, had abetted a shameful conspiracy to control the mind of a vulnerable old lady.

The negative publicity was a sharp embarrassment

for the industrialist, who didn't always enjoy a favorable business press but who had never before had his character impugned, even indirectly. Even when the stories outlining his role in the scandal were cautiously written, as was a three-column piece in the March 11, 1968, issue of *Newsweek*, there was the stain of association, amplified by a photograph of him placed next to one of Sarita and also a shot of Brother Leo taken at Martinique, depicting the blank-faced monk, clothed in a light pajama-like outfit, standing with his right hand resting on a shovel.

Nor did Peter Grace's troubles subside after Judge Edwards's verdict. He remained one of the prime targets in Leo's still-pending (if dormant) bill of review. And Frank Nesbitt wasn't through with him, either. After discovering Grace's detailed correspondence in Cardinal Spellman's files and placing the letters into evidence, the Turcottes' lawyer still wanted Peter Grace's deposition for the next trial, to begin in 1970 before Judge W. R. Blalock in the central jury room of the Nueces County courthouse, in Corpus Christi. That March, Nesbitt, along with Pat Horkin, Ken Oden, Denman Moody, Burch Downman (the lawyer for Andy Turcotte and other members of the Turcotte family not contesting the entire 1960 will, as Frank Nesbitt's clients were), Eldon Dyer (Walter Groce's associate, there on behalf of Tom East), and Joe Day, filed into the Cahill, Gordon conference room to interrogate the corporation chairman.

Nesbitt had been to New York once before in connection with the case, in 1965, when his client Pat Turcotte had received a mysterious telephone call from an attorney in New York who claimed to represent unnamed principals in the case who could work out a solution for him. Much later, as Nesbitt recalls, he discovered that Dom Columban Hawkins was behind the initiative.

"He said, 'My client would like to talk to you, and we know that we can fix you and Tom East up.' Well, immediately I was suspicious because my clients hated Tom East, and Tom East and my clients both hated that New York crowd.

"And when we got up there, this lawyer had all the allegiances mixed up. He had to have heard it all from Dom Hawkins, who obviously had no more idea of who was who in this thing than the man in the moon. The ol' dom must have heard it all from Leo, who I imagined described everyone down here the way he wanted them, not the way they actually were. But Dom Hawkins apparently believed in Leo so strongly that he thought maybe he'd straighten this whole thing out.

"Anyway, Dom Hawkins or the fella who was supposed to talk for him never showed up. We hung around for a couple hours, and finally it was called off. So we went back to Texas."

Five years later, at about 9:30 A.M. on Monday, March 9, 1970, Nesbitt led the party of south Texas lawyers into the conference room at Cahill, Gordon, Reindel & Ohl, at 80 Pine Street, in lower Manhattan.

"Of course, they had impressive offices," he remembers. "Great big rooms, you know. And we were all sittin' around that conference table waitin' for Grace. All us country hicks.

"So the time came, and all of a sudden these two great big *tall* church-like doors opened wide and in comes Lawrence McKay, a *big* fella, and dark, yellin', 'Gentlemen! *Mister* Grace!'

"And every one of us jumped up like, 'Oh boy! Here's the president,' or something. Peter Grace strode in and sat down, and we just stood there a moment lookin' at each other, asking,' 'What the hell did we do that for?' Then we started laughin', you know. They didn't bring him in that way anymore."

Whereas he showed a genial tolerance toward

Brother Leo, Nesbitt didn't like J. Peter Grace. "I guess I thought he was just another big shot trying to impress us Texas hicks," he says. "Grace was one of the most overbearing individuals I ever met in my life." Yet the attorney found Peter Grace, in his way, as skillful at handling a deposition as the monk. "He was extremely sharp. Not that he was adept, like Leo, at avoiding questions. Grace would just tell you no."

Nesbitt had hoped to draw Peter Grace out about his undue-influence chart.

"That was a good chart, that one," Grace opined early on in the deposition.

"You prepared that yourself?" Nesbitt asked.

"Yes, I did," answered Grace. "I think it's terrific. That is one I'm proud of, that chart. I am looking forward to discussing it with you."

At this point Larry McKay interrupted. The New York lawyer had obtained a court order preventing any discussion of events subsequent to Mrs. East's death: damaging episodes like the name-calling fracas in Paris would not come to light. In particular McKay did not want any avoidable mention made of the undue-influence chart.

"Not at this time," he said.

"No?" Grace asked. "I say, I am looking forward to that day. I understand we may have a lot of fun with that."

"We may," replied Nesbitt, who never would get the chance to do so.

On the strength of the bill of review, and Leo's testimony, Nesbitt did know of the rift between Grace and Brother Leo. He tried to exploit it by asking the executive if he and his wife had named a son for the monk.

"His name is Christopher Gregory," Grace replied, "and I guess we named him Christopher and my wife wanted to add the Gregory. So I guess you would say he is named after him, although we have always called our son Christopher.''

Thereafter, Grace was a stone wall. When Nesbitt probed for reasons why the W. R. Grace travel department extended Sarita so many courtesies, Grace answered, "Let me explain to you, because you are a great lawyer but not a businessman. [It] was a service department to serve any friends of the firm or friends of the officers of the firm. . . . This was sort of a friendly thing. In other words, if I liked you and you might say to me, 'I'm going to South America, can I use the W. R. Grace & Company transportation department?—remember the song, 'If the madam likes you, the lessons are free'?—if I like you I say, 'Yes, call Bill Creamer and tell him to give you a nice trip, give you VIP treatment.' Yes, the transportation department was serving Mrs. East, along with other friends of the company.''

On the question of the apparent haste with which Grace's team assembled all the documents for Mrs. East to sign, he told Nesbitt that he was still smarting from the same query put to him by Pat Horkin in 1962. "I said, 'You ought to be ashamed of yourself, as a lawyer for a bishop, asking such an inflammatory question . . .' If he had been familiar with the need for money of the church, which had just gone down the drain every year that Mrs. East did not give her full capability, based on her taxable possibilities of using royalties, income, and foundations, [Horkin would have understood that this] was money taken out of the mouths of starving children. . . . Mrs. East wanted to help.

"When I am involved, I feel I have an obligation if somebody comes to me and says, 'How can I get more money to poor, starving priests who can't get out to their parishioners? They don't have money for a motor scooter?' And I say, 'See me next month, toots'?

"I think that is a sin. I have the power to show them how to get the money to the priest. We are sitting in great luxury. It looks like the Versailles Palace here. And we tell these poor people, 'Drop dead'? I will certainly move forward very rapidly to get money in the hands of any poor people who are only prevented from having that money by my ineptitude."

When confronted with Father Tiblier's memo of the December 1959 meeting at La Parra in which the priest wrote that the board of Sarita's foundation was to be made up of prelates, including her bishop, Grace reacted by calling the idea "nutty George," a term he had heard on a Bob Newhart comedy album. "I can't believe it was discussed without my making serious reservations as to the wisdom of such a thing," he said. "In the first place, she would limit the beneficiaries of the foundation to certain [ones] named as of that moment. The superiors of those beneficiaries would get together and fight over how much they would get, with the bishop refereeing. I don't recall that at all. It sounds so stupid I just don't believe it."

He returned to this argument at another point in the deposition, recounting how he later advised Sarita that to confer foundation membership on a reliable bishop or cardinal did not ensure that his successor would be equally suitable for the position. "We don't know who will come up in that job the next time," he explained, adding, "a good example is Philadelphia." Grace, at the time, was still angry with his treatment by the new cardinal of Philadelphia, John Krol.

The industrialist also swore he knew nothing of Sarita's account in the Grace Bank (opened by his assistant Tom Doyle, with $50 of Grace's money), or of Leo's power of attorney over it, or of the special instructions that canceled checks and statements be sent to Doyle's home address, until much later. "There would be no reason for me to know about it," he testified. "There was nothing unusual, people using the Grace Bank. There certainly was no big deal with me, as far as I was concerned. The money went in and out pretty fast. The Grace Bank probably lost money on it."

Grace stated that he was the "author of all of the financial conceptual thinking that was embraced in the will and the foundation" but that he had exercised no direct influence on Sarita's plans. "I only discussed tax aspects with Mrs. East," he said. Furthermore, he elaborated, "I purposely stayed away from personalities or any of that stuff. I did broad, conceptual thinking. I didn't think it was my business having anything to do with where she left the money, to whom, that sort of stuff. That is why I deeply resent these charges and these ten years of publicity about my alleged role in this matter. Utterly ridiculous! I just came in as a financial man, that is all."

Not quite. Nesbitt caught Grace in a straddle on the issue of his dealings with Jake Floyd. It would undercut Grace's credibility as Sarita's supposedly disinterested adviser to admit that covert warfare had been waged for command of her trust. But the industrialist also had to explain the necessity for his own active part in seeing to it that her new will and foundation papers were executed.

Without naming Floyd, he repeatedly described the quality of the attorney's advice to Mrs. East as "phony" and "baloney." Elsewhere in the questioning, however, he professed warm regard for Floyd. "Every dealing I had with Mr. Floyd I would have nothing to criticize," he said. "I had admiration for Mr. Floyd. He was an outstanding man, from what I could see, in his community. I had no trouble with him at all. He was a man whom I respected very much. I have no reason not to respect him today."

Grace then acted surprised to learn from Nesbitt that

Floyd had warned Sarita against the possible interim use of the industrialist's Serra Fund while she waited for an IRS ruling on the tax-exempt status of the Kenedy foundation, because she might never see her money again. "If," said Grace indignantly, "he was making statements like that, he was really a complete hypocrite, because he was writing me, 'Thank you so much for everything you have done. It was so nice of you. It was great to meet you.'

"I don't know if he did do this. I don't accuse him. . . . If he said this, it would be completely hypocritical."

But since Grace claimed respect for Floyd, and ignorance of his underhandedness, why had he felt it necessary to be on hand personally, with Lawrence McKay, for the signing of the new will and foundation?

"All right," Grace replied. "I come down there. I am president of a big corporation. I am well known throughout Latin America. I am providing a backdrop for any questions that may come up. I am there. I am sure there was confidence indicated. There was nothing Mr. Floyd could have raised. I had a number of discussions with Mr. Floyd during the meeting. He raised certain points. I would say, 'Just a minute, Mr. Floyd. Do you know this? Do you know that?' I mean, just in case Mr. Floyd was about to tell Mrs. East that Brother Leo was a complete nut, there are a couple guys there that might step on his toes, you know. Just in case he tried."

"Well, did Mr. Floyd attempt to do this in any respect?"

"No, he didn't. You never know what people . . . I have learned, you know, if I weigh 180 pounds, see, a lot of people who weigh 160 pounds don't start anything with me. But if I was 140 pounds, I would get the feeling that some of those people might, you know.''

"What would that have to do with Mr. Floyd?"

"Well, you never know what Mr. Floyd . . . Here he had been playing around with this idea for ten years. He had never made any progress on it. So he was probably a little embarrassed. So you never know what he might have in mind if there hadn't been big shots in the room. That is what I mean.''

Peter Grace's testimony directly contradicted Leo's twice. He indicated his firm understanding that the Trappists were to be beneficiaries of Sarita's foundation after her death; the monk insisted the order had no claim on any of the money. Grace also testified that Mrs. East's deathbed appointment of Leo as a co-member of the foundation—the position the monk said was permanent and placed him in full control of the foundation—was in fact a temporary move, *according to what Grace remembered hearing from Leo himself at the time*. Here was Grace's payback to Leo for trying to shove him and Father Peyton aside.

"Did Mrs. East discuss the appointment of Brother Leo as a member with you at any time prior to the time that it was prepared and signed?'' Nesbitt asked.

"Not that I recall,'' Grace answered.

"Did Brother Leo discuss the matter with you prior to the time it was signed, or Mr. McKay?''

"I don't think either of them did,'' said Grace.

"Were you aware that she was about to appoint someone as a member with her?''

"I am going to amend my answer,'' Grace announced. "I now recall, as you continue the questioning, that Brother Leo mentioned to me that Mrs. East wanted someone to assist her during her illness, so she wouldn't have as many papers to sign, that she wanted to appoint him to do this. So he did mention this to me; whether it was before or after, I don't remember.''

What papers were there for Mrs. East to sign? Nesbitt wanted to know. ''I haven't run across any formal actions taken by the foundation during this period of time,'' he said. ''I can't understand what official business was contemplated that would require somebody. I guess you can't help me with that?''

''I can't help you at all,'' said Grace, who, after having set Leo up, was more than ready to let suspicion fester. ''I would have to know a lot more than I know today to help you. The word 'require' wasn't used either. It might have been she felt more comfortable having someone who is also a member. I just don't know. I presume Brother Leo would have much better knowledge of this. Was he able to throw any light on this?''

''Frankly, Mr. Grace,'' Nesbitt replied, ''I don't recall at this date what he said.

''I haven't read his deposition,'' Grace added. ''So I don't know either. I would be interested in what his answer would be to that.''

Otherwise Peter Grace defended the monk's conduct, much as it might have galled him to do so. ''Mr. Grace,'' asked Joe Day, ''you describe Brother Leo as peripatetic and as a very friendly person. I wonder if you would agree with me that he is and was during this period prior to Mrs. East's death a particularly aggressive, personable person?''

''Well,'' Grace answered, ''there are two adjectives there. Aggressive?''

''Yes,'' said Day, ''how about that first?''

''We will leave 'personable' alone for the moment?''

''Yes.''

''He is aggressive.''

''Would you also say when he wants to be, or has

reason to be, that he also may be a very personable person?''

"I would call him personable at all times," Grace replied, despite his contrary experience with the monk. "Again, how do you define the word 'personable'? I assume someone who identifies with the other person and gives them the feeling he is interested in what they are interested in. He is interested in them, not impersonal toward them. I found him that way toward all people. Not just when he wants to be. I really feel that very strongly.''

"He is," asked Day, "the sort of person that can so relate to another person that they feel very, very close to him, right?''

"Very, very close to him? I say, he can so relate to another person so they feel he had a genuine interest in them.''

"Would you say that he is very persistent in the pursuit of his goals?''

"Yes.''

"And in that regard he can be very persuasive?''

"He is a persuasive individual.''

"Would you also describe him as an ambitious person?''

"No, I would not.''

"Ambitious in the pursuit of his goals," Day corrected himself. "Not personally.''

"I would not call him ambitious," Grace repeated. "For the reason that I have never seen him try to get anything for himself. There is a big difference here. I think this is one of the problems that confuses a lot of people here. I say this from many years of experience with him, long before he was working with Mrs. East.

"I have seen Brother Leo fly all night, or drive all night, or sit up all night to save a soul, some poor person in a hospital that nobody ever heard of. He is absolutely, completely self-sacrificing by way of meals, or sleep, or personal inconvenience to do something that he thinks ought to be done.''

"I will tell you what I was thinking about," Day went on. "I sat through some of his very long deposition, and after a few weeks I had the impression that Brother Leo in the back of his mind, maybe subconsciously, rather aspires to be a future saint. Would you have ever gotten that same impression? Saint Leo of South America, you know?''

"I don't think so, I really don't," Grace answered. "And I know him pretty well from that viewpoint. I find his appraisal of himself consistent with the attitude of most monks; that is, they feel that they are terrible sinners. If you say to the average monk, 'You are a good man. You don't drink. You don't smoke. You don't eat any meat. You never get out of the monastery. You are a great guy.'

"Gee whiz, no!" [he'd say]. "I am a sinner.''

The questioning of the magnate, with many interruptions so that he could see to his heavy business schedule, stretched for seventeen days and filled 610 pages of transcript. In the end, almost no new damage was done to Ken Oden's defense of the will and foundation—except for the entry of a number of exhibits Frank Nesbitt planned to use before Judge Blalock—and Denman Moody had an easy time of rounding off Grace's testimony.

The Houston lawyer asked if, given the same circumstances, he would help another person such as Sarita set up a Catholic foundation. This was just the softball Peter Grace had been waiting for a chance to hit.

"I may sound very conceited," he answered. "But I was sufficiently dedicated to my Catholicity and sufficiently concerned as to the needs of the church that I felt it was the least I could do. . . . Therefore, I thought I was doing something for her that very, very few, if anybody, else would do.

"And in answer to your question, I would do exactly the same thing if Mrs. East appeared on the scene, or if anybody else did, and wanted this kind of help. I see no difference [now], no change in either the need of the church for money or in the utter ridiculousness of people paying taxes with money that they can use to help the people they want to help with that money. I think that is ridiculous."

"Now, Mr. Grace," Moody continued. "When you gave this financial advice to Mrs. Sarita East, did you have any motive of personal gain to get any of her money or anything like that?"

"The only personal gain I had in mind, Mr. Moody, was to maybe save my soul, which is very important in the long run. But other than that, it was the same personal gain I have when I go to church in the morning, or stop in at church on my way home at night. I like to try to make up for all my deficiencies.

"We both had the same interest. She wanted to save her soul, and I wanted to save my soul. And the best way to save your soul is to think of God and your neighbor, and that means to help them. That was her interest."

"It has been alleged in this will-contest suit that you tried to gain possession and control of Mrs. East's estate," Moody stated, not adding that Brother Leo alleged a Grace power grab, too. "Is that true or false?"

"It is very humorous and untrue," Grace responded. "I must be the greatest salesman in the world if in a meeting in my home with all my children, my wife, Brother Leo, and Lady East, or in a meeting at the ranch with Father Tiblier, or meeting with lawyers in New York, or in the hotel in Texas and up in Maine—the maybe ten times I met Mrs. East—that I could get control of her, always surrounded. I had enough of a hard time getting one girl to marry me. It is such a ridiculous statement. I would feel a little complimented that anybody would think that I was that good.''

THIRTY
✦ ✦ ✦

Deal-Cutting

For all the accusation, acrimony, and scandal surrounding Sarita Kenedy East's relationship with Brother Leo and J. Peter Grace, nearly a decade after her death the ostensible reason for the litigation, the issue of right and wrong, had become moot. On the record, the two men were guilty; Judge Edwards had so ruled. But from the day of his decision forward, the only legal issue that would matter was the money; who would get it, and how much?

Brother Leo, a shadow presence in the litigation since his 1966 deposition, continued to contend, through Marshall Boykin, that the Kenedy Memorial Foundation belonged exclusively to him as keeper of the flame, Sarita's late-awakening desire that her estate should serve the poor of the world. J. Peter Grace had agreed to take $14.4 million (for his Serra Fund, renamed the Sarita K. East Foundation) when, and if, the lawsuits ceased.

The south Texans were divided, according to their contentions, into five major blocs: the bank and foundation (subsuming Elena Kenedy, Lee Lytton, and Tom East, although East remained as an independent litigant); Bishop Drury, still arguing the legality of the first codicil; the Oblate fathers, who were trying to regain their mineral royalty under the ten thousand acres they inherited; the "Mexican" heirs (joined by some members of the Turcotte family); and Frank Nesbitt's clients, Louis Edgar Turcotte's five sons.

None of these contestants, or their twenty-odd attorneys, were anywhere close to an accord as to how they would divide up the fortune wrested back from Leo and Grace. And the amount they were fighting over was staggering.

Oil and gas production was expanding at both of Mrs. East's ranches, and new discoveries were being made almost weekly. Within three years the Arab oil embargo would bump oil prices up 400 percent, leading to guesses that the ultimate total value of the mineral reserves under Kenedy land easily might exceed half a billion dollars. The Kenedy Memorial Foundation alone, being fed solely by royalties from Mrs. East's inter vivos gifts, had swelled to $30 million in assets by 1970, all on deposit at the Alice National Bank.

Ken Oden, as lead attorney for the bank, found himself in the same position that his old mentor Jake Floyd had been in when Brother Leo had first wandered onto his territory more than twenty years earlier. The object of all Ken Oden's efforts was to preserve and protect the bank's control of the Kenedy fortune. And, like Jake Floyd, Oden recognized the virtue of patience. A hasty conclusion to the will contest was the last thing Ken Oden wanted.

Jury selection for the second trial before Judge Blalock didn't begin until July 19, 1970, and then abruptly stopped two weeks later. At 3:30 P.M. on August 3, hurricane Celia blasted up from the Gulf of Mexico just east of downtown Corpus Christi. With winds clocked at 180 mph before the measuring instruments were blown away, Celia killed eleven Texans and caused an estimated $454 million in damage.

Metropolitan Corpus Christi took the brunt of the ferocious storm, but the plaintiffs' attorneys didn't believe the local destruction was so great as to justify a two-week recess in the trial. Before the first word of disputation, they had been given a glimpse of Ken Oden's strategy and a taste of how W. R. Blalock intended to conduct his courtroom. "I am absolutely certain," says Joe Day, "that the other side had him in their pocket."

Joe Day, Frank Nesbitt, and the rest of the plaintiffs' attorneys' perceived disadvantage in front of Judge Blalock was offset by a second, sound perception that a panel of peers in Corpus Christi, where Sarita was born, would agree with Judge Edwards's verdict. At least insofar as the charges of undue influence were concerned, there was little doubt that Leo and Peter Grace would be convicted again. Still, Ken Oden had the resources to sift carefully through the jury pool in search of the most favorable panel possible. The defense retained private investigators who produced dossiers on each member of the pool. During voir dire, the oral examination of potential jurors, the bank and foundation lawyers honed their questions from the investigative reports and identified those who were acceptable, as well as the persons they would dismiss before agreeing to a final twelve. It required another three weeks, until September 9, 1970, to finish the process.

Judge Blalock, an elderly, retired district court judge from Mission, a little town in the Rio Grande Valley, flew home for long weekends in the private plane of one of the defense attorneys, a neighbor. He kept the workdays short in court, too. Nine in the morning until four in the afternoon was as long as any trial day went, with frequent recesses, leisurely lunch hours, and an early-afternoon end of business each Friday.

Even after the case had ground into its third month, he gladly stopped proceedings so that one of the foundation lawyers could go to Austin to see his son sworn in as a member of the Texas State bar. Every holiday was observed; the Thanksgiving break lasted seven days and the Christmas break eighteen. Because of a juror's illness, and then an accident involving one of the attorneys, in January the court was in session for but a single day.

The snail's pace told on the jury, three members of which were openly complaining of the tedium by the turn of the year. But what infuriated the plaintiffs' attorneys was not so much the stalling as the content of the proceedings. Joe Day and Frank Nesbitt concluded from the start that Oden was slowing the case in the hope of wearing them down as he searched for a break or a misstep. They were enraged, however, to see that Oden's willing confederate in this strategy was none other than one of their own, William Wright. Bill Wright and his group, including Johnny Fitzgibbon, had at last come to see that an accommodation with Oden was all that might rescue them from Nesbitt's taking everything.

The Laredo attorney, by virtue of having originally filed Cause 348 in July of 1962, was the first lawyer to present evidence. After him, each of the succeeding intervenors would offer his case in turn until it came to Nesbitt and then Day, the last of those to enter the case—and the two lawyers who had developed most of it.

"I watched 'em," remembers Frank Nesbitt. "Oden and Wright. I don't know what kind of arrangement they had, but I do know that they sat across from one another. Bill would look up at Oden and ask him what page to turn to in a deposition he was reading, and then he'd offer that as evidence. This went on day after day. It was obvious that Kenneth Oden was tellin' him what to put on."

Bill Wright is deceased. But his associate, Johnny Fitzgibbon, confirms that the team representing the Mexican heirs had come to understand that Frank Nesbitt was a threat to them. "I wouldn't say we got together [with Oden]," Fitzgibbon says with a laugh. "We were putting on evidence, and they had reason to object to it. It was part of the ploy that we had to do to iron out a settlement."

After a while, says Joe Day, "we were jumping up and objecting to Wright's evidence. It was like he was putting on the defense case. He didn't go near the letters or Peter Grace's chart. It was all junk. It got so that the rest of us lawyers would have serious sessions each day after trial, trying to figure out what to do about it." At one point, several of the plaintiffs' attorneys were considering an open accusation of unprofessional conduct against Bill Wright.

Wright and his team didn't conclude their presentation until March of 1971, almost eight months from the day jury selection began. They left Frank Nesbitt to face a jury both bored and mutinous, and a trial record so convoluted that to appeal the case, if necessary, would strain a battery of lawyers to assemble a coherent attack on it in the short time allotted for such motions.

Nesbitt's case was nonetheless salvageable, and he furthermore appeared to have dodged the issue of his clients' right to come to court at all. According to Texas law, any challenge had to come in the form of a pretrial motion for a hearing, to be conducted before the actual trial began. Since no one had properly raised the question, Frank Nesbitt felt sure that he could go on with his evidence. He was wrong.

In early March, Ken Oden offered three motions,

one to dismiss Brother Leo (entered as a party to 348 by Marshall Boykin), one to knock out Bishop Drury, and a third to estop the Turcottes for lack of standing. Judge Blalock accepted the motions and granted all three. "That slovenly old bastard!" says Nesbitt. "He didn't give a damn what the law was. He just went with 'em. He's the only one I really hated comin' out of that thing."

Nesbitt instantly scrambled to the Texas Supreme Court in pursuit of a writ of mandamus to reinstall him in the suit. Meanwhile, Blalock adjourned the trial to give Ken Oden time to negotiate settlement terms with his remaining adversaries. Everyone fell into line behind Bill Wright except Joe Day. "When Nesbitt's neck went, it just scared the shit out of all of 'em," he says. "I was the only one left who could try the thing."

Day, in fact, believed himself in a position to hold out. He had been certain for some time that even if Nesbitt had been able to make his case, the jury would have trouble agreeing with his position—that is, to jettison the entire 1960 will in favor of the 1948 document. "You see," he explains, "Nesbitt would have disqualified all those cowboys [the dozens of vaqueros whose debts were forgiven under the 1960 will and others who were given their houses under it] and all those relatives of Mrs. East and all the other people who worked on the ranch. The jury would have been sympathetic toward them and to all the charities in Corpus Christi who would lose out of Nesbitt won. If the Turcottes won, they and the Easts were the only winners."

So Joe Day dug in his heels. "I told 'em what I would take," he says. "They had a bullshit story about how the estate tax had built up so that if they gave me what I was asking for there wouldn't be anything to give the foundation at all. That there would be more estate tax than they could pay.''

In the end, two of the other plaintiffs' attorneys conceded parts of their prospective shares in the settlement to Joe Day and his clients, which satisfied him. With Frank Nesbitt having lost his bid for a mandamus writ (and now reconciled to an ordeal in the appeals courts), the settlement was agreed to on June 1, 1971. The Oblate fathers accepted partial restoration of the mineral royalty beneath their ten thousand acres in exchange for surface rights to nine thousand of them. These became the Kenedy foundation's property. The rest of the plaintiffs and their lawyers, 135 people in all, split a royalty under thirteen thousand acres of La Parra, the same parcel of land that the bishop of Corpus Christi would have inherited had the 1948 will stood.

The exact shares were determined by the degree of each contestant's blood kinship to Sarita. Raúl Trevino, one of Wright's clients, whose distinction it was to be the lead plaintiff (and thus have his name carried on each pleading and judgment and every other piece of paper generated in the nine-year-long case), received .061 percent of the settlement, which was then estimated to be worth $10 million or more. This meant, at the time, that Trevino could look forward to about $61,000 in oil royalty payments over the coming years, which turned out to be an accurate forecast. The 13,000-acre tract is still producing oil and gas, and the litigants' share of its revenues, if put on the market today, might fetch anywhere from an additional $2 million to as much as $20 million.

Burch Downman's Turcotte clients fared much better than did anyone else's. The least amount any of them received was .625 percent; together with their attorney, they were granted a full quarter of the royalty income, or least $2.5 million. Tom East, Jr., who was not a blood relative of Sarita's and therefore, technically, should not have received anything under the terms of the settlement, did so anyway. Along with his brother and sister, East was given a 2.5 percent interest. Downman was the highest-paid of the lawyers. He received 5 percent. Bill Wright took 2.77 percent, as did his associate, John Fitzgibbon. Joe Day was awarded a 3.337 percent share.

A *Corpus Christi Caller* headline writer captured the raw essence of what had happened in Blalock's court. "Deal Reached in East Will," the paper reported in its June 2, 1971, editions. "Heirs to Get Millions in Oil, Gas Royalties." The judge, however, tried to paint a soothing portrait for the jurors, who correctly felt that the many months of droning testimony had been a complete waste of their time. "You have become part of our judicial family," he told them. "You were always here ready to determine the facts if the lawyers did not settle their differences."

To the attorneys standing before him, Blalock was expansive. "Possibly," he said, "you will be able to tell your grandchildren that you had a part in what probably was the most important civil case ever tried in this state. I am going to miss you all. I have never known a group of lawyers who conducted themselves with more respect, more sincerely, and more cooperatively."

Blalock's remarks, of course, were not directed toward the absent Frank Nesbitt, who had received nothing except the wrath of his clients and the marathon challenge of trying to reverse his ouster from the case in the Texas appeals courts. Until that process was complete, and the will-case settlement made legally final, the divided royalty income would continue to accrue, in escrow, where all the money always went, into the Alice National Bank. So, too, would the 1964 settlement pend, as well as Brother Leo's bill of review to undo it. Peter Grace would have to continue waiting for his $14.4 million, and the burgeoning treasury of the Kenedy Memorial Foundation would burgeon on, unavailable for distribution to the poor or anyone else for years to come.

Ken Oden had done his job well.

THIRTY-ONE

✝ ✝ ✝

A Goat Spurned

On July 19, 1970, the day Judge Blalock gaveled the will contest into session, Brother Leo was half a world away from Corpus Christi in Darjeeling, India, at the foot of the Himalayas, discussing Buddhism with the younger brother of the Dalai Lama, the exiled Buddhist theocrat of Tibet. The monk had begun an Asian pilgrimage two weeks earlier in the Holy Land, where Leo, with his broadening view of spirituality, had accepted the gift of a beaten-silver Star of David, which he proudly attached to the scapular he wore beneath his travel mufti. "I love the Jews!" he exulted in a description of his journeys.

He visited Cana, Mt. Carmel, Jericho, and the Sea of Galilee; then he went south by bus into the Sinai before flying farther eastward to Delhi, India, where he made an homage to Mohandas Gandhi's memorial. Thence north to Kashmir, south to Calcutta, north again into the Himalayas, and finally westward to Damascus and Beirut, where he caught a plane to Zurich for a visit with Dr. Yolanda Jacobi, from whom he would later take his instruction in Jungian psychology.

On Wednesday, July 29, the monk was in Washington, D.C., where he conferred with the counsel William R. Joyce. The purpose of the call was to discuss how, if possible, Joyce together with one of Leo's many financial backers, Mel Budish of Worcester, Massachusetts, might recoup part of their investments in the monk's legal battles. Leo owed Budish outright; Bill Joyce had never been paid for any of his work. He promised Joyce he would have Marshall Boykin enter his name in the will-case record to protect Joyce should any money become available in a settlement. Leo promptly forgot to do so, leaving Bill Joyce to ask Sissy Farenthold directly for the favor. It was a slim hope in any event. Bill Joyce says he has never been paid for any of his help to Leo. Neither has Sissy Farenthold.

Yet Brother Leo has never lacked for funds when he has needed them. "He knows where to go for money," says Francis Verstraeten, Jr. "People give him things. For instance, for my wedding in 1968 he gave me a Hertz car rent credit card from some company in Massachusetts and told me I could use it whenever I wanted. 'Just don't go crazy,' he said.

"Everyone who knows him helps him. Not always in incredible amounts. But ten dollars, thirty dollars. An airplane ticket. A suit. He knows he can have zero in his pocket and still get whatever he wants or needs."

In early August of 1970 Leo jetted south to Argentina to visit the Verstraetens and to consult with Francis Verstraeten on the construction of a new hermitage for the monk, a cell Verstraeten offered to design and build on property he owned near the Argentine summer resort city of Córdoba. Verstraeten had been appalled at the conditions at Fond Canot, on Martinique, and hoped to make his friend Leo more comfortable as he pursued his solitary life and settled down, as Leo said he was going to, to work on a commentary on the life of St. John of the Cross.

Leo's subsequent letters to Francis Verstraeten, written from various points in the United States and from Martinique before he left in the spring of 1971 for Switzerland, were composed in a chatty, earnest voice, brief (for Leo), full of news as well as gentle exhortations that Verstraeten amend his character faults (Leo thought his friend too dictatorial toward his family, in the Latin stereotype), and sprinkled with suggestions for the building of the new hermitage. He wanted the structure simple, and inexpensively made.

But to Rachel Verstraeten—another "Carissime," like his mother and Sarita and many of the women Leo wrote to—he typed long, intimately worded messages, laced with mysticism, spiritual advice, and homiletic lectures that he encouraged Mrs. Verstraeten to reflect upon.

"My mother," says Francis Verstraeten, Jr., a stockbroker in Buenos Aires, "is a very provincial woman, like Sarita was. She is also very spiritual."

Leo credited Rachel Verstraeten for introducing him to "Helen." Apropos his Jungian researches, he sent her a letter in late November of 1970, quoting to her at length from *The Way of Individuation*, recently published by Dr. Jacobi in Switzerland. Specifically, it was a dream described by Jacobi that the monk wished to share.

The reverie, as Leo transcribed it verbatim for Mrs. Verstraeten, begins with the dreamer, a woman, bound on her back to the revolving parquet floor in an empty twelve-sided room, the walls and ceiling of which are lined with mirrors. The floor spins more rapidly, and the dreamer's clothes fall away. Then she finds herself naked, still on her back, in a freshly plowed field with her lover sitting next to her. They begin to mate, but are transformed in the act; she becomes one with the earth beneath her, and he melts as if to become part of the sky. "Thus," wrote Dr. Jacobi, "they celebrated the marriage of heaven and earth, the union of the masculine and feminine principles."

Leo spent six weeks with Dr. Jacobi in Zurich and

then came to Córdoba in the summer of 1971 to claim
his new hermitage. "It was really a wonderful place,
a very elegant hermitage," recalls Sylvia Sola Claret,
a Russian-German widow and friend of the Verstraetens, who owned a holiday retreat in Córdoba. She
remembers the handsome white altar Francis built according to Leo's specifications, the cell's library with
a built-in desk, and the monk's marble-floored
kitchen—"Out of this world!' as she describes it.

Sylvia Sola Claret also remembers how impressed
she was, at first, by Brother Leo. "He was a very
tender person," she says. "I felt he was really interested in me. I liked him personally very much. Very
charming."

She often spoke with the monk about the church but
never in the context of his own troubles. "He thought
Rome was out of touch," she recalls, "that they should
take measures to come to terms with modern life, and
that sort of thing. He was very much against the Curia,
and once he really got going against Pope Paul VI.
And the hierarchy! He was *absolutely* against it. He
thought it was something terrible."

Mrs. Claret pauses. "You could talk to Brother Leo
about anything, really," she goes on. "Brother Leo is
a very pleasant and agreeable man, unless you ask him
to take care of your goat."

The goat incident shocked Sylvia Sola Claret. One
Christmas, which she always spent in Córdoba, she
was given a caramel-colored goat, a gift meant for her
dinner table. "But I couldn't possibly eat it," she says.
"It was like a little pet. My dog started protecting it.
It quickly became part of the family—and it was growing."

March arrived, the beginning of the rainy Argentine
autumn, and Sylvia Claret prepared to return to her
apartment in Buenos Aires. "So I went to see Brother
Leo, considering him to be a good man. I'd never

asked a favor of him. And I said, 'Brother Leo, could you please look after my little goat for me?'

"And he said no.

" 'How can you say no?' I asked.

" 'Because,' he said, 'I must not have any senti-mental attachments. I must write my book.'

"I was very upset. I just couldn't understand it.''

She later went to the monk with a second question, which occasioned another unsettling response. Mrs. Claret, a Catholic, was considering marrying a di-vorced man.

"Before I decided on that step,'' she says, "I went to see Brother Leo because, as I told you, you could talk to him. And I said, 'Brother Leo, what do you think I should do?'

"He said, 'You can't marry, it's impossible. He's a divorced person. That's out of the question. Why can't you just love him?'

" 'What do you mean by that?' I asked.

" 'No sex. Just love. Love is God. Love is the world. No sex at all.'

"I said, 'Well, Brother Leo, maybe you can do that, but I'm afraid that isn't a possibility in a normal life.' He surprised me, though. Wasn't that a sort of funny thing for him to say?''

Francis Verstraeten, Sr., was for twelve years one of Leo's closest friends and admirers and a key ally in the monk's successful campaign to deny the Trappists control of Los Laureles. In 1963 Verstraeten helped engineer the dismissal of Los Laureles board mem-bers—including Dr. Cosme Beccar-Varella and J. Pe-ter Grace—who were sympathetic to Dom Keating. He later assisted Leo in disposing of Sarita's property at Entre Ríos. But by 1971 Verstraeten was beginning to puzzle, unhappily, over what he thought was the monk's meddlesome interest in Mrs. Verstraeten. Francis was displeased by the six framed photographs of Leo that his wife had hung in their bedroom. And though he acknowledges, without elaboration, that there were other strains on his marriage, he blames Leo for exacerbating the situation.

Another point of irritation between Francis and the monk was the hermitage. Leo bridled when Verstraeten tried to add a guest bedroom beneath it, a place for Francis and Rachel to stay when they came to visit the monk. Harsh words were exchanged over a fence Verstraeten wished to construct at one end of the property, and there were recriminations over the noise and distractions of construction, which Leo said interfered with his solitude.

But the underlying issue between them was Rachel, and it first came to a confrontation in early 1972. One day in February, as Mrs. Verstraeten was about to board a plane for the short flight back to Buenos Aires, she was stricken with severe abdominal pains. Leo, who was taking her to the airport in Córdoba, at first suspected an ulcer and then learned from Rachel that she sometimes suffered debilitating menstrual cramps. On his advice, and against her husband's wishes, she postponed her flight in order to rest.

Francis Verstraeten flew up from Buenos Aires the next day to bring his wife home, deeply angered by Leo's presumption, as he saw it, and further upset that although Rachel's pain was temporary it could have been very serious, requiring the superior medical attention she might have received in Buenos Aires had Leo allowed her to depart.

In a letter dated February 12, 1970, two days after the incident, Verstraeten vented his anger. "First of all," he wrote,

> I am very sorry indeed that I lost my temper, but frankly you ought to know by now that I strongly resent [interference] by anyone whomsoever in matters

pertaining exclusively to my wife and me. If, as her husband, I decided it was best to travel 1,000 miles to fetch her, because her health was not what it ought to be, no one has any right whatsoever to interfere in the matter, specially if unasked. Furthermore, I do not believe you are qualified to give a medical opinion of her condition, and even less to talk about her menstrual cycle. I am sorry, but you are way off side there. As you must understand once and for all, Rachel is, today at least, still my wife, and as such I am the only person responsible for her.

Further down in the typed note, Verstraeten moved his complaint from the specific to the general:

If your understanding of our friendship is that you [are] to run my life and my home—I realize fully it is done "ad maiorem Dei gratiae"—you can keep it. I want no part of it. After reading Freud, Jung, Frankl etc. . . . you should realize people are to be accepted as they are. Why do you insist on converting everyone, and trying to change everyone? Maybe you have a special pattern all your own which would explain somehow what happened with Peter [Grace], Pierre [Jacomet], and Harry [Gibbons]. You can probably add me to the list if you care to.

Francis and Rachel Verstraeten's marriage did not mend; in 1976 they were finally separated (divorce was then not legal in Argentina). Francis Verstraeten believes—and Leo adamantly denies—that in this period the monk induced Mrs. Verstraeten to withdraw more than half a million dollars from an account, originally set up for Francis's father in a Bermuda bank, to help defray Leo's legal expenses.

The squabbling over the hermitage lasted for several years, too. At one juncture, Verstraeten sought access to Leo's water supply for his own, quite grand summer villa that he built nearby. The monk refused to consider the request unless Verstraeten returned to him a pair of .38 revolvers, weapons he claimed that he and Sarita had exchanged as gifts long ago. By 1977 Leo had deserted, and sold, the hermitage.

"I cannot help but smile," Verstraeten wrote Leo in a bitter parting letter, "when I remember reading TIME's article about you, and I asked you what 'Svengali' meant? Really, that reporter was a pretty sharp potato. From now on, I leave you in complete control of your 'experiment,' Rachel, your Pygmalion No.? I admit freely you have won, you are probably the better man. Frankly, I can say without any sort of mental reserve, 'I'm sorry I ever met you, Brother,' as maybe a few others have said in the past."

Several of the Verstraetens' eight children took sides for or against Brother Leo and their father, painful family divisions that persist to this day. But their eldest son, Francis, Jr., now forty-four, who was a close observer of Leo's whole history with his parents, has mixed feelings toward the monk. "I wouldn't be so strong as to say Brother Leo stole money from my father [who actively considered murdering Leo]," explains Francis, Jr. "And I don't believe Brother Leo is evil. He is wrong-minded. My father is a very drastic person. He hates or loves, never in the middle. So now he's angry with Brother Leo with just reason, because he was hurt."

He adds, "Brother Leo has always been strange to me. I don't know what he gets out of what he does. He is a very funny mixture of Rasputin and the pope. I don't know. He's a strange mixture. He's transparent, and he's black. He's ingenuous, and he's complicated. He's kind, and he's bad. He has all these personalities."

Although it has been more than ten years since he

last saw the monk, Francis, Sr., still cannot bring himself to even this equivocal view of his former friend. In 1987 he flew to Texas to inform attorneys there of what he knew about Leo, and sat for an informal, videotaped statement. "I believe Brother Leo's a very dangerous man," the elder Verstraeten said into the camera. "And I would go out of my way to see that he does as little damage as possible to others."

THIRTY-TWO

✛ ✛ ✛

Laughlin's Verdict

Throughout most of the 1970s Brother Leo was seldom seen and nearly forgotten in south Texas, where the prime focus of attention was Frank Nesbitt's battles up and down and in and out of the appeals courts. Nesbitt did not enjoy the process of trying to get the Turcotte brothers reinstated as legitimate will-case plaintiffs. He had been in litigation as their attorney—without compensation, except for expenses—since 1963 and would have preferred that his truculent clients settled with Ken Oden when they had the chance. But since the five Turcottes would at no time consider a settlement, Nesbitt had no choice but to keep pursuing the increasingly unlikely chance that somewhere in the Texas court system he would be given the opportunity to lay out his compendious case against Brother Leo and J. Peter Grace.

Ironically, Frank Nesbitt wanted to give Brother Leo what the monk had been asking for since 1966 in his bill of review, a full hearing on the charges against him as originally contained in Lee Lytton's 1961 lawsuit, Cause 12071. It remained the consensus wisdom that any Texas jury, once it heard the evidence against Leo and Peter Grace and read the monk's letters to Mrs. East, would easily be persuaded that a fraud had been committed. However, once Judge Blalock accepted the will-case settlement—Cause 348—there no longer was any interest in Texas in adjudicating the monk's guilt or innocence. Everyone, except for Frank Nesbitt and Leo himself, had too much to lose if one or both of the settlements were upset.

Nesbitt suffered no illusions about his prospects for success in the Texas appeals courts. He warned the Turcottes, he says, that if they did not settle before the case went up on appeal, they would certainly lose everything no matter how strong, or well argued, their evidence was. "After that ol' bastard Blalock gutted me," the attorney explains, "I knew what all the judges upstairs would think and what our opponents would tell 'em. My clients' reputation was going to hurt us, because they were so tough. And those judges were going to say, 'Jesus Christ! It's all agreed on and settled out except for this bunch of bastards. Isn't there some way we can get rid of Nesbitt?' "

Not without a fight.

For what it was worth, Nesbitt firmly believed that he had the law on his side, an assumption ratified on September 24, 1973, by a unanimous vote of a three-judge court of civil appeals, sitting in Corpus Christi. The judges ruled that a hearing must be held on the matter of the Turcottes' legal standing to sue and remanded the case to district court. Two years later Judge Joe Wade in Beeville, near San Antonio, listened to three weeks of argument and then decided that the Turcottes did not have standing.

The Texas Supreme Court refused Nesbitt's application for a writ of error, but the court of civil appeals reversed Judge Wade in 1976, agreeing with him that Louis Edgar Turcotte's acceptance of his inheritance did estop his family from challenging the will, but also holding that the share of interest Turcotte's sons purchased from the Putegnats was completely legal, and gave them standing to sue. Bill Wright, on behalf of his "Mexican heirs," appealed this decision back up to the Texas Supreme Court (which would be the last court of appeal; the federal judiciary rarely will take up probate cases, which are considered local matters), where the question rested for another two years.

If the supreme court judges (who are elected officials in Texas) required added incentive to finally dispose of the Turcotte challenge, they might have borne in mind a $7.5 million grant that had been announced for St. Mary's University Law School, in San Antonio, by the Kenedy Memorial Foundation once it was free to begin making donations. The huge gift, at first glance, appeared to have been a blatant sop; several of the judges were St. Mary's graduates, and the newest member of the court, Charles Barrow of San Antonio—now dean of Baylor University Law School, in Waco—was a close friend of the university president.

According to Lee Lytton's personal friend (and later attorney) Davis Grant, however, the gift was long planned and had nothing to do with the Kenedy foundation's hopes that Frank Nesbitt would finally be muzzled. The St. Mary's Law School dean, claims Grant, had cultivated both Elena and Sarita, hoping for just such a gift someday. Lee Lytton had proposed the donation, says Grant, because he felt that it was something Mrs. East would have wished done.

Nevertheless, the donation was contingent upon Frank Nesbitt and the Turcotte boys being disposed of as contenders for the Kenedy estate. While Charles Barrow was still a district judge, Nesbitt says, "he was runnin' down this lawsuit something terrible. How it was awful we were holding up that money, which we were, all right." On March 15, 1978, when the supreme court ruling came down, Justice Barrow was its author.

"I've known Charlie for years and years," says Nesbitt. "We used to be pretty good friends back when we were young. And I knew his father real well. Ol' man Barrow was on the court of civil appeals, and he once wrote an opinion in my favor that sure gutted the other side in a big case. But ol' Charlie evened it up."

Justice Barrow, writing for the majority, affirmed the court of civil appeals opinion that Louis Edgar Turcotte's acceptance of his inheritance estopped his sons from suing as interested heirs, pointing out in his decision that Louis Edgar, Sr., had received about $1.3 million in property and income under the 1960 will and that his family since his death had realized almost $1 million more.

He had a lot more trouble with the Turcottes' purchase of interest from Robert Putegnat and Putegnat's sister, Mrs. Walker. The judge admitted that he couldn't find any Texas case law that directly addressed the issue. This left Barrow in the fuzzy realm of equity, forcing him to rule, in essence, on the basis of what seemed right, whether or not he had the law to buttress his decision. He noted that the Turcottes' pro rata share of the Putegnats' award under the 1971 settlement was negligible; for $4,400 Pat Turcotte's return was about $400. "We conclude," he wrote,

> that it would be inequitable and unjust to allow [the Turcottes] to assert standing as interested parties by virtue of the minute interests acquired through the assignments purchased for the purpose of defeating the will under which their father elected to take [his inheritance]. Furthermore, to permit standing under such circumstances is against public policy in that it would breed litigation and deprive the real parties at interest of their right to compromise and settle their controversies.
>
> Therefore, the court of civil appeals erred in holding [that the Turcottes] are entitled to contest the 1960 will. The judgment of the court of civil appeals is

reversed and the judgment of the trial court is affirmed.

An incredulous dissent was written by Justice Jack Pope, for himself and Justice T. C. Chadick. "The majority," noted Pope in his opening paragraph, "recognizes that [the Putegnats] had an interest and standing, but in some mysterious manner, a part of their interest and standing vanished by their assignment to the Turcottes."

"In other words," the judge wrote, "[the Turcottes] lawfully bought the interests . . . and the majority holds the lawfulness of the purchase. We thus have the situation in which [the Turcottes] bought an unestopped interest; however, this court denied them the right to assert that unestopped interest."

Pope then went beyond the narrow point of estoppal to lay bare the larger question, "I," he said, "would permit [Nesbitt] to make [his] proof about the testamentary capacity of Mrs. East and on the issues of fraud, undue influence, and duress. That issue will now never be determined."

"And that," says Frank Nesbitt, "was that. Period. After fifteen years, my best years as a lawyer, they just gutted me. They didn't have a damn bit of law on their side, and they knew it. About a year later, I ran into Charlie Barrow at one of those big political barbecues they have every year over in Beeville. He said, 'Frank, I want to talk to you.' And I said, 'Charlie, you don't have to talk to me about anything.' I just waved at him. That's the last time I ever talked to Charlie."

"Ruling," declared the *Corpus Christi Caller* headline on Thursday, March 16, 1978, "may be final word in fight over East will." Indeed, Nesbitt's debacle in the Texas Supreme Court seemed at first to have concluded all but the marginal issues in the long battle for control of the Kenedy fortune. The stage appeared set for the will-case plaintiffs to receive their $10 million settlement and for J. Peter Grace finally to be given his $14.4 million.

Most important, the Kenedy Memorial Foundation would at last emerge from under Judge C. W. Laughlin's seventeen-year-old injunction and could begin to distribute the $80 million of its money that had accumulated in the Alice National Bank since 1960. Henceforth, the foundation would directly manage these assets, along with Sarita's 200,000 acres of La Parra (worth $30 million) and the future oil income. Its ultimate value has been difficult to set because of rapidly changing oil prices, variable rates of production at La Parra and San Pablo, and imprecise knowledge of how much oil and gas remains beneath the two ranches. The foundation attorney Richard Hatch today guesses that at current prices the minerals under the foundation's lands are worth between $20 million and $200 million. Others estimate the oil and gas to be worth twice that amount.

As of 1978 the Kenedy foundation's five-member board remained as it had been since 1964 with the local bishop, now Thomas Drury, Elena Kenedy, Lee Lytton, Ken Oden, and Bruno Goldapp, who had become president of the Alice National Bank.

Everything was in readiness until Brother Leo, rising up like a phoenix from the ashes of his many past defeats, came again to Texas to rejoin the fray. The monk's attorney Marshall Boykin had hoped that the confrontation would come much sooner. Once his attempt to file his bill of review had forced Judge Laughlin and the higher Texas courts to pronounce, unambiguously, that the 1964 settlement was interlocutory (that is, still pending the outcome of the will contest), he was free to attack it with a motion to set it aside, which he filed in 1968.

Then, for a decade, Leo's attorney tried to have his motion set for trial by jury, a full judicial proceeding to decide if the 1964 settlement had been legitimately concluded. "Every time I went over to Alice," says Boykin, "the foundation attorney, Kenneth Oden, went in and said, 'Judge, we're not ready.' And Judge Laughlin said, 'Passed.' He wouldn't try it."

From the Alice bank's perspective, the judgment could have remained interlocutory forever; until it became final, Peter Grace could not receive his money, nor could the Kenedy foundation begin to function. The status quo sustained the bank in full control of all assets, on much of which it paid no interest.

On July 24, 1979, however—sixteen months after Frank Nesbitt's defeat in the state supreme court—the office of the Texas attorney general, Mark White, filed its own motion for entry of a final judgment in 12074. This action forced Judge Laughlin to schedule a hearing and thus the opportunity, Marshall Boykin thought, for his client to present his case.

The hearing was set for late September. Unbeknownst to Boykin, Kenneth Oden was now in favor of giving Leo his trial, certain that the monk's contentions would never sway a Texas jury. More important, Oden explains, he feared that if Leo didn't get his jury trial there would be later constitutional problems in the federal courts. "I knew it might come back to haunt us," he says. "I wasn't afraid of giving Leo his day in court; I knew he'd lose. There was no way, at any time, that he was going to win. But I thought he should have a jury listen to him. Legally, it was not a frivolous claim."

Yet according to the Alice lawyer, both Peter Grace's attorneys and the Texas attorney general wanted, in his phrase, "to shut down any testimony, try to take no depositions, and get rid of him strictly on a law motion without any factual determination.'' Oden acceded to this strategy.

With Judge Laughlin thus informed, the hearing proceeded. Boykin brought Leo to court on September 21, 1979, and put him on the stand for an hour. The monk declared that he did not agree with the settlement, and then his attorney asked that a trial date be set. When asked what happened next, Marshall Boykin shrugs. ''I wish I knew,'' he says. ''I thought we were having just a hearing. But Judge Laughlin said, ''The judgment is final, and I'm entering judgment on the basis of the interlocutory judgment. And that's final!' ''

With a rap of his gavel, Laughlin consigned Leo to the appeals courts and, just as Ken Oden had anticipated, opened for him a route into the federal courts. Until that lengthy tour through the higher courts was complete, there still would be no charity dispensed from the John G. & Marie Stella Memorial Foundation and no final disposition of Sarita's estate, both remaining in the care of the Alice National Bank.

THIRTY-THREE

✛ ✛ ✛

Awkward Questions

One of the curious witnesses to Leo's appearance in Judge Laughlin's courtroom was the twenty-five-year-old Amie Rodnick of the Texas attorney general's charitable-trust division. At that time, there were only three state lawyers assigned to charitable-trust work. One had just quit. Another, named Frances Frederick, was about to quit. The third was Amie Rodnick, who had passed her state bar examination the preceding May. "Here I was," she remembers. "I had been licensed for all of four months, and I was now the person who'd take over this obscure division of the attorney general's office. So the last thing that Francie did before she left was take me down to south Texas for this hearing."

Rodnick was a girl of seven when Sarita East died, and she knew little more about the litigation over the Kenedy fortune than any other young Texas lawyer who had read about the case in the papers over the years. The dominant character in these reports, of course, had always been Brother Leo, who now was in his early sixties. From what she had heard of the accusations against Leo, Amie Rodnick was looking forward to sizing him up for herself.

"I thought," she says, "he was going to look like Rasputin, with wild hair and crazy eyes." But Leo's turn on the witness stand disappointed her. "He was a pretty ordinary-looking guy."

Rodnick took a more personal—and professional—interest in Ken Oden, whose appearance did make an impression on her. The attorney, then fifty-five, suffers from various medical conditions that have required frequent stays in the hospital. As a result, Oden had by 1979 begun to lose much of the nervous élan that once had marked his courtroom demeanor.

"He's pretty amazing," says Rodnick. "Oden's color is very pale. He's got just a few strands of white hair on the top of his head. And he wears these thick, black horn-rimmed glasses. He just looks like a snake-oil salesman, in my opinion."

Rodnick discovered that Ken Oden's role in the Kenedy foundation's affairs was pretty amazing, too. She learned he was a member and secretary of the foundation board, as well as the foundation's attorney. He also separately represented the Alice National Bank (still executor of Sarita's estate, as well as foundation depository), Elena Kenedy, and Tom East, who had acquired a controlling interest in the Alice bank stock. "I didn't pay much attention to Brother Leo's case," she says, "but I recall being very concerned about all the different hats Mr. Oden was wearing. I thought this was pretty strange, that this guy obviously had a serious conflict of interest. But being very, very low on the totem pole at the attorney general's office, and being fairly inexperienced at that time, I was really not in a position to trigger some enormous investigation of this foundation and the Alice bank, or the estate executor, which was also the bank."

It would be two years before Amie Rodnick's attention was redirected to the workings of the Kenedy Memorial Foundation. She was in Houston, representing the state's interests in another will dispute, and came to know one of the lawyers in the case, Taylor Moore.

One day in his office, Moore mentioned to her that he had once been involved in the Kenedy foundation case. His client was Pat Horkin, who had been fired by Bishop Drury in 1974 and then engaged Taylor Moore to sue the Corpus Christi diocese for allegedly unpaid fees. In the course of settling Horkin's claims, Moore had learned a great deal about the Kenedy foundation from his client. According to what Moore told Rodnick, Horkin suspected the Alice bank was fleecing the foundation. "Horkin may not have been pure of motive," Rodnick recalls, "but he was absolutely convinced that something rotten was going on."

Pat Horkin was himself in ill health by this time and "kinda out of it," as Rodnick remembers; he died in 1988. But the substance of his long-held suspicions was contained in documents Taylor Moore made available to her. Moore encouraged Rodnick to initiate a state investigation, but she remained reluctant to do so, for two reasons.

It appeared to her from what she read that Bishop Drury, a member of the foundation, had been notably passive toward Ken Oden and the Alice bank, doing little to oppose their control over sixteen years. "I just assumed they were all crooks," she says, "and that the bishop was just out of it, or didn't care. Or there was something wrong with him, too. I was kinda cynical about the whole bunch. And my attitude was, 'Well, the Catholic church doesn't care, and they're getting 90 percent of the benefits from this foundation. Why should we care? If they're not willing to take the initiative and protect this foundation, should we really be spending taxpayers' money to do this?' I had problems with that."

Her second concern was with the low probability of a successful investigation if none of those connected with the foundation were willing to talk. "In a lot of these cases," she explains, "the only way you can do them is if you have someone on the inside who's going to cooperate.''

Nor did Rodnick as yet know exactly how the Alice bank and Ken Oden were manipulating the foundation, where Tom East fit into the equation, or, once the facts were known, whether she would find hard evidence of wrongdoing behind the outward look of impropriety. She did consult, without success, with the Internal Revenue Service and with the Dallas office of the U.S. Comptroller of the Currency. She even flew to Washington to meet with officials of the National Conference of Catholic Charities. "I said, 'If you people have any power to do anything, step in and do it.' They were very friendly and very nice. But they pretty much said to me, 'The bishop is lord over his own domain. We don't have a whole lot of control over it. Bishop Drury is the guy in charge there.' ''

Since repeated official requests for information from Ken Oden had also netted Rodnick nothing, the practical prospects for launching a full-scale investigation of the Kenedy foundation were glimmering by 1982 and might have died altogether but for a surprise telephone call she received from an Austin lawyer, Davis Grant. His name was familiar to Rodnick; Davis Grant was a former first assistant Texas attorney general and had served for twenty years as general counsel to the Texas State Bar Association. He was widely respected and influential in both legal and legislative circles in Austin. Grant was also, as he explained to Rodnick, a good friend and personal attorney to Judge Lee Lytton, Jr. And Davis Grant had a story to tell.

Now retired and in his mid-seventies, Grant remembers that his involvement with the Kenedy foundation began in early 1979 after a conversation with Judge Lytton. The judge explained that with great hesitation he had come to believe that the Kenedy foundation, of which he remained a member, was being run by Ken

Oden exclusively for the benefit of the Alice bank and Tom East, Jr., the bank's largest stockholder.

It had taken many years for the scales to fall from Lytton's eyes, but a spring 1979 meeting had, in Grant's phrase, "broken the camel's back with Judge Lytton." He told his attorney that Tom East was about to take over management of La Parra—not as a bank employee (the arrangement under which he had run the ranch since 1964) but as a lessee. Lytton knew at that time that similar leases—for grazing and hunting rights—were being let for between five and six dollars an acre in the region. But Tom East had bid only two dollars for grazing rights and proposed a total ban on hunting. Ken Oden had called the offer "generous" at the meeting.

Davis Grant and his client thought this arrangement would be tantamount to theft, and the two began to consider how they might prevent it. The first necessity was for Grant henceforth to accompany Lytton to all foundation meetings. When Lytton told Oden of this decision, says Grant, the foundation attorney replied, "Oh, no. We don't want anybody but members of the family at these meetings. This is confidential."

"When the judge told me that," Grant recalls, "I said, 'That's a bunch of bull. If you want me there, I'll be there.' "

Davis Grant would wait until 1982 before informing the attorney general's office of what he knew about the Kenedy foundation. Beginning at about the time of Brother Leo's 1979 testimony before Judge Laughlin, Grant attended every foundation meeting, as did attorneys who came each time with Bishop Drury. Together, they managed to force open bidding for the La Parra lease. One keenly interested party was the King Ranch. In 1980 the foundation received an offer of $5.65 an acre for grazing and hunting rights from the King Ranch. (Bob Kleberg had died six years before, and the King Ranch corporation chief executive was now John B. Armstrong, Tobin Armstrong's brother and nephew of the aged Major Tom Armstrong and his late wife, Henrietta, who died in 1969.)

Tom East countered with a bid of $5.50—this time for both grazing and hunting rights—but added that he would match any other offer. As Davis Grant recalls the meeting when the bids were opened, Ken Oden read them both and declared, "Well, it's obvious that Mr. East's bid is the better bid. And I move that we accept it." Bruno Goldapp and Elena Kenedy voted with the attorney in favor of East's offer. Bishop Drury abstained. Only Lee Lytton voted against it.

"I knew at that time that the attorney general was a necessary party," says Davis Grant. "So I decided that I would involve them, encourage them to come to the meetings." Beginning in 1982 Amie Rodnick and her new colleague in the charitable-trust division, Lance Beversdorf, began their own steady attendance at all meetings of the Kenedy Memorial Foundation.

"The first meeting we attended, Oden asked us to leave," says Rodnick. "We just sat there. So he went on and did business as usual. After a while, he seemed to accept the fact that we were going to show up for the meetings."

Each session was held in Elena Kenedy's parlor at a big table, at whose head Mrs. Kenedy, the president of the board of members, was seated. Ken Oden sat to her immediate left between her and Bruno Goldapp. Bishop Drury, vice-president of the foundation, always took the seat to Elena's right. Next to him and on down the table were Judge Lytton, Davis Grant, Amie Rodnick, and Lance Beversdorf. Once in a while, Bruno Goldapp's successor as president of the Alice bank, Jim Mayo, also attended the meetings.

Goldapp, eighty, who always voted with Ken Oden and Elena Kenedy, was no mystery to the outside attorneys. Rodnick remembers Goldapp arriving at the ranch, in Ken Oden's car, with a pocketful of cigars that he would offer to everyone. And then "Bruno would sit there, just kinda staring blankly straight ahead," she says. "He was always neatly dressed, but I noticed a lot of his suits had holes in them. One time, Oden passed him a waiver and gave him a pencil. He signed it and then tried to give it to me to sign! I handed it back to him, and he handed it to me again. I handed it back, and then he handed it to Lance! Bruno didn't know what to do with it."

Rodnick and Beversdorf soon discovered what Davis Grant also recognized about Bishop Drury, that he was a diffident prelate who usually kept his own counsel no matter what he thought of the proceedings. According to his far less reticent successor as bishop of Corpus Christi, Rene Gracida, Drury instinctively feared that to assert himself might necessarily entail litigation, a prospect the bishop constitutionally could not bring himself to face, partly out of respect to Mrs. Kenedy.

He did try on at least one occasion, says Gracida, to dilute Ken Oden's power by pushing for an expanded board. Drury had a candidate, an area Catholic dairyman named Dan Meaney, and privately secured Elena's support for his election. But the moment she voted yes, making a majority with Drury and Lytton, Oden interrupted the meeting. "I'm told," says Gracida, "that Kenneth Oden asked Mrs. Kenedy to leave the room with him. They were gone for fifteen or twenty minutes, and when they came back she changed her vote. No one knows what he told her."

Mrs. Kenedy, who turned ninety-two in 1981, struck Amie Rodnick as being every bit as mentally disengaged as Bruno Goldapp. Elena had endured an extended old age of gradual decline, although she had been alert and ambulatory enough into the late 1970s to remain as the National Weather Service's official Kenedy County rain-gauge keeper. Dutifully, after every rainfall she would check the exact amount of precipitation and note the amount in written reports to the service's regional center in Corpus Christi. But she suffered the first of several incapacitating strokes in 1978 and underwent cataract surgery, after which she was forced to wear extremely thick-lensed glasses.

"She was very small and frail," Amie Rodnick recalls. "She just kinda sunk into her wheelchair. You know when you're drivin' along, and you see some little old person who can barely peer over the edge of their dashboard? She was like that. She could barely peer over the edge of the table."

Rodnick remembers Elena Kenedy often nodding off and snoring through meetings. On at least one occasion Mrs. Kenedy affixed her signature to the tablecloth, not being able to distinguish it from the documents Ken Oden pushed under her hand. But Rodnick also had the impression that Oden deliberately conducted the meetings so as to lull Mrs. Kenedy into stupors of boredom.

"After one meeting she'd slept through, Lance and I went up to her and shook her hand, and she apologized for falling asleep. She said, 'I'm so sorry I fell asleep, but I thought that Mr. Oden was a television set. He just kept droning on and on and on like a television set.'"

Amie Rodnick found the fifth member of the foundation, Judge Lee Lytton, both personally agreeable and, as Frank Nesbitt had observed, worthy of respect. Lytton, she recalls, was a big man, "craggy-faced" in his mid-sixties, with a full head of snow-white hair and wearing horn-rim glasses. She appreciated that he had struggled with his decision to expose Ken Oden's behavior. "If there's a hero in this story," she says, "it's Judge Lytton."

Davis Grant explains his client's long reluctance to directly question Oden's management of the foundation's resources as a product of Lytton's strong friendship for the Alice attorney, as well as his respect for Oden's able handling of Brother Leo's repeated legal sorties and Frank Nesbitt's eleventh-hour defeat. Problems first arose, says Grant, when Lytton began to doubt Tom East's stewardship of La Parra.

Sarita, Lee Lytton knew, placed more emphasis on pride than on profit in the cattle business. She had striven hard to make La Parra a showplace operation. Lytton therefore objected when Tom East allowed La Parra's fences to rot away as he began to run the ranch cattle in huge pastures. East fired vaqueros, says Davis Grant, in favor of herding by helicopter. And, as Lytton saw it, La Parra was being overgrazed.

Furthermore, the judge had always believed that his aunt had truly intended for the bulk of her fortune to benefit primarily her local church—not himself, or the Turcottes, or Brother Leo's schemes, or Tom East and the Alice bank.

"Insofar as Judge Lytton is concerned," says Davis Grant, "this was not a vendetta. He was concerned about Tom East exploiting the ranch, and Oden manipulating that board for East's benefit, and the benefit of the bank and his law firm, rather than his true client, the foundation. The judge had taken about as much as he could stand of Oden running that foundation, even though they had been very close friends.

"Tom East, of course, was part and parcel of it. I don't know if this can ever be established beyond a shadow of a doubt, but I don't think that Tom East was calling the plays. He didn't have to. Oden and his predecessor knew what Tom East wanted. And Tom East could have fired them from representing that bank any time he wanted to. He controlled the Alice bank."

Attending the foundation meetings provided the attorney general's representatives with an inside look at *how* Ken Oden operated, but Rodnick and Beversdorf heard nothing in Elena Kenedy's parlor that of itself warranted civil action, or indictment, against Oden. Besides the attorney's well-documented attempt to lease Tom East the ranch for two dollars per acre, the only other information they had was Lee Lytton's account of how the board had voted the Alice bank a fee of several hundred thousand dollars for managing foundation funds it was holding in non-interest-bearing accounts, a sort of double dip for the Alice bank.

What was required, they realized, was a full accounting from the Alice bank, information that Rodnick would force from the bank in a lawsuit she filed in 1982. But this was just a preliminary move. While the state of Texas waited to learn what the Alice National Bank had been doing with Mrs. East's money for the past two decades, Rodnick would lay the groundwork for Oden's removal from control of the foundation itself.

She and Davis Grant first addressed the obvious impracticality of trying to obtain a judgment against the Alice bank and Ken Oden in Jim Wells County. "We were terrified of that," says Rodnick. "Why even bother?"

Their solution was to prepare an amendment to Texas's charitable-trust statutes, "providing," as Grant explains, "that where there are accusations of misconduct on the part of a trustee of a charitable trust, any suit resulting from it shall be tried in Travis County" in Austin. Davis Grant suggested the names of representatives to sponsor the bill in the Texas state legislature, which passed the measure at its 1983 biennial session. "It just sailed through," says Grant. "I don't think Oden and the rest of them even knew it was being done."

But 1983 also brought a change in Texas attorneys

general. The preceding year, Mark White ran successfully as the Democratic candidate for the governor-
ship. His elected replacement as attorney general was
the Dallas congressman Jim Mattox, best known to
that point for his refusal to wear a suit coat on the
floor of the House in the summertime. For this act of
defiance Mattox was publicly chastised by House
Speaker Tip O'Neill.

A liberal Democrat on most substantive issues, Mattox came to his new job as the Texas attorney general
with a reputation as a tough and, most people agreed,
fearless campaigner—"short on tact, long on balls,"
as a Dallas lawyer describes him. Yet it was hard to
know what to expect of him in such a complicated
affair as the Kenedy Memorial Foundation fight. Two
years after assuming office, for example, Mattox took
a major political gamble by questioning (and then, in
effect, halting) the Texas Rangers' investigation of
Henry Lee Lucas, a one-eyed, snaggle-toothed drifter
with a mid-double-digit IQ who had convinced certain
credulous Rangers that he is the most prolific serial
killer of all time. Logic, to Jim Mattox, dictated otherwise.

All that Amie Rodnick knew in 1983 was that her
new boss seemed to have an independent turn of mind.
"I got real excited when Mattox came in," says Rodnick, who reports that the White administration had
given her only tepid support. "I thought, 'This guy
sounds like the kinda guy who'd really be interested
in an investigation like this.' "

However, Rodnick quickly found that the pursuit of
Ken Oden wouldn't be that simple. After filing her suit
demanding an accounting and passing the new statute,
she says, "I went back to my division chief and requested permission to file a suit to remove Ken Oden
from the foundation. I had a petition drafted. And I

was told, 'No, because we don't know who might be friends of Jim Mattox down there. Don't file it.'

"Now, I don't know if the division chief *knew* if there were any friends of Jim Mattox involved, but I was told not to do anything until we made sure there weren't. I was *never* told something like that in the White administration."

Angered at what she was told, and already restless to open her own private practice after four and a half years in the charitable-trust division, Amie Rodnick submitted her resignation in late 1983. She gave Jim Mattox two months' notice in order for the new attorney general to find a suitable replacement for her. No one had been hired by the time she left, nor had the suit she had drafted been filed. It appeared, at that moment, that Ken Oden and the Alice National Bank had weathered the most serious challenge yet to their management of Sarita's fortune.

Then the redoubtable bishop Rene Gracida arrived on the scene.

THIRTY-FOUR

✠ ✠ ✠

The Bishop's Gambit

Age and ill health forced Bishop Thomas Drury to announce his retirement in early 1983. His departure would close a quiet, eighteen-year interregnum in the diocese of Corpus Christi, and it offered the Catholic Church a propitious moment to install a more dynamic presence in the Corpus Christi chancery. "The word was out," the *National Catholic Reporter* quoted an anonymous source in 1987, "that the next bishop would be a Hispanic who could count."

Rene Gracida is physically compact, trim for his years, with dark features and a candid mien. He speaks in measured tones lightly inflected with Spanish, especially his consonants. He was born in New Orleans in 1923 and raised in Texas City, Texas. Like Ken Oden, Rene Gracida served as a bomber pilot in World War II. Like Brother Leo, he is a former monk, a member of the Benedictine community at St. Vincent's Archabbey, near Latrobe, Pennsylvania, from 1951 until 1961. Gracida left the Benedictines, voluntarily, and moved to south Florida, where he became a parish priest in the Miami archdiocese. In 1972 he was elevated to bishop. Three years later, he took over the diocese of Pensacola-Tallahassee, where he served until being called to Corpus Christi in the summer of 1983.

According to the *National Catholic Reporter,* priests and lay Catholics in Corpus Christi found that their new bishop had a manner similar to that of a corporate CEO—businesslike and aggressive—and showed little interest in pastoral responsibilities. When asked about his image, Gracida reflects silently for a moment before responding in full, well-considered sentences.

"The fundamental charism of the office of bishop always has been—is even more so today—the charism of administration," he says. "We are ordinarily deprived of the opportunity to engage in the kind of one-to-one ministry that priests are able to do in parishes. Our responsibility is to coordinate the activity of a lot of different people, to keep their operations on a sound fiscal basis, to identify their charisms and to call them forth in service, validate them. The diocese of Tyler, Texas, has 25,000 Catholics. The bishop of Tyler, I'm sure, does not have to be as much of an administrator as I do with 325,000 Catholics. He has ten to fifteen priests. I have a hundred and fifty. Obviously, personnel problems, priest personnel problems, lay personnel problems occupy a great deal of my time. So I think that the *National Catholic Reporter* erred in portraying my administration as being unique to me, to this diocese. It's fairly typical of every diocese of any size. As to the description 'hard-driving,' well, maybe I am a more zealous bishop than some. Naturally, some people who would have liked to continue at the same leisurely pace [at which] they had been living and working in the past considered me to be hard-driving."

Rene Gracida was at St. Vincent's Archabbey when he first read of the Kenedy foundation controversy in *Time.* As a Catholic monk and Texan, he says, he found the story intriguing. Over the ensuing years in Florida, he continued to read articles about Leo and Sarita from time to time. "But I hadn't the foggiest idea I would ever, at any time in my life, be personally involved with the case. When I came here to Corpus Christi, I really didn't know the status of it. I thought it had long since been resolved and the whole thing was settled. I was shocked to discover that it was still very much alive."

Unlike Bishop Drury, Bishop Gracida had no compunction about challenging Ken Oden for control of the Kenedy Memorial Foundation. But he is not an incautious man. Patiently, the new bishop familiarized himself with the foundation's tortuous legal history and its current management and satisfied himself that some sort of action against Oden was going to be necessary. Events, he decided, would dictate when, and how, he would proceed.

The first of these was Bruno Goldapp's death, in August of 1983. Whoever replaced Goldapp on the board, Gracida recognized, would become the swing vote, the key to control of the membership, and the bishop was not about to risk what he calls "a golden opportunity to change the situation dramatically." Aware that Ken Oden intended to replace Goldapp with a clone, and uncertain whether he could thwart the attorney with only his own and Lee Lytton's vote, Gracida stalled Oden when he asked that a meeting to select Goldapp's successor be held. "I begged off," says Gracida. "I told him that I needed time to get settled in as bishop of the diocese."

Meanwhile, he got to know Elena Kenedy on visits to La Parra and also to her bedside at Spohn Hospital, in Corpus Christi, where Mrs. Kenedy was a frequent patient. He says that when he discussed with Elena her feelings about the foundation, she told him several times, "I don't know why the Lord is keeping me involved in all this at age ninety-four. I think it's time the Lord took me to Himself and gave me peace. I'm so sick and tired of all this."

If she were to resign, the bishop asked her, whom

would she like to see replace her on the foundation board? Elena's answer was Sister Bernard Marie Borgmeyer of the Sisters of Charity, who was a former administrator at Spohn Hospital and had become a close friend. Bishop Gracida did not know the sister.

"I met Mrs. Kenedy first when she was a patient at the hospital," says Sister Bernard Marie, who joined the Sisters of Charity in 1939. "She seemed to take a liking to me. And I liked her. She was a very interesting person, a lovely person.

"She had always, repeatedly, said to me, 'I want you to take my place [on the foundation] when I give it up.' I didn't agree to do it, then. I didn't really want it.'"

Before leaving Spohn, in 1981, the nun finally relented. "I said yes. I felt that she wanted, sincerely wished this and that she wanted it settled before she died."

His interview with Elena Kenedy convinced Bishop Gracida that he might succeed where Bishop Drury had failed to place Dan Meaney on the foundation board. "I felt," says the bishop, "that I had gained sufficient knowledge of the situation that I could propose Dan Meaney for membership and get Mrs. Kenedy to agree to it again, and to stick to it this time."

Gracida also knew that in Austin Attorney General Jim Mattox had in hand Amie Rodnick's draft petition to remove Ken Oden from the foundation. The bishop's plan was to arrange for Dan Meaney's election at the annual meeting of the board, usually held in January, but he hoped the attorney general's suit would be filed before the meeting took place.

"Jim Mattox procrastinated for reasons known only to Jim Mattox," he says with an edge in his voice. "He did nothing and did nothing and did nothing. I wanted to give him enough time to make up his mind; was he going to do it, or wasn't he? Finally, I decided he was not. So I asked Mrs. Kenedy if I could send out notices to everybody. I went ahead and set the date for the annual meeting, arbitrarily, on February 13, 1984. The date had no significance.''

But it would.

To the surprise and delight of Davis Grant, Amie Rodnick, and especially Bishop Rene Gracida, on Wednesday, February 8, 1984, Jim Mattox's office at last sued for Ken Oden's removal from the Kenedy Memorial Foundation board, alleging conflict of interest and questioning a range of actions, from the $1.9 million in non-statutory executors' fees the Alice National Bank had collected from Sarita's estate to the $2.5 million in legal fees Oden's firm and Baker, Botts had charged the foundation.

As part of the attorney general's filing, Mattox requested a ten-day restraining order barring Oden from participating in foundation matters until the judge in the case, Joseph H. Hart, could decide if he would grant a full injunction to the same effect. Davis Grant, Lee Lytton's attorney, expected that Judge Hart would set a hearing for perhaps the seventeenth or the eighteenth. Instead, and by a stroke of what Bishop Gracida regards as divine providence, Hart set Monday, February 13, as the date he would hear arguments in his Travis County courtroom. On the day that Gracida hoped to install his ally Dan Meany on the foundation board, his adversary Ken Oden would be 220 miles north in the state capital defending his administration of the foundation.

Knowing that Judge Lytton would also be in Austin, where his testimony against Oden might be required, Bishop Gracida decided on Thursday, the ninth, to drive to Sarita the following day to secure Lytton's proxy for the Monday meeting. With Bruno Goldapp's death and Ken Oden's forced absence, the bishop would have a clear majority no matter how Elena Kenedy voted.

But there was still the possibility of mischief from Tom East. So Gracida then called Mrs. Kenedy that Thursday and made an appointment to visit her at her house the following morning. After that he telephoned the foundation attorney, Richard Hatch, and asked him to draft a proxy for Elena to sign, as well as a letter of resignation.

Gracida had seen and heard enough in his brief acquaintance with Elena Kenedy to realize that while her servants were intensely loyal to her, they were even more afraid of Tom East, La Parra's de facto *patron*. The bishop therefore assumed that a member of Elena's household staff would alert Tom or his wife, Evelyn, of his impending visit. He was right.

"When I arrived at the ranchhouse that morning," he says, "I found the door was opened by Evelyn East. It was obvious that she was very annoyed and was reluctant for me to visit with Mrs. Kenedy. But there's no way she could have prevented it."

Gracida asked Elena if they might meet in private. She showed him to her second-floor sitting room, dismissed her private-duty nurse, and then sat at silent attention.

"I explained to her," the bishop continues, "that the meeting on Monday was of critical importance to the future of the foundation. And that she really needed to think about the possibility that others—I didn't name them, I trusted that she would know who I was referring to—might try to prevent her from being present. Would she therefore be willing to give me a proxy in the event that she could not be present?" Gracida also explained to Mrs. Kenedy, he says, that his intent on Monday was to elect Dan Meaney, the dairyman, to the board.

"I read the proxy to her, and then I handed it to

her. She took her time sitting by a round table with a lamp, a bright light, right there. She took her time, and she read it *very* carefully. And after she finished reading it, she signed it and gave it to me.''

Bishop Gracida, of course, was sensitive about the scene's uncomfortable similarity to one nearly a quarter of a century earlier in a New York hospital room. There he was, a Catholic man of the cloth alone with an aged and physically infirm widow, asking her to sign over effective control of a vast fortune. Still, with no alternative means for achieving his intentions, he pressed on with the interview.

''Then I broached the subject of resignation,'' he recalls. ''I said, 'Now, Mrs. Kenedy, we need to think of the future. We need to think of the possibility that at your age you are going to be less and less able to participate in board meetings. Maybe at this time you'd like to consider doing what you've discussed with me several times before—that is, resigning in favor of Sister Bernard Marie Borgmeyer. Would you want to consider that?'

''She said, *'Yes, very much,* Bishop!'

''In anticipation that you might,'' Gracida replied, ''I brought a letter of resignation for you to sign.'' He read it to Elena, he says, ''and she signed it and gave it back to me.''

According to Gracida, he informed Mrs. Kenedy that he thought it imperative that Sister Borgmeyer be on hand for the Monday meeting and that he would contact her as soon as he could. He also discussed with her the need to satisfy a stipulation to the foundation charter. As per a condition imposed by the Texas attorney general in 1964, at least one member of the Kenedy Memorial Foundation had to be non-Catholic. Gracida's candidate was Elena's personal physician, Dr. Ben Groner.

"She said, 'Yes,' " he reports. " 'That would be a good choice.' "

The bishop is quick to point out that both Borgmeyer and Groner were strangers to him. "No one can say they were my stooges, so to speak," he says. "These two people were totally unknown to me, and I had no idea if they would be hostile to me. But I figured that since she knew them and respected them, they must be good people. I felt in all probability that they would not vote with the bank."

Gracida drove from the ranch directly into Sarita, where he spoke with Lee Lytton and obtained the judge's proxy. It was by now early afternoon on Friday, February 10.

By midafternoon he was back in his chancery and on the telephone trying to locate Sister Borgmeyer, who he learned was living at her order's Santa Rosa Convent, in San Antonio. To Bishop Gracida's momentary distress, the San Antonio convent informed him that Sister Bernard Marie was in Amarillo, attending a board meeting for the hospital that the Sisters of Charity ran in the Texas Panhandle city. They weren't sure if she could be reached. The bishop left his private number for Sister Borgmeyer to call, and drove home to his official residence.

Meanwhile, Mrs. Kenedy had also been trying to reach Sister Bernard Marie. "At first," the nun remembers, "I got an urgent call from my office in San Antonio telling me that Mrs. Kenedy was trying to get in touch with me." When Elena finally got through to Sister Bernard Marie, she announced her decision to resign from the Kenedy Memorial Foundation and her intention to hold the nun to her promise to replace her on the foundation board. Furthermore, Mrs. Kenedy told Sister Borgmeyer that it was imperative she attend the board meeting set for the coming Monday.

The first call Bishop Gracida received when he got

home came from Judge Lytton in Sarita. "You no sooner left my house, Bishop," Lytton reported, "than I happened to look out my window and I saw this big black Cadillac belonging to Kenneth Oden. He was in it with Tom East and Mrs. Kenedy's secretary, Juan Cuevas, and they were heading toward the ranch. An hour or so later they came back into Sarita and they went to Juan Cuevas's office. After about half an hour there they went back to the ranch, and then a half hour later they all came out again."

On Sunday, February 12, Bishop Rene Gracida received a hand-delivered letter from La Parra, typed on Elena Kenedy's stationery. It read,

Dear Bishop Gracida,
In connection with the annual meeting of the John G. & Marie Stella Kenedy Memorial Foundation which has been set for February 13th, 1984, at 2 o'clock at my residence on the Kenedy Ranch, I revoke any written proxy heretofore executed by me, and I wish to cancel the meeting until such time as litigation involving the attorney general of Texas, Mr. Kenneth Oden and others and the Foundation is resolved and concluded. Until Mr. Oden can be present at any future meeting of the Foundation, I ask that you not set or call any meeting of the members or directors.

Faithfully yours,
Elena S. Kenedy

"I can only suppose what happened in that meeting at the ranch," says Gracida. "They must have put her under a tremendous amount of pressure, demanding to know what I was doing there. And they must have asked her specifically, 'Did you sign anything?' And she must have said yes. And they must have then asked her, 'Did you sign a proxy?' And she answered yes.

"So they went back over to the office and drafted a

revocation and got her to sign it. But with all the pressure they put her under, she never told them that she had resigned! They asked if she had signed a proxy, and she said yes. But she never *volunteered* the rest. It never *dawned* on them that she might have resigned! So they left confident that they had checkmated me in this little game.''

Having resigned from the foundation, Elena Kenedy legally could not cancel one of its meetings. But there was another development just as important to the ultimate success of Bishop Gracida's plan, and to his credibility. He thinks it was the hand of providence again intervening in the affair when his telephone rang for a second time. It was Sister Bernard Marie Borgmeyer calling from Amarillo.

"I proceeded to explain to her why I had called," he recounts, "and she stopped me. She said, 'Bishop, I know all that.'

"I said, 'How do you know all this?'

" 'Mrs. Kenedy called me this afternoon,' she said.

"I was flabbergasted! I said, '*You* are telling *me* that Elena Kenedy called you *this afternoon* and told you she had *resigned* in your favor and that I was going to nominate and elect you to be, in her place, a member of the foundation on Monday?'

"She said yes and explained the whole thing to me.

"I cannot exaggerate the importance of that. Number one, it proves to anyone that Mrs. Kenedy acted of her own free will. I did not exert any influence on her. Secondly, she knew what she was doing. She was fully lucid, comprehending. Third, she not only knew, but she was determined not to let others undo what she had done, because she *didn't* tell them! But after they left, she called Sister Borgmeyer to make *sure* that she got down here by Monday. She knew that it was important, and she was determined to see that it happened.

"When Sister Borgmeyer told me that, I said, 'Thank God!' Now I had an independent witness that I had not done with Elena Kenedy what Brother Leo did with Sarita East. I *did not* go to her deathbed and while she was heavily sedated get her to sign a document that she couldn't read or know what was in it. *I did not do that!*"

On Monday, February 13, Gracida assembled his team in Corpus Christi. Besides himself, Sister Bernard Marie, Dr. Groner, and Dan Meaney, he asked that a member of Richard Hatch's law firm join the group; Hatch, who was in Austin for Ken Oden's hearing, sent his son Richard Hatch, Jr. Also, the bishop wanted a representative from the attorney general's office on hand. Because everyone in Mattox's office then connected with the case was in Austin, too, an associate attorney general from McAllen, in the Rio Grande Valley, was brought up to accompany the bishop's party to the meeting.

Just before two o'clock that afternoon, they pulled up at the main gate at La Parra. "The gateman," remembers Gracida, "was in an obvious state of embarrassment. He said, 'Bishop, why are you here?'

"I said, 'I'm here to attend a meeting at Mrs. Kenedy's house.' "

The cowboy informed Gracida that Elena was not at home.

" 'Oh,' " I said, " 'where is she?' And he said— these were his exact words—'Bishop, I don't know. They have taken her away.' "

Gracida inferred from the cowboy's manner that he had been ordered not to let the party onto the ranch. But before the vaquero had a chance to refuse the bishop entry, Gracida told him that he needed to visit the old Headquarters house, which had been turned into a prayer retreat by the Oblates. This was church business. As bishop of the diocese, Gracida could not be refused access to a place of prayer under his authority.

He and the rest of his group drove on around the Headquarters and back to Elena's clapboard house, old Mifflin Kenedy's original residence. He remembers standing on the porch as a servant came to the door, eyeing him with fear. "Mrs. Kenedy's not at home," he was told. "She's gone to Corpus Christi to have her hearing aid checked."

When the bishop asked if he and the rest could come inside, the servant said no. Tom's wife, Evelyn East, had given orders, she said, that Bishop Gracida was not to be allowed in the house.

But Rene Gracida was not to be foiled. He looked around a moment and was inspired with a solution. "The notice of meeting did not say *in* the house," he explains. "It said *at* Mrs. Kenedy's residence."

He turned back to the servant at the door. "I don't want to get you in trouble," he said. "So here's what I'm going to do. You close the door and lock it. We're going to have a meeting out here on the porch."

Within a few minutes it was all over. Gracida opened the meeting, read Elena's resignation to the group, and then nominated and elected Borgmeyer, Groner, and Meaney to the foundation board of members. Then the group elected itself both directors and officers of the foundation—another brief formality concluded as Tom East's accountant drove up to the house. It didn't take long for her to relay word to Austin of what was happening.

When this news arrived in the courtroom, Oden's attorney (and law partner), Buster Adami, stood up and asked that the proceedings be dismissed because, Adami announced dramatically, at that very moment an illegal meeting of the foundation was being held. Mrs. Kenedy, he said, had canceled the meeting and was not even at home. Furthermore, the proxy that

Bishop Gracida apparently believed was valid had been revoked by Mrs. Kenedy.

Then it was Richard Hatch's turn. The foundation attorney answered, "Your Honor, the point they raise is moot. The matter at issue is not Mrs. Kenedy's proxy but her resignation, because on the tenth Mrs. Elena Kenedy resigned as a member of the board!"

According to what Bishop Gracida was later told, "Oden and his attorneys just about had a stroke at that point." The next morning, says Davis Grant, Oden was ready to deal. "There was some blusterin' that went on," Grant recalls. "But they capitulated." In return for a promise of no future litigation against himself, or his law firm, Ken Oden agreed to resign from the foundation. And except for a sad coda, the Alice bank's long reign of complete control of Sarita's fortune was over.

Shortly after Kenneth Oden's resignation on February 14, Tom East contacted Jim Mattox, who in turned called a meeting in Austin. As Davis Grant remembers the day, Mattox directed his remarks mainly to the bishop. "I know you and the foundation are tired of litigation," Grant recalls the attorney general's saying in his office. "And to avoid any further litigation, Tom East says he won't sue the foundation if you will permit him to name a member to take Oden's place."

"There was no expression made one way or the other by Bishop Gracida, or anybody else in the room," says Grant. "We just listened and thanked him and left. But in my own mind as soon as he said it I said, 'How in the *hell* can Tom East sue the foundation? He's got absolutely no justiciable reason.' "

If East's threat was a bluff, his next act wasn't. He again spoke to Jim Mattox, who decided to fly personally to south Texas to interview Elena for himself. "I think," says Bishop Gracida, "that what Tom East decided was that they might be able to attack the validity of her resignation, and therefore the validity of the meeting, by accusing me of undue influence just as they had successfully accused Brother Leo of undue influence twenty years before. I'm not sure that she ever revealed to them that she had called Sister Bernard Marie. I don't know what she told them. But they must have felt so confident that they could pin that on me and make it stick that they invited the attorney general to come to interview her."

"I wanted to see the situation firsthand, up close," says Mattox in explanation of his decision to go visit Elena. "There were a lot of people talking for her, you know. And there were different rumors about the state of her mental stability. I decided I was going to resolve this issue, and the best way—really the only way, I guess—was to see for myself what she had to say, and if she understood and knew what she was saying."

As for the suspicions that he previously had stalled the state's investigation of Oden and the Alice National Bank, Mattox counters, "Actually, I was being very aggressive about trying to resolve the matter. They were at loggerheads; they'd been at loggerheads for quite some time. The bank was making a vast amount of money. There were obvious conflicts of interest surrounding the process, and I decided it had been let slide too long. It looked to me like it had been improperly dealt with, because of the fear of stepping on the toes of some very powerful people."

According to Richard Hatch, the attorney for the Kenedy Memorial Foundation, Jim Mattox gave him another reason why he decided to visit La Parra. "He did not tell me the purpose was to visit Mrs. Kenedy," says Hatch. "He said that he came because Morris Atlas [one of Tom East's attorneys] asked him to. He said he talked to East and basically that Tom was concerned that the new board was going to cancel his lease. He was also concerned that the new board was going to sell the ranch.''

Hatch did not inquire further why a Texas state attorney general would take a state aircraft from Austin to Kingsville to hear a private business complaint. But whatever Mattox's reason for traveling to La Parra, Bishop Gracida is persuaded that Tom East's last-ditch effort to regain his, and the Alice bank's, command of the foundation and the ranch broke Elena Kenedy's heart. As Gracida understands the story, on March 2, 1984, as Mattox was being driven to La Parra from the Kingsville airport, Elena Kenedy died. Mattox recalls only that when he got to the ranch he was told Elena was too ill to see him. ''They basically said she was sleeping, resting or something, and was not available to see me,'' says Mattox. It was only later in the day, he recalls, ''that somebody informed us she had passed away.''

''I hate to say this, but I will,'' says Gracida, leaning forward at his massive chancery desk, his voice rising slightly and his hand formed into a fist. ''In my opinion, that killed her. In my opinion, Mrs. Kenedy was not able to sustain the prospect of being interrogated by the attorney general of the state of Texas regarding a false accusation that her bishop had exerted undue influence over her.''

Elena Kenedy was taken to the mortuary of Andy Turcotte, Jr., in Kingsville, and then buried three days later at La Parra. Her simple headstone, next to that of her husband, Johnny, completed the tidy row of graves laid out by Sarita fifty-two years before. Nine months later, Tom East, Jr., sixty-seven, suffered a fatal heart attack while driving in a truck on his ranch. He, too, was taken to the Turcotte mortuary and buried on his ranch.

''Crud'' was how Kenneth Oden later described to the *Corpus Christi Caller* the attorney general's suit that led to his resignation from the Kenedy Memorial Foundation. "The words 'conflict of interest,' " he told the newspaper, "are something that uninformed people attribute to busy people."

But another veteran of the foundation wars, Frank Nesbitt, sees the allegations and the rest of the events of February 1984 in a different light. "That new bishop!" exclaims Nesbitt. "That fella's got some *guts!* I've got to admire him. He set it up where he held his own little private meeting there on the porch and kicked everybody off the board and took over! From my standpoint, I can't say justice wasn't done. Accidentally. The money's back in the hands of the Catholics, which I guess is probably what Sarita wanted. It's not being chewed up and thrown away by that bunch at the bank, at least. And I'll tell you, it would have been a different story if that ol' bishop had been around here in the sixties."

Bishop Gracida was not satisfied with Ken Oden's removal. Late in 1984 the Kenedy Memorial Foundation joined in a damage suit originally filed by the attorney general against the Alice National Bank. Oden and his law firm, under the terms of his resignation, were immune from litigation. But the Alice bank itself was not. In the suit, which by late 1989 was unresolved, the state and the foundation allege conflicts of interest, mismanagement, self-dealing, and gross negligence on the bank's part and specify the damages allegedly done. They include the following:

- failure to place estate and foundation assets in income-producing accounts—$3 million
- failure over several years to lease La Parra for hunting—$4 million
- "acts or omissions" by Tom East to adequately maintain the ranch and the quality of its cattle—$3 million

- breach of fiduciary trust and overcharging for commissions and fees—$2 million
- the bank's failure to assert claims to La Parra's coastal mud flats, a tidal area under which, according to the suit, as much as $35 million worth of gas and oil remains unexploited

While this litigation pends, the fortune Bishop Gracida wrested from Ken Oden's control has finally been put to work. The money wasn't free of legal entanglements until mid-1981, when the U.S. Supreme Court refused to hear Brother Leo's appeal of Judge Laughlin's 1979 decision changing the 1964 settlement agreement from interlocutory to final.

Under federal law a charitable trust must distribute 10 percent of its net available assets in every calendar year. But because the Kenedy Memorial Foundation had donated next to nothing over the twenty years of legal warfare, the government applied a retroactive formula to its giving, requiring of the foundation that it give away about $34 million almost immediately.

Before Bishop Garriga arrived in Corpus Christi, $7.5 million was given to St. Mary's University Law School to refurbish its law library. Another $10 million had been promised, but not yet delivered, to the Spohn Hospital, in Corpus Christi. That left about $16 million more to give away, and fast, to meet the federal deadline.

In the summer of 1984, just a year after Gracida became bishop of Corpus Christi, the Kenedy Memorial Foundation announced $16.3 million in grants. Limited by the terms of the 1964 settlement to making disbursals exclusively within the state of Texas—10 percent of which was reserved to nonsectarian causes— the first batch of donations fell into two general categories. The bulk of the money was earmarked for church and classroom construction and renovation in eight Texas dioceses. A lesser amount went to educational programs and to Catholic media centers. In Corpus Christi, where about $7.5 million was spent, the diocese built a state-of-the-art television and radio production facility.

The nonsectarian grants ranged from about half a million dollars for the local public television station, KEDT in Corpus Christi, to nearly $350,000 for books and furniture for the new Corpus Christi public library. The United Way was given $75,000 to buy a new computer. The Food Bank of Corpus Christi received $122,500 to buy some land.

The reconstituted Kenedy Memorial Foundation board, led by Bishop Gracida, has been criticized for this pattern of spending, which does not focus on the basic needs of the poor, the homeless, the sick, and the dispossessed—the people, according to Brother Leo, whose welfare Sarita came to see as her special responsibility in the last year of her life. On the other hand, the foundation grants do broadly match Sarita's history of giving as reflected in her records, including the last year of her life, except for the million dollars funneled through the Grace bank accounts to the Trappists and to the monastery that never was, Los Laureles.

THIRTY-FIVE

The Free-Roaming
Trappist

Brother Leo spent two years in fruitless appeals of Judge C. W. Laughlin's 1979 ruling that the 1964 settlement was final and beyond the monk's power to change. Even after the U.S. Supreme Court refused to hear the case in 1981, the monk did not quit. He went to the Boston law firm of Hale & Door and hired its most famous partner, James St. Clair, Richard Nixon's lawyer during the Watergate affair, to file a federal lawsuit. In it, Leo would argue that his civil rights had been violated in the Texas courts.

J. Peter Grace, who received his $14.4 million once Leo lost the state-level round of appeals, spent $1.3 million of the money retiring the Sarita East Foundation's legal bills. Then, when he heard that Brother Leo had hired a high-profile lawyer like St. Clair to begin a new round of litigation, Grace took the occasion of a business trip to Chile to make the monk an offer.

Father Richard Gans, one of the original twelve monks to be sent from the Spencer mother house to Chile in 1960 and one of Leo's closest allies in the order, was present for the meeting between Grace and the monk. "To be very truthful," says Father Gans, "I was a little scandalized at Peter."

As he explains the episode, Father Thomas Keating

called Gans from the United States and asked that he arrange the "reunion," as Gans calls it. "Peter said that he wanted to have breakfast with Brother Leo. And Brother Leo, who was in Argentina, was just a little offended that Peter would want him to come over from Argentina just for breakfast.

"Well, finally Peter was on the scene. He was down here in Chile to see the president [Pinochet], and so he had all the security men—about three cars of them—one coming out ahead of him, one behind and one on the side. All of these people suddenly appearing at the monastery.

"I was superior at the time, so I went out to see him and took him into the guesthouse. While we were waiting for Brother Leo to come out from Santiago, Peter started kind of pushing me around, saying that this whole thing of Brother Leo still trying to fight for his rights and things of that sort was really ridiculous. That brother should have no problem just forgetting about the whole thing and just letting a dead dog lie. Trying to pooh-pooh the thing, you know.

"I said, 'If that's all you know about Brother Leo, I would say you know very little about the case.' Peter didn't like that at all. He kind of tried to belittle me, like I belittled him. From then on I kept silent."

According to Gans, the meeting between Grace and Leo was polite but tense. The industrialist, he recalls, showed them a recent surgical scar on his abdomen. Then Grace got down to business. If Leo would drop his federal lawsuit and desist from stirring up any further publicity, he said, Grace was prepared to split the Sarita K. East Foundation three ways among the monk, Father Peyton, and himself. Each of them would administer his equal third of the divided foundation as he saw fit. Father Gans recalls that the specific amounts Grace mentioned were $4 million apiece.

"Well, look," Gans remembers the monk's saying

to Grace. " 'I'm going to have to think this thing over. I'm going to have to consult and everything like that.' We talked about it afterward, and Brother Leo told me he had no intention of going along with Peter. He was just looking for a nice way to say that he would not accept the deal.''

Thus rebuffed, J. Peter Grace proceeded to invest and distribute the Sarita K. East Foundation assets in a way that he believes reflects Mrs. East's wishes as expressed in her third codicil, naming Peter Grace, Father Peyton, and Leo her foundation management troika. "I knew she liked the Trappists and Father Peyton," says Grace. "I have no evidence that she ever changed her mind, and I would doubt that she did. I would justify every one of [our donations] as something she would be in favor of.''

In 1981 Grace gave $191,000 to the Trappists, $36,000 to Father Peyton's Rosary Crusade, and $100,000 to the U.S. Military Vicarate, which provides priests to American armed forces and which was a special interest of the late Francis Cardinal Spellman, who once headed the organization.

The next year, out of about $1 million in total giving, Grace's foundation gave the Trappists $320,000 and Father Peyton $142,000. Beginning in 1983 Covenant House, Father Bruce Ritter's New York City–based shelter program for homeless and runaway youths, also became an important charitable cause to Peter Grace, as custodian of Sarita East's wishes. In all, of the $6 million donated by the Sarita K. East Foundation between 1981 and 1985, $700,000 was given to the Trappists and an equal amount to the Rosary Crusade. Covenant House received $300,000. The foundation's largest single donation, $1 million, was made in 1985 to AMERICARES, a relief organization that specializes in bringing food and medical supplies to disaster victims.

Brother Leo does not approve of this pattern of giving, any more than he does of the way in which Bishop Gracida in Corpus Christi spends the original Kenedy Memorial Foundation's assets. Nor are his relations with Gracida any more cordial than they are with J. Peter Grace.

Shortly after the bishop's porch meeting at Elena Kenedy's in February of 1984 (and while Brother Leo's civil rights suit was pending on the federal court docket in Corpus Christi), Gracida decided he would contact the monk to discuss the litigation. Gracida had been told, he says, that the only reason Brother Leo was persisting in his legal battle was to combat the usurpation of the Kenedy Memorial Foundation by the Alice National Bank. The source of this information was Stephen Dougherty, of the Beeville Doughertys, with whom Brother Leo had been close for more than forty years. If this was true, Bishop Gracida reasoned, then he had personally taken care of the problem for the monk.

Through a series of intermediaries, the bishop sent a message to Stephen Dougherty. Was what he heard about Leo true, Gracida asked, and if so, would Mr. Dougherty have time to meet with the bishop? A short while later, they met at the bishop's residence in Corpus Christi. Gracida cooked breakfast for the two.

"I enjoyed meeting him," Gracida recalls. "It was obvious that he thought very highly of Brother Leo. The bottom line was that I asked him, 'Will you contact Brother Leo and ask him to come see me? Tell him that I'd be interested in discussing this idea now that the Alice National Bank group no longer controls the foundation, would he be willing to stop the litigation?' Stephen said he'd be very happy to do that. And he did."

A short time later, Leo appeared at Gracida's door, accompanied by Father Richard Gans. Waiting for them, along with the bishop, was his vicar for canonical affairs, Monsignor Leonard Pivonka, who took notes on the meeting.

Father Gans remembers the start of the meeting as "very, very friendly." He adds, "I would say without any tension whatever. So then we finally came to the point. He [Gracida] said, 'Well, Brother, what really do you want? What are you expecting of this case?'

"So Brother Leo tried in as nice a way as possible to say, 'Well, basically what I want of the thing is what Sarita East asked in the first place—that her money, a great part of her money, go for the poor of Latin America.'

"Of course, when he mentioned that," Father Richard goes on, "the bishop said, 'Well, I'm sorry. But we just can't do any of that for you.' "

Bishop Rene Gracida admits he was very curious about the monk. "Leo, I knew, has the power to bring people under his control and keep them under his control," he explains. "I was hoping when he came to my house and sat down in the living room that I would see someone who exuded a charisma that would explain to me why so many people are under his spell."

But the bishop found both his guests disagreeable, especially Brother Leo. "His personality," says Gracida, "just turned me off the moment he opened his mouth and started talking. His manner was repellent to me.

"Right off I told him my purpose, that I had been led to believe that he was suing only because of the bank. I asked, 'Is it true?'

"He said no, that wasn't his only reason.

"And so I asked, 'Why do you persist in the litigation?'

"He answered, 'Because I feel that I was cheated out of my right to run the foundation, and I feel that I have a right to do so.'

" 'What,' I said, 'would it take for you to drop your litigation?'

"He proposed a division of the assets. I don't think we ever got into specific amounts or figures. But I was certainly appalled to hear that he wanted the foundation assets divided, with him taking a significant portion of the assets to set up another foundation 'to help the poor of South America,' in his words."

The bishop and the monk soon exhausted the topic; never, willingly, would the former part with a portion of the Kenedy fortune, and the latter inflexibly insisted that he should. "Oh yeah," adds Father Gans. "There was also a little incident in there. The priest with the bishop [Monsignor Pivonka] started speaking up, saying, 'For the love of God,' telling Brother Leo, 'for the love of God, why can't you forget about this thing?' So then I said a few things, that it was Leo's contention 'for the love of God' to do what Sarita really wanted to do with her money and to help the poor of Latin America."

In this atmosphere the bishop then decided to probe Leo's standing within the church.

"I am a Trappist monk," he told Gracida.

"Well," the bishop replied, "I have difficulty understanding that because I've seen a copy of a letter from your abbot dismissing you from your monastery. Also, as a former Benedictine, I know that the Trappists belong to a monastery, or they don't belong. There's no such thing as a free-roaming Trappist.

"I said that I noticed he wasn't wearing a habit, and he said, 'No, but I will be able to wear a habit once this litigation is settled.'

" 'Oh?' I said. 'You've been dismissed from your monastery, yet you've been told that your vows remain? That's highly unusual. When I left the Benedictines, I was dispensed from my vows. I don't understand how it's possible for you not to be a member of the community at St. Joseph's Abbey, yet still have vows.'

"He said, 'Well, I'm a hermit.'

Gracida conducted a hostile interrogation of Leo on this point, too. "The conversation just was downhill all the way," he says. "It ended up with him leaving, and the parting was not particularly friendly."

Subsequently, the bishop received two scathing letters from Stephen Dougherty, which he keeps in his hate-mail file. Dougherty accused Gracida, according to the bishop, of being the Antichrist. He has received similarly antagonistic missives from Father Richard Gans.

"Father Richard," he says, "seems to have almost as ferocious, *tenacious* an interest in this whole thing as Brother Leo. Let me tell you how they operate. A year or two went by after that meeting, and one day my secretary tells me that a bishop so-and-so called and he's staying at the Sheraton and he'd like to see you. She gave me his name, and I looked it up and saw that he was from Chile. Immediately, alarm bells went off in my head. What is a bishop from Chile doing in Corpus Christi, unannounced, no letters, no telephone calls telling me he's coming? And he's here at the hotel and wants to see me.

"I decided, 'Well, I'll see him *there* at the Sheraton, not *here*. I can always leave *there*, but I can't very well throw him out of *here*. That wouldn't be protocol. I can't physically evict him from my office.' "

Gracida had his secretary make a lunch appointment for him and drove over to the Sheraton, where he encountered not one, but two, Latin-American prelates waiting for him in the lobby. The first one, Bishop Carlos Gonzalez, of Talca, hesitated for a moment and then spoke. "Would you mind," asked Gonzalez, "if a companion joins us?"

"I said, 'Well, who is the companion?'

" 'I think you know him. It's Father Richard Gans.'

"And with that, Father Richard steps out from behind a partition! Naturally, I'm dumbfounded. I'm being set up, you understand? I mean, this is cloak-and-dagger stuff. But I figured, 'Well, I've come this far. I might as well hear what they have to say.'

"So we go up to the rooftop restaurant and order, and the conversation begins. In a nutshell, Father Richard had brought these two bishops up to do a number on me, as they say in the street. They tried to intimidate me. How could I be so unconscionable as to deprive the poor of Latin America of all this help which Sarita Kenedy East obviously intended be given them? Didn't I have any feelings for the Third World? How could I possibly not be sensitive to it? And why wouldn't I agree to the proposition Brother Leo made, a division of the foundation assets?

"I said, 'It's unthinkable, impossible. The court settlement provided that the foundation was to make its contributions in Texas. The attorney general's a party to it now. There's *no way* on God's green earth that I could ever succeed in doing such a thing, because the state of Texas would intervene and prevent it!'

"At that point Gans said, 'Well, Bishop, that's not true.'

"As if I'd been sitting there lying to them!

" 'You know as well as I do that if you wanted to get the settlement changed you could go to court and get it changed.'

"I got up and walked out: I hadn't even eaten yet. Without even saying good-bye I just got up and left the table and the hotel, and that was the end of that. I wasn't about to stay there and be subjected to any further abuse."

Father Gans confirms Bishop Gracida's depiction of their rooftop luncheon. "He was totally unwilling to listen to us," says Father Richard. "But he did pay the bill."

Another target of Brother Leo's (and thus Father Gans's) active displeasure has been Father Thomas Keating, who retired as abbot at St. Joseph's Abbey in Spencer in the early 1980s and has since lived as a choir monk at St. Benedict's in Snowmass, where he was the original superior before being elected in 1961 to replace the ailing Dom Edmund Futterer.

Brother Leo professes great love and respect for Dom Keating. "He's highly intelligent, and he's a good monk," says Leo. "I would look upon him as one of the best monks I've ever known. But I would say that he caved in to a lot of fears."

Dom Thomas, for his part, remains tolerant of Leo. "He's a fighter, you know," says the former abbot. "On his trips to South America he saw the plight of the poor, who definitely have his loyalties. And he convinced himself that he knew Mrs. East's wishes. I don't blame him for trying to meet the challenge; the foundation was his baby. But I do think the greater act would have been to let go of it and accept what I argued was the 'supernatural view,' that maybe God was asking me, and him, for this sacrifice."

Brother Leo's complaints against the Trappists and Father Thomas have their roots in the period before Keating became abbot when the alleged exchange of letters between Dom Edmund and Sarita took place. These notes, says Leo, established a contractual relationship and obliged him, under his vow of obedience to Dom Edmund, to resist Dom Keating's directives to desist in his legal fight to win back the Kenedy Memorial Foundation. In September of 1981, he wrote to Dom Futterer, then in his early eighties, at the monastery in Estancia Acosta, in Argentina, saying to the aged dom,

As I recall in early January 1960 you showed me a letter, written in hand by Sarita East, and sent to you, in which she offered to underwrite our South American expansion program (the purchase of Chile and building the Church, etc. at Azul) if you would permit me to help her set up and give direction to her proposed Foundation. I also recall that you showed me your reply, a typed letter of perhaps two pages, in which you consented to let me work with her while pointing out that this was indeed a rare permission.

Futterer responded that he did remember an exchange of letters, although their dates escaped him. "You and I," the old abbot wrote just months before his death, "well know how Sarita had written to me on one occasion a personal letter asking me if she might continue to make use of you in the work of setting up a foundation in the interest of the poor and underprivileged of Latin America. I replied in the affirmative in consideration of all that she had done in befriending us financially and otherwise. . . ."

Abbot Futterer's letter did not corroborate Leo's story. Dom Edmund said nothing about a deal or any resultant obligation on Leo's part to fight for Sarita's foundation. The abbot's only extant pronouncement on this is the October 1960 memo signed by Futterer, Leo, and Brother Luke Roberts at Spencer. It indicated that Leo might be allowed to spend a restricted amount of time with Sarita because of the future money she, or her foundation, were expected to give to the Trappists. As for being an officer of the foundation itself, Futterer reserved the right to name someone else from Spencer.

In 1966 Father Raphael interviewed Dom Futterer's former assistant secretary, Brother Simon, who typed the October 1960 document. "He told me," Father Raphael notes in his written recollection of the interview, "that Dom Edmund was very much surprised to discover . . . that Brother Leo was a director of the Kenedy Memorial Foundation. . . . He [Dom Edmund] did not consider that the permission he gave Brother Leo to help Sarita East with her foundation included permission to be a member or director of the foundation."

The monk's next complaint is that with his silencing in 1961 he was denied access to the canonical advisers of his selection. Both Dom Keating and Father Raphael insist that Leo was offered his choice of experts, but that he declined.

Leo also claims that his resignation of May 1962 was revoked before the interlocutory settlement of 1964 was entered. This is one of several arguments he uses in his claim that the settlement was illegal. However, Kenneth Oden insists that he never received Leo's resignation, only notification, by telegram, from Bill Joyce in Washington that the resignation was being revoked and that confirmation would follow. Oden says that confirmation did not follow, at least not before September 1, 1964. Bill Joyce does not contradict Oden's version of events.

In the same vein Leo argues that the settlement should not have been completed, because his signature, in Chile, in 1963 to the settlement papers was conditional upon Pope Paul VI's accepting moral responsibility for contravening Sarita's will. Father Thomas Keating relied upon assurances from Archbishop Krol that Brother Leo's condition had been fulfilled.

As for the July 1964 letter of capitulation sent from the monastery in Calvaire, Leo in 1979 was able to produce a letter from the former Father Dominic Hughes, who by then had left the priesthood and married. Like Dom Futterer, Hughes would be dead just months after writing his note for the monk.

According to Hughes, the 1964 letter from Calvaire was "never interpreted authentically." Unequivocal as it had been—"I shall initiate no further action whatever concerning the Kenedy Memorial Foundation," it read in part—Hughes characterized it as written by himself and "signed by Brother Leo in such circumstances as would preclude a thoughtful and totally free exercise of his judgment." The letter was "intended as a denial, a positive act of rejection of an unwritten, unwarranted demand." Hughes added, "Brother Leo was led to believe—on my sole advice, since no other was available to him—that he was saying, 'I do not hereby renounce any of my obligations and rights to anyone and in particular to the person making the demand. . . . An interpretation allowing for a concession of power of attorney, however stated in his message, is clearly contrary to Brother Leo's intent previous to that time and on that very day."

Dominic Hughes was a thinker of perhaps too-refined subtlety. Father Keating had read the letter as the monk's earnest attempt to restore himself to his vocation. In his own written explanation of his actions, Father Keating quotes a second letter he received from the monk just five days after the first. "With a fairly quiet mind," wrote the monk, this time on his own,

> I can forget Mrs. East's two poor foundations and concentrate at long last on trying to become a good monk. I certainly have a tremendous way to go. Your strong actions during the past two weeks have done *much* to cut me off from ties that were hurting me. For that you'll have my *lasting* gratitude. Coming here to Rogersville has been a tremendous help! Trusting in your prayers and God's mercy, I still hope to yet become a monk before dying.

Abbot Keating then heard by telephone from Lawrence McKay that the settlement was ready to be filed. McKay indicated it would be useful, but not imperative, for the monk to sign another resignation with a more current date on it. "I called Brother Leo," writes Father Thomas, "and intended to raise this possibility with him when I thought better of it. I knew that he was at peace at the moment but that every reminder of the case tended to start his mind working again, and I wanted to avoid raising matters that would needlessly disturb him. I ended the call without asking for any further authority from Brother Leo.

"After obtaining all the canonical and legal advice that I could get in the brief time given me to reach the decision, I decided that Brother's July letters emphatically affirming his intention to leave everything in my hands, empowered me to act. I authorized the filing of the settlement papers in virtue of 'the understanding' described in these letters.

"Within days of my authorizing the lawyers to continue to act on his behalf, I received a further letter from Brother which stated, in part: 'As my Abbot, I realize that you feel both a right and a duty to take whatever steps you can to bring the case to an end, acting in my stead as my canonical Superior. I assure you that I do not resent such actions on your part, and of course shall never question them nor even seek to know them.' "

THIRTY-SIX

✦ ✦ ✦

Poetic Justice

Brother Leo describes his desire to conform—and reform—as expressed in his 1964 correspondence to Dom Keating as symptoms of what he now sees as a "very serious spiritual defect." Once he recognized and overcame this flaw, Leo explains, he let his conscience be his guide. It is this psychically liberated Brother Leo who for the past quarter of a century has publicly denounced his abbot's actions and who for twenty-three of those years has had a lawsuit pending against someone, somewhere, in his nonstop campaign to regain control of Sarita's lost fortune.

The monk's 1981 civil rights suit, which listed as defendants the Texas attorney general (then Mark White), the Alice National Bank, the bishop of Corpus Christi (then Thomas Drury), and Lee Lytton, Jr., alleged that the group had conspired to deprive him of a full and fair trial, violating his constitutional rights under the Fifth and Fourteenth amendments. Federal District Judge Carl O. Bue, Jr., however, didn't see it that way. Bue, sitting in Corpus Christi, ruled against Leo and his Boston lawyers in 1985.

Then the monk lost on appeal in the Fifth Circuit Court in New Orleans. "The full story of this Texas-size will contest," wrote Circuit Judge Patrick E. Higginbotham in February of 1987, affirming Judge Bue, "would challenge the imagination of even Larry McMurtry and has a cast that rivals his epic, *Lonesome Dove*. But we [the three-judge circuit court] enter at the very end of this legal saga, the end despite the entry of fresh counsel with ingenious arguments who try to salvage too much, too late, and with too little." In brief, the circuit court ruled that Leo had been given ample opportunity to make his case and had lost, fair and square, in the Texas courts. However, as Kenneth Oden had predicted, the federal judges did not find Leo's case frivolous and denied defense requests for court costs and counsel fees from the monk. Some months later the U.S. Supreme Court refused to grant Leo's petition for a writ of certiorari, a kind of general review of the case.

In the meantime Brother Leo created another legal tangle. In October of 1985 a pro forma suit was filed in Corpus Christi state district court to free a large portion of the Kenedy Memorial Foundation's funds for dispersal. A legal technicality required the foundation to file the court petition, and, according to law, it was published. Brother Leo read the official notice as an opportunity to jump back into the fray.

His lawyers first tried to intervene the monk as an interested party in the petition. When that plea was denied by the state district judge, Leo's attorneys filed an appeal. Since this action would hold up the distribution of money until its merits were finally adjudicated (and therefore possibly work an undue burden on the intended recipients of the suspended foundation donations), civil law required that Brother Leo post $300,000 to cover the recipients interim costs should his appeal be denied. In August of 1986 the Texas State Court of Civil Appeals upheld the trial court's decision that Leo could not intervene. The following year an array of south Texas charitable causes, mostly Catholic, from the Mary Help of Christians Mission to St.

Andrews Convent—and including the Guadalupe Church in Sarita itself—sued Brother Leo to recover their attorneys' fees, court costs, and interest payments on the money lost in the year his court action held it up. This suit is not likely to be settled soon, but Leo stands to lose his $300,000 bond, which was guaranteed by Stephen Dougherty.

With this setback and the Supreme Court's decision, Leo appeared to have run out of legal arguments, or at least legal arguments that seemed to stand any chance of success in court. But even before he had exhausted his legal remedies, the monk had opened warfare in another arena. Much as he abominated the press for what he believed was highly biased coverage of his case during the 1960s and 1970s, Leo agreed to discuss the controversy, on camera, for a 1984 series of Cable News Network broadcasts. He spoke, as well, with a *Wall Street Journal* reporter, who wrote two long, front-page articles on the affair in October of 1986. Then Leo sat down with a writer at the *National Catholic Reporter,* who produced a three-part series published in early 1987.

The press attention, sympathetic to the ever-persuasive monk, was not welcomed by J. Peter Grace, who at first declined all requests for interviews to explain his role in the story. Nor were the Trappists at St. Joseph's Abbey in Spencer gratified to see themselves treated in a negative light, or by the audience response as reflected in a representative letter from a CNN viewer. It roundly condemned everyone connected with the case who didn't agree with Brother Leo. "This story," the typewritten note read, "stripped away any of the last shreds of comfortable feelings I used to have about Church authority—'obedience' etc. It showed me that those who occupy the highest positions of authority in the Church are no better than the evil men who run our own military dictatorships, they are sometimes those who are least principled, the least passionate for justice, and the least orthodox in the literal sense of that work [*sic*]. . . . God is *not* praised by the stuff that T.K., Grace, Krol, et al. has [*sic*] done to Leo and even *more* to the poor of Latin America.''

Leo did not immediately accept every reporter's invitation to discuss his convoluted saga. We first tried to contact him in the summer of 1987 by tapping into his extensive network of attorneys, past and present. In Corpus Christi, we found Curtis B. Dyer, who had worked on Leo's civil rights appeal. Dyer referred us to the monk's friend Stephen Dougherty, who did not return our telephone calls.

In Worcester, Massachusetts, there was a lawyer named Richard Simonian, who had also represented Leo in part of his federal case. Simonian tried to discourage us from continuing with the project but did inquire whether we had considered writing a book *for* the monk, rather than *about* him.

At Hale & Dorr in Boston, James St. Clair's firm, we spoke to his partner Tom O'Connor. He didn't want to discuss the case, which had just been refused for review by the U.S. Supreme Court. There was some concern within the law firm that the litigious monk, disappointed that the case had failed, might next decide to sue Hale & Dorr. O'Connor did say he liked and admired Brother Leo.

In Washington, D.C., we introduced ourselves to William Joyce, Leo's most patient and loyal advocate. Bill Joyce, a much-decorated Catholic layman (he says he has been awarded more honors than has Peter Grace), strongly believes that Brother Leo was wronged by both the Trappists and the Vatican, not to mention by J. Peter Grace, Cardinal Krol, and the Texas courts. Joyce dismisses most of Leo's antagonists within the church as ''cheap professional Catholic frauds, mostly Irish.'' But Bill Joyce also has a sense of humor about his client. ''Leo had a very engaging personality,'' says the lawyer, ''particularly if you were an older woman. 'Oh, this lovely boy! How much can I give him today?' You know. He could be extremely gushing when talking to the old gals. 'My dear, how *are* you?''

Joyce agreed that if and when he heard again from the monk—their contact was sporadic—he would pass along our request for an interview. He didn't think Leo would refuse another opportunity to make his case, although Leo did not seem to be in any hurry to talk to us. We waited until late October of 1987 and then went looking for him in Argentina. In Buenos Aires, Francis Verstraeten, Sr., told us that his ex-wife, Rachel, and her two elderly sisters often shared a house with Leo, in the town of Tanti, not far from Córdoba. If he wasn't in the United States and wasn't at the monastery in Chile, he probably was in Tanti. The telephone there was not answered.

Next, we spoke to Verstraeten's son Xavier, whom Francis describes as being as estranged from him as Xavier is close to Leo, his godfather. Xavier declined to be of help to us. So, after winding up the rest of the interviewing in Buenos Aires and visiting the impressive brick monastery in Estancia Acosta, we typed up a note for the monk and slipped it under Xavier's door the morning of our flight back to the United States.

Some weeks later Bill Joyce called to say that his client would entertain written interrogations. It was a start.

In our first batch of questions, we asked Leo if he knew how we might find copies of the alleged correspondence between Dom Futterer and Sarita, the letters that the monk claimed established his contractual, moral, and religious duty to defy Dom Thomas Keating's authority. In his written reply, Leo claimed that he had given both letters to the late Lawrence McKay. "I suppose," he wrote, "they have been returned to the monastery file at Spencer." The answer seemed disingenuous; we knew that Leo had long before accused McKay of losing the letters, a charge that the attorney strenuously denied.

We asked what, if anything, the monk would have done differently in his fight for control of Sarita's foundation. "My mistake," he wrote back, "was in not taking the case to Court before the end of 1961 while Mrs. East's many loyal friends were still alive. Had this been done I'm sure the Foundation would have been saved."

Was he bitter over his many defeats? "No, I'm not bitter. My responsibility was to do what I felt was right and necessary, and then leave the results to God, and I've followed this principle. If I have been obliged [sic] to resist certain orders from my Superiors, I have never doubted that they were sincere in following their own lights."

What, in Leo's view, had been the net effect of all the legal turmoil on the church? "Within the Catholic Church," he wrote, "there are of course many millions of individuals, most of whom have never heard of this case. Those who do know of it have been effected [sic] in different ways. Bishop Gracida today must be pleased that my efforts to set aside the 1964 Settlement have failed. I myself of course am very disappointed that Mrs. East's clearly expressed wishes have been frustrated, and I am also sorry that the many poor whom she wanted so much to help have been left unaided."

After his recent defeat at the U.S. Supreme Court, did Leo contemplate any further legal action? "I have finally dropped all Court proceedings in regard to Mrs. East's Foundation," the monk declared in his typewritten reply. "As far as I am concerned, the case is finished." Elsewhere in his response, Leo added that he expected to rejoin the Trappists soon.

We then sent a second set of queries. Question Number two read, "Recently published reports notwithstanding, the available evidence that Mrs. East wished her foundation to aid the Universal Church and the poor of Latin America specifically is confined to your testimony. . . . Can you direct us to concrete evidence Mrs. East did not want her money spent in the main in Texas?"

It seemed like a fairly obvious question to ask, a chance for Leo to make his case. But it was soon just as clear to us that Brother Leo does not suffer skeptical inquiry gladly. Once again through Bill Joyce, we were informed that he was coming north and would meet us at Joyce's Washington law office on the afternoon of April 19, 1988.

At about one-thirty on a dappled and breezy spring Tuesday, Leo stepped into Joyce's spacious office, not far from the White House, clad in a light blue turtleneck, a gray suit jacket, deep blue-gray trousers, and black loafers. On television, our only view of him until that point, Leo had looked crabbed, bloated, and old. In person he was trim and vigorous for a seventy-year-old. His hair, close-cropped, was nearly white.

Leo greeted his lawyer and gave us a curt hello. Then he attacked. "I assume," said the monk, his bright eyes lit with anger and his voice pitched somewhere between a growl and a hiss, "that you people aren't morons. I mean, you've supposedly been working on this case for some time. For investigative reporters to come up with a question like this! It's a stupid question! And unless you can go out and get some information that will allow you to rephrase it, I don't think there's any purpose to my answering any further questions."

Bill Joyce appeared to be as surprised by Leo's outburst as were we. "Uh, Brother Leo . . . ," he began.

The monk ignored him.

"If you can't find evidence that she wanted to help
the poor in South America, you're either awfully poor
investigators or you're orientated in a way that I suspect you two are."

"And how's that?" we asked.

"Well," the monk replied. "Your interest in this
story really stems from twenty years of near libelous
stuff that's been printed in south Texas. Rasputin
monk! Svengali monk! And all the stuff that has been
printed in Corpus Christi."

Leo elaborated on his suspicions. He accused us of
being in league with his supposed enemies within the
mother house at Spencer. "You assured them," he
accused, "that you would write a book that would be
a lot more pleasing to them."

"Pleasing to them?"

"Sure! Spencer and Grace and that little bishop."

We told the monk that no one had been given any
such assurances and that he ought to double-check his
sources. We also asked who at Spencer Leo thought
was plotting against him. He answered that it was Father Raphael Simon and the present abbot, Dom Au-
gustine Roberts. We protested that both men seemed
to care very deeply for the monk and had said so to
us.

"Yes, well," Leo replied with a little hoot. "I know
them better than you do. Much better. I know exactly
their mentality."

"And what's that?"

"That all that Spencer has done up to date has been
the proper thing to do."

"And you naturally disagree?"

"Sure I do."

The bickering went on for more than an hour.

"You know virtually nothing about what *really* went on between Mrs. East and me!" he nearly shouted at one point. "Why don't you fellas do a little legwork and then come back when you have some facts?"

Leo did, at last, stop referring to question number two as "stupid"—then denied that he had done so in the first place. It required another half an hour to get him onto a new topic. He did, at that time, apologize for his tantrum.

"You'll forgive me for blowing my top," he said. "I have a lot of sensitive areas."

Leo had several things to say about Peter Grace, none complimentary. "I'll tell you a little story about Peter," he said. "He can't *stand* disagreement. When he makes up his mind, he wants everybody to say, 'This is the way we'll do it.'

"Poor Peter! He hardly knew Mrs. East [and she] indicated to others, not to me, but to others who told me, that she didn't trust Mr. Grace. I didn't learn that until after she was dead. But she went along with him because he seemed to be such a good friend of mine.

"Of certain things, I'm certain. The foundation was *never* meant to help the Trappists. That's a twist that originated with Peter and others. Peter Grace had ignorantly assumed that because a Trappist lay brother helped her to found the foundation—because I was on as a director and a member—that that ensured the Trappists should receive substantial help over the years. Such was never, never intended to be the case."

We asked Leo about the confrontation with Grace in Paris. His recollection—which the monk acknowledges is often faulty—was that he had called Grace a megalomaniac in Rome. "And I didn't call him a megalomaniac, either. I said, 'The way you're going, you could become a megalomaniac.' And he really blew up."

"And his answer," we asked, "was what he was

going to do with the settlement? Shove it down your throat?''

"Right," Leo answered. "He was hypersensitive to that. Poor Peter.''

Archbishop Krol, the monk went on, "was an amazing man. He was very powerful, had hands like a blacksmith. He exuded power. You knew when you spoke to him that he was an important person. I remember asking him to put some of his threats in writing, and he sort of smiled [Leo laughed], which impressed me. Dom Thomas *did* put his warnings in writing, repeatedly. You won't find anything in this case, I don't think, that's been written or signed by Krol that puts him in a difficult situation at all.

"He was shrewd, powerful, and intelligent. He gave the Holy See what they wanted. I think his settlement was atrocious, abominable. But he was clever enough to get credit for it and make it look like it was a good settlement for the church when, in fact, he turned over entire control of the estate to the Alice bank.''

"Grace says Krol told him that you were a crook," we pointed out.

"Right," Leo answered. "And they both agree that now that I'm out of the way there's no reason why they shouldn't be the best of friends.''

At mention of the late Bishop Mariano Garriga, Leo claimed, "I hardly remember him. I felt sorry for him. He was sort of an old man full of his own importance and not too smart.''

"How about when he summoned you to his chancery in 1961? He warned about some 'hothead' filing a suit, and you told him to go ahead.''

"Well," said Leo, "that was a sort of foolish statement like I made to you earlier.''

"Garriga later testified that you then kissed his ring and asked his blessing.''

"I may have. I don't remember. But I was *terribly*

annoyed. It was *unbelievable* that this man who had received the largest gift his diocese had ever received from this woman would despise her intentions that way. Incredible! She was free, white, and twenty-one. She had a right to do whatever she wanted to do with her money.

"Sarita wanted to adopt me. Had I wanted what the good bishop wanted, I really could have had it. Had she lived. If she hadn't died as quickly as she did, there never would have been a lawsuit. If she had lived for three years, this suit never would have taken place. It was just very bad luck."

We told Leo that we had interviewed Francis Verstraeten, Sr.

"Poor Francis," he replied. "He has suffered a great deal. Enormously wealthy through his mother, and he had a lot of money, too. He's gone through, I think, three fortunes. Four fortunes. Now he has very little. Now the poor man is a bitter, unhappy man."

"Very bitter," we agreed.

"It's a tragedy. Of course, it's not nice to have someone say unkind things about you. Particularly if they are not true. But I feel more sorry for him than I do for myself."

"Is he a liar, would you say?"

"I never said he was a liar."

"We thought you did."

"No. No. No. I would never say he's a liar. He makes a good story better. Some people, you know, you can feel you're right close up to the real facts. And other people, the way they describe a situation, you can sense you're at a distance from the facts."

"Well, he does level one accusation against you: that you drained the bank account in Bermuda."

"How did I drain it?"

"Through his ex-wife, Rachel."

"I, I wasn't involved in that. It was worked out by her brother and another attorney."

"For your information, [Francis] alleges that at the time they split up, you were involved as an agent provocateur and, secondly, that there was an account of some $600,000 in the Butterfield Bank of Bermuda. According to him, through your Svengali-like machinations she was induced to drain all but $2,000 out of this account."

"I don't know about that," Leo answered evenly. "I don't believe there was ever $600,000 in that account."

"That's the allegation."

"Yeah. I would find out about that."

"Why did you move out of your hermitage that he built for you?"

"I didn't like it over there [in Córdoba]. It was overrun with tourists."

"Lack of solitude?"

"Yeah."

"And Francis breathing down your neck?"

"Yeah."

"Verstraeten also pointed out how you've angered other friends [like Pierre Jacomet and Harry Gibbons]. Everyone over the years seems to either love Brother Leo or hate Brother Leo. There seems to be no in-between. What makes it that way?"

"Uh," Leo laughed. "I don't know. Must just be bad luck! One of the reasons maybe showed today. I shouldn't have gotten so, un . . . I try not to judge people, especially people I'm tempted to judge harshly, like the two of you. I'm *sensitive* about this case, you know. I did a lousy job. But I don't know. It's my fault, I'm sure, that [some] people hate me. Most people hate another person for a reason."

We covered as broad a range of subjects with Leo as we could, giving him the chance to explain his actions and to answer the allegations of others, such as those of his former friend Francis Verstraeten. But the only subject that the monk really wanted to discuss that first day was one he raised—the recent decision to sell the six hundred hectares of property Sarita had bought for the Trappists in Chile for $300,000 in 1960.

As he had anticipated, Leo explained, the city of Santiago has spilled westward toward the monastery lands, driving local real estate values to unprecedented highs. The monastery, he continued, was no longer a Spencer daughter house; its property was owned by a Chilean foundation (similar to Sarita's Argentine foundation) whose members were all monks. Faced with having to move anyway—the scenic valley in Chile was filling up with people—the community voted to sell the land and, after building a new monastery elsewhere, to donate all the remaining proceeds to the homeless of Santiago.

As Father Richard Gans later explained to us in more detail, the monks in Chile are buying house lots for the poor along a river near the monastery. Each family contributes what it can to the acquisition and construction of each dwelling. The rest will be paid for by the Trappists.

It is the program's scale that is amazing. Depending upon the rate at which the monks sell off their property and whether it goes in small pieces or large chunks, they expect to realize at least $20 million in profit, and perhaps ten times that much.

"Life's full of little ironies, isn't it, Brother Leo?" we asked after he told us of the land sale.

"Yeah, it certainly is," he replied. "But I wouldn't call it irony. I'd call it poetic justice. This will all go to the poor of Chile."

On our second day of conversation, which continued in New York, Leo returned to his first theme—our shallowness and lack of proper perspective—again and again. It became a bit tedious. And he often compared us, unfavorably, with a journalist he had recently spent a great deal of time with.

"My own feelings," said the monk, "are that you reveal yourself a little bit in your questions. In a sense, I'm very glad to hear them. Ah, you're welcome to your own way in which you see the case, [but] it's not a point of view that I would be interested in bending over backwards to help further. I'm *trying* to be kind."

"Thank you, Brother Leo. You've been very forbearing," we replied. The note of irritation didn't faze him.

"As far as I can see," he said, "I'll probably not be too much interested in reading your book."

"Is that because some of our questions are derived from what others have had to say about you . . . ?"

"Sure."

"If we don't [bring them up], we're being dishonest."

"I agree with you," he said. "[But] I've tried over the years in the monastery to not judge people, and certainly not to defend myself when others attack me. It's against my religion. I probably would have been wiser had I remained silent [to you]."

"George," Leo went on, in reference to the newsman he admires, "handled me much better. And I appreciated him much more. When he asked me these questions, I think I was a little more humble and virtuous, and I didn't justify myself. There's a whole long list of facts—impressive facts—that I mentioned to George that I am not going to mention to you. We'll leave it there."

In the last hour of our talks, Leo addressed the central issue of his saga—his conscience. "Some obligations are relative," he said. "A sacred obligation means that there's nothing relative about it. And there are other obligations that are more or less absolute.

"Now, Mrs. East unfortunately chose me—entrusted [to] me—something that meant a great deal to her. It was almost a continuation of her life. And I saw, furthermore, that that trust would have allowed me, in her name, to give to poor people, for example, things that they desperately needed, things they die from if they don't receive them. And that's not an overstatement. [Others] will grow up with warped brains because of malnutrition. The *need* is tremendous!

"These people would have received this help had the foundation been permitted to take its natural course. So I certainly looked upon my obligation to *that* commitment as being just as important as my obligation to conscience and to obedience. I defended my obligation to Sarita because I thought it was the right thing to do. It was the honest thing to do."

"But in the process," we observed, "you alienated sympathetic people and isolated yourself."

"Very true."

"Didn't you feel some self-doubt?"

"That's true. Three or four years of it."

"And then, you tried to see the thing as your cross to bear?"

"Right, and something therapeutic, too. I realized somewhere along the line, maybe when I was at Calvaire, that this bitter portion could be therapeutic, too. Because it was setting me free from that naturally instinctive role that I played of taking a lesser . . . letting others pretty much run my life."

It was in that obedient frame of mind, said Leo, that he accepted his exile to Calvaire. "You know, when I submitted to going up [there] I said, 'Well, this is gonna be hard, but they can't do anything without me.' I never dreamt that they'd be able to effect a settlement. I never dreamt that that was possible."

"What about Father Dominic Hughes's role at this time? He had sort of an elfin sensibility, didn't he?"

"Absolutely," answered the monk. "Absolutely."

"He enjoyed tweaking the establishment?"

"Right. Right."

"And he was offended by the treatment you'd received?"

"It was the lack of liberty of conscience which was terrible."

"He was fairly contemptuous of Peter Grace?"

Leo paused a moment. "Perhaps," he said. "Dom Thomas, too."

"And Hughes," we continued, "wasn't necessarily interested in your vindication in the foundation affair? His first issue was to protect you as an individual. Do you think he patronized you?"

"Yeah," Leo replied. "Yeah. He felt superior, and he was superior. An incredibly high IQ."

"What about that memo of July 9? That seems to pretty plainly signal your capitulation."

"Father Hughes promised me that he needed it," Leo answered with animation. "I wasn't convinced. I said, 'Okay, dammit!' I don't know why the hell he wrote it."

A month afterward, the monk went on to recount, he nearly lost his mind from the frustration and vexation of life at Calvaire. "I'll never forget that date as long as I live. August 10. My birthday. Oh God! I was in the hothouse watering these damn little plants, whatever they were—cabbages or tomatoes or something—and boy, I thought my head was gonna blow up. It was frightening.

"It was at Calvaire, I think, that I began to see that this experience was going to put me in the limelight. Number two, it was going to put me in a negative limelight. And number three, it would put me in direct confrontation with the highest authority of the church.

You couldn't, as a Catholic, stand up against more power structure.

"And here's another thing. This story from one point of view is much bigger than I am. You would have had to have the courage of seven superheroes, maybe, to have done what I did. But what I did came more or less naturally. For example, to live alone is much more congenial [for me] than living in a community. To be dismissed from the order was a godsend! I wound up right where I had a natural orientation. To live alone."

"That's fascinating," we remarked.

"Yes," the monk answered. "I'm no hero. I mean, I've just gone my way. I'm sort of a crazy guy with a—I've always been more or less of a loner. It's just the way I'm built. And the other thing is that I needed to grow up. I can see now that had I remained in the monastery as a shoemaker, as a brother, or a choir monk, going along with my superiors, I think I today would be a little less mature than maybe, by the grace of God, I am. I think it's been a good experience for me."

With that, Brother Leo finished a helping of pecan pie and grabbed his coat. There wasn't much more to be said. As we walked out onto the street, he observed, as he had before, how much he hated big cities and cold weather. It was especially brisk that Sunday afternoon. Wind gusts were tossing bits of paper up into the trees. Brother Leo pulled his lightweight overcoat tighter to his chest.

At the corner of Eighty-first and Columbus a light rain began. Quickly, the monk hailed a cab and popped into it. With the briefest of handshakes he thanked us for dinner the night before, and the homemade pie. Then, as the cab drove away, he turned back and gave us a parting wave.

The following spring Brother Leo wrote to the current Trappist abbot general, Dom Ambrose Southey, in Rome. The olive branch had been extended by the Cistercians. Despite everything, if Leo would only forswear any further litigation (as he wrote to us that he had), then he was welcome back into the order. On Father Gans's suggestion, and in line with his own instincts, Leo could not bring himself to do it.

"I was dismissed," he wrote Southey, "for opposing this Settlement and perhaps you are right in saying that no great injustice has been done to me, but I am sure as are many others that a very great injustice has been done to Mrs. East and the poor in South America and elsewhere whom she intended to help. You ask me to send you a letter that in effect would say I am in accord with this Settlement, and I ask you how in good conscience I can do so?"

As of late 1989 Brother Leo still has not rejoined the Trappists.

✣ ✣ ✣

Index

ABOUT THE AUTHORS

Stephen G. Michaud is the author of six books, four of them with Hugh Aynesworth. Mr. Michaud also has written for *Newsweek*, *Business Week*, *People*, *The New York Times Magazine*, *Smart*, and *The Smithsonian* among many other publications. At present he lives with his wife, Susan, in New York City.

Hugh Aynesworth is a veteran investigative reporter. Besides his collaborations with Michaud, Mr. Aynesworth has been a correspondent for ABC-TV's "20/20," a bureau chief for *Newsweek*, an editor at several daily newspapers, and a private investigator. He is a foremost authority on the assassination of President John F. Kennedy. Aynesworth, currently a national correspondent for *The Washington Times*, lives in Dallas with his wife Paula.

Together they have written the bestsellers *The Only Living Witness* and *Ted Bundy: Conversations With a Killer*, about serial killer Ted Bundy, and *Wanted for Murder*.